National Accounts at a Glance 2015

This work is published on the responsibility of the Secretary-General of the OECD. The opinions expressed and arguments employed herein do not necessarily reflect the official views of the OECD or of the governments of its member countries.

This document and any map included herein are without prejudice to the status of or sovereignty over any territory, to the delimitation of international frontiers and boundaries and to the name of any territory, city or area.

Please cite this publication as:
OECD (2015), *National Accounts at a Glance 2015*, OECD Publishing.
http://dx.doi.org/10.1787/na_glance-2015-en

ISBN 978-92-64-24679-9 (print)
ISBN 978-92-64-24678-2 (PDF)

Series: National Accounts at a Glance
ISSN 2220-0436 (print)
ISSN 2220-0444 (online)

The statistical data for Israel are supplied by and under the responsibility of the relevant Israeli authorities. The use of such data by the OECD is without prejudice to the status of the Golan Heights, East Jerusalem and Israeli settlements in the West Bank under the terms of international law.

Photo credits: Cover © Yahia LOUKKAL – Fotolia.com.

Corrigenda to OECD publications may be found on line at: *www.oecd.org/about/publishing/corrigenda.htm*.

Foreword

This 2015 publication presents information using an "indicator" approach, focusing on cross-country comparisons. The aim is to make the accounts more accessible and informative, whilst taking the opportunity to present the conceptual underpinning and comparability issues of each of the indicators presented. The 2015 edition is an abbreviated version of the regular publication since it only includes tables and metadata. The next full edition will be released in 2016.

The range of indicators is set deliberately wide to reflect the richness of the national accounts dataset and to encourage users of economic statistics to refocus some of the spotlight that is often placed on GDP to other important economic indicators, which may better respond to their needs. Indeed many users themselves have been instrumental in this regard. The report of the Commission on the Measurement of Economic Performance and Social Progress (Stiglitz-Sen-Fitoussi Commission) is but one notable example.

That is not to undermine the importance of GDP, which arguably remains the most important measure of total economic activity, but other measures may better reflect other aspects of the economy. For example, net national income may be a more appropriate measure of income available to citizens in countries with large outflows of property income, and household adjusted disposable income per capita may be a better indicator of the material well-being of citizens. But certainly from a data perspective more can and remains to be done. The Stiglitz-Sen-Fitoussi Commission for example highlights the pressing need for the provision, by official statistics institutes, of more detailed information that better describes the distributional aspects of activity, especially income, and the need to build on the national accounts framework to address issues such as non-market services produced by households or leisure. It is hoped that by producing a publication such as this and thereby raising awareness, the momentum from this and other initiatives will be accelerated. The publication itself will pick up new indicators in the future as they become available at the OECD.

The publication is broken down into eight chapters: The first provides a general introduction focusing on indicators of GDP. The second focuses on income and presents a number of important indicators such as net national income, savings and net lending/net borrowing rates. The third chapter looks at indicators related to the expenditure approach to GDP estimation, with information on the key components of demand and imports. The fourth chapter looks at indicators from a production perspective. The fifth chapter on households provides a more detailed approach on household sector indicators. The sixth chapter focuses on general government, presenting several indicators such as total expenditure or gross debt of general government. The seventh chapter looks at the health of corporations. The eighth and final chapter focuses on capital. Finally the annex provides important reference indicators, important in their own-right but also because they are used in the construction of many of the indicators presented elsewhere in the publication. It also provides further background on the 2008 System of National Accounts, *which is the basis of data published here, with the exception of Chile, Japan and Turkey who still present data on the 1993 SNA basis. It is important to note however that differences between the 2008 SNA and the 1993 SNA do not have a significant impact on the comparability of most indicators presented in this publication. The annex at the end of this publication describes the key changes from the 1993 SNA that may impact on the indicators presented.*

Table of contents

Reader's Guide

Main feature

Each indicator is preceded by a short text that opens with an explanation of what is measured and why. This is followed by a more detailed description of the underlying concept (Definition) consistent with the 2008 System of National Accounts (SNA). The final paragraph (Comparability) highlights those areas where some caution may be needed when comparing performance across countries or over time. Some issues relating to comparability, or the care that should be taken when making comparisons, cut across a number of subject areas. Rather than refer to these each time they arise these generic cases are described below.

2008 SNA – Changes from the 1993 SNA

Since 2014, the majority of OECD countries publish data according to the 2008 SNA. Data included in this publication are compiled according to the 2008 SNA "System of National Accounts, 2008" with the exception of Chile, Japan, and Turkey who still present data on an 1993 SNA basis. Key changes from the 1993 SNA are presented in the annex.

Impact on GDP due to the incorporation of the 2008 SNA

The incorporation of the 2008 SNA and benchmark statistical revisions increased the GDP level for the OECD total by 3.8% for the year 2010. Therefore, every indicator where GDP is the denominator will be affected. But in some cases, both numerator and denominator have been revised leading to a minor variation in the previously published indicator. It is important to note that since the level of GDP was revised for all years it did not have much impact on the percent changes.

Moreover, when changes in international standards are implemented countries often take the opportunity to implement improved compilation methods- therefore also implementing various improvements in sources and estimation methodologies. In some countries the impact of the "statistical benchmark revision" could be higher than the impact of the changeover in standards. For example, the Netherlands increased their level of GDP by 7.6% for 2010, but only 3 percentage points are related to the implementation of the 2008 SNA.

For more information refer to "New standards for compiling national accounts: what's the impact on GDP and other macro-economic indicators? "Statistic brief:

www.oecd.org/std/na/new-standards-for-compiling-national-accounts-SNA2008-OECDSB20.pdf

Questionnaires and source data

Unless otherwise specified all data have been provided by countries via standardised OECD questionnaires.

Statistical conventions

- All growth rates refer to constant prices (or real) data.
- Ratios, percentages and shares are derived from current prices data.
- Contribution of Y to the growth of X (Y being a component of X) is defined as the growth rate of Y (chained or fixed constant prices or previous year prices) weighted by the share of Y in X at current prices (period t-1).

Signs and abbreviations

..: Missing values, not applicable or not available.

e: OECD estimates.

|: Break.

Countries and zones

Data are available for most indicators for all OECD countries. Where data are not available or have not been provided to the OECD, estimates are as much as possible produced.

OECD total

OECD total refers to all OECD countries unless otherwise specified.

Euro area

Data for the zone "euro area" are taken from Eurostat databases.

Data in euros

Data for all member countries of the European Economic and Monetary Union (EMU) are expressed in euros.

Data relating to years prior to entry into the EMU have been converted from the former national currency using the appropriate irrevocable conversion rate. This presentation facilitates comparisons within a country over time and ensures that the historical evolution (i.e. growth rates) is preserved. However, pre-EMU euros are a notional unit and are not normally suitable to form area aggregates or to carry out cross-country comparisons.

OECD accession countries

In 2007 the OECD Council opened membership discussions with five candidate countries, as a result of which Chile, Estonia, Israel and Slovenia became members in 2010. *Discussions with the Russian Federation are currently postponed.* In May 2013, the Council decided to launch a new wave of accession discussions with Colombia and Latvia; in April 2015, it invited Costa Rica and Lithuania to open formal OECD accession talks .The OECD is also engaging key global players in its work, such as Brazil, China, India, Indonesia and South Africa. Data for these countries are part of this publication whenever available.

General comments on concepts and comparability

The list of comments described below relates to cross-cutting issues and is provided here to avoid repetition in the sections that follow.

Purchasing power parities (PPP) for GDP and for actual individual consumption

PPPs are the rates of currency conversion that equalise the purchasing power of different countries by eliminating differences in price levels between countries. When converted by means of PPPs, expenditures on GDP across countries are in effect expressed at the same set of prices, enabling comparisons between countries that reflect only differences in the volume of goods and services purchased. Simplistic comparisons of economic activity using exchange rates should generally be avoided as such comparisons will embody these price differences, and, moreover, exchange rate series tend to be more volatile than PPPs, presenting difficulties when comparing across countries and time.

However, a caveat related to international comparisons still remains in the context of PPPs. When countries are clustered around a very narrow range of outcomes, it may be misleading to establish a strict order of ranking. As is often the case with statistical information, there is a level of uncertainty associated with the data sources and procedures on which PPP computations rely. Relatively minor differences between two countries' PPP adjusted indicators, such as PPP adjusted GDP or NNI, may not be statistically or economically significant.

PPPs for GDP are used in all tables and graphs using PPPs as conversion rates except in the following tables and graph where PPPs for actual individual consumption are used: Table 14.1 (Household gross adjusted disposable income per capita), Figure 8.2 for household actual individual consumption, Table A.5 (Actual individual consumption, current PPPs) and Table A.6 (Actual individual consumption, 2010 constant PPPs).

1999, 2002, 2005, 2008 and **2011**: PPPs for all OECD countries are triennial benchmark results calculated jointly by the OECD and Eurostat. The 2011 benchmark results introduced Chile for the first time.

More information is available on the PPP Internet site: *www.oecd.org/std/prices-ppp/*.

Exchange rates

The exchange rates used in this publication have been calculated by the International Monetary Fund (IMF), and are published in International Financial Statistics (IFS). They are market rates averaged over the year.

Per capita indicators

Many of the indicators that follow are shown on a per capita basis. It is important to note therefore that the underlying population estimates are based on the SNA notion of residency: namely they include persons who are resident in a country for one year or more, regardless of their citizenship. Diplomatic personnel, defence personnel, together with their families located abroad, and students studying and patients seeking treatment abroad, are considered as residents of their home country, even if they stay abroad for more than one year. The "one-year rule" means that usual residents who live abroad for less than one year are included in their "home country's" population and foreign visitors (for example, holidaymakers) who are in the country for less than one year are not included.

An important point to note in this context is that individuals may feature as employees of one country (contributing to the GDP of that country via production), but residents of another (with their wages and salaries reflected in the GNI of their resident country).

Calendar/fiscal years

Unless specified below, or in the text accompanying the section, all data are on the basis of calendar years.

For non-financial indicators, data for Australia and New Zealand refer to fiscal years – 1 July of the year indicated to 30 June for Australia and 1 April of the year indicated to 31 March for New Zealand. Financial data refer to fiscal year for Japan, 1 April of the year indicated to 31 March.

Volume (constant price) estimates

Most OECD countries now produce their accounts using annual chain volume series. Mexico however currently produces fixed-base volume estimates with the base year updated, at present, less periodically with links created to earlier base year estimates.

The SNA recommends the production of estimates on the basis of annual chain volume series. These produce better estimates of growth as the weights used for the contribution of different goods and services are more relevant to the period in question. There is one downside to (annual) chaining however: aggregates may not equal the sum of their components in volume terms.

Gross and net values

The term "gross" is a common means of referring to values before deducting consumption of fixed capital. But not all references to "net" are necessarily in the context of net of depreciation. The reference to "net lending/borrowing" is the relevant example in this publication where "net" is not in the context of "depreciation". The same holds for indicators such as "gross debt" and "net worth".

Industrial classification (ISIC Rev. 4 International Standard Industrial Classification of All Economic Activities)

Currently, the reference classification is ISIC Rev. 4. All OECD countries provide their industrial classification according to ISIC Rev4.

The ISIC Rev. 4 classification is broken down into 10 activities.

ISIC Rev 4 classification and its correspondence are available on UNSD website: *http://unstats.un.org/unsd/cr/registry/regcst.asp?Cl=27*.

Households and NPISHs

A number of countries are not able to provide a breakdown of Households and Non-Profit Institutions Serving Households (NPISHs) in their sector accounts. As a consequence, to ensure the highest level of comparability, unless otherwise specified, the accounts for the households sector include NPISHs in this publication.

Stocks and flows

Most of the data presented in this publication refer to flows, which are production, generation and distribution of income, and the net acquisition of assets and net incurrence of liabilities. Stock data refer to balance sheet accounts, which present values of assets and liabilities and the net worth of the sector at the end of the accounting period.

Tables mentioned below refer to stocks data:

- 18. Non-financial assets of households
- 19. Composition of household portfolio

- 20. Household debt
- 21. Financial net worth of households
- 22. Total net worth of households
- 29. Adjusted general government debt-to-GDP
- 30. Financial net worth of general government
- 31. Non-financial corporations' debt
- 32. Debt to equity ratio in financial corporations
- 33. Leverage of the banking sector
- 35. Net capital stock

Important equalities in the SNA

Gross domestic product (GDP) at market prices

= Final consumption expenditure
+ Gross capital formation
+ Exports of goods and services
- Imports of goods and services
= Gross value added at basic prices
+ Taxes less subsidies on products

Net National Income (NNI) at market prices

= GDP at market prices
+ Taxes less subsidies on production and imports (net, receivable from abroad)
+ Compensation of employees (net, receivable from abroad)
+ Property income (net, receivable from abroad)
- Consumption of fixed capital

Net National Disposable Income (NNDI)

= NNI at market prices
+ Current taxes on income, wealth, etc. (net, receivable from abroad)
+ Social contributions and benefits and other current transfers (net, receivable from abroad)

Saving, net

= NNDI at market prices
- Final consumption expenditure
+ Adjustment for the change in net equity of households on pension entitlements (net, receivable from abroad)

Net lending/net borrowing

= Saving, net
+ Capital transfers (net, receivable from abroad)
- Gross capital formation
- Acquisitions less disposals of non-produced non-financial assets
+ Consumption of fixed capital

Further reading

Useful references for "further reading" are available at the bottom of most sections.

For all sections, general information on methodology and detailed definitions can be found in:

- European Commission, International Monetary Fund, Organisation for Economic Co-operation and Development, United Nations, World Bank, New York, 2009, System of National Accounts 2008, *http://unstats.un.org/unsd/nationalaccount/docs/SNA2008.pdf*.
- Commission of the European Communities, International Monetary Fund, Organisation for Economic Co-operation and Development, United Nations, World Bank, Brussels / Luxembourg, New York, Paris, Washington, D.C., 1993, System of National Accounts 1993, *http://unstats.un.org/unsd/nationalaccount/docs/1993sna.pdf*.

Additional information and complementary tables can be found in:

- OECD (2014), OECD Factbook 2014: Economic, Environmental and Social Statistics, OECD Publishing, Paris. DOI: *http://dx.doi.org/10.1787/factbook-2014-en*.

Online data

National Accounts at a Glance – Database edition

The database edition of National Accounts at a Glance is continuously updated on line and contains longer time series than the publication: *http://dx.doi.org/10.1787/data-00369-en*. Data are available as far back as 1970 for some countries.

Detailed National Accounts data

The National Accounts at a Glance dataset is published as part of the OECD National Accounts Statistics online database which can be accessed via *http://dx.doi.org/10.1787/na-data-en*. This database includes very detailed information from the annual national accounts, non-financial as well as financial, many of which are also available on a quarterly basis.

The following is a list of the datasets which are available:

Aggregate national accounts

- Gross domestic product.
- Disposable income and net lending/borrowing.
- Population and employment by main activity.
- PPPs and exchange rates.

Detailed national accounts

- Balance sheets for non-financial assets.
- Capital formation by activity.
- Final consumption expenditure of households.
- Fixed assets by activity and by type of product.
- Labour input by activity.
- Non-financial accounts by sectors.
- Simplified non-financial accounts.
- Value added and its components by activity.

Financial accounts

- Consolidated financial accounts (flows).
- Non-consolidated financial accounts (flows).
- Consolidated financial balance sheets (stocks).
- Non-consolidated financial balance sheets (stocks).

General government accounts

- Government expenditure by function.
- Maastricht debt.
- Main aggregates.
- Taxes and social contributions receipts.

Website

OECD National Accounts, *http://www.oecd.org/std/na/*.

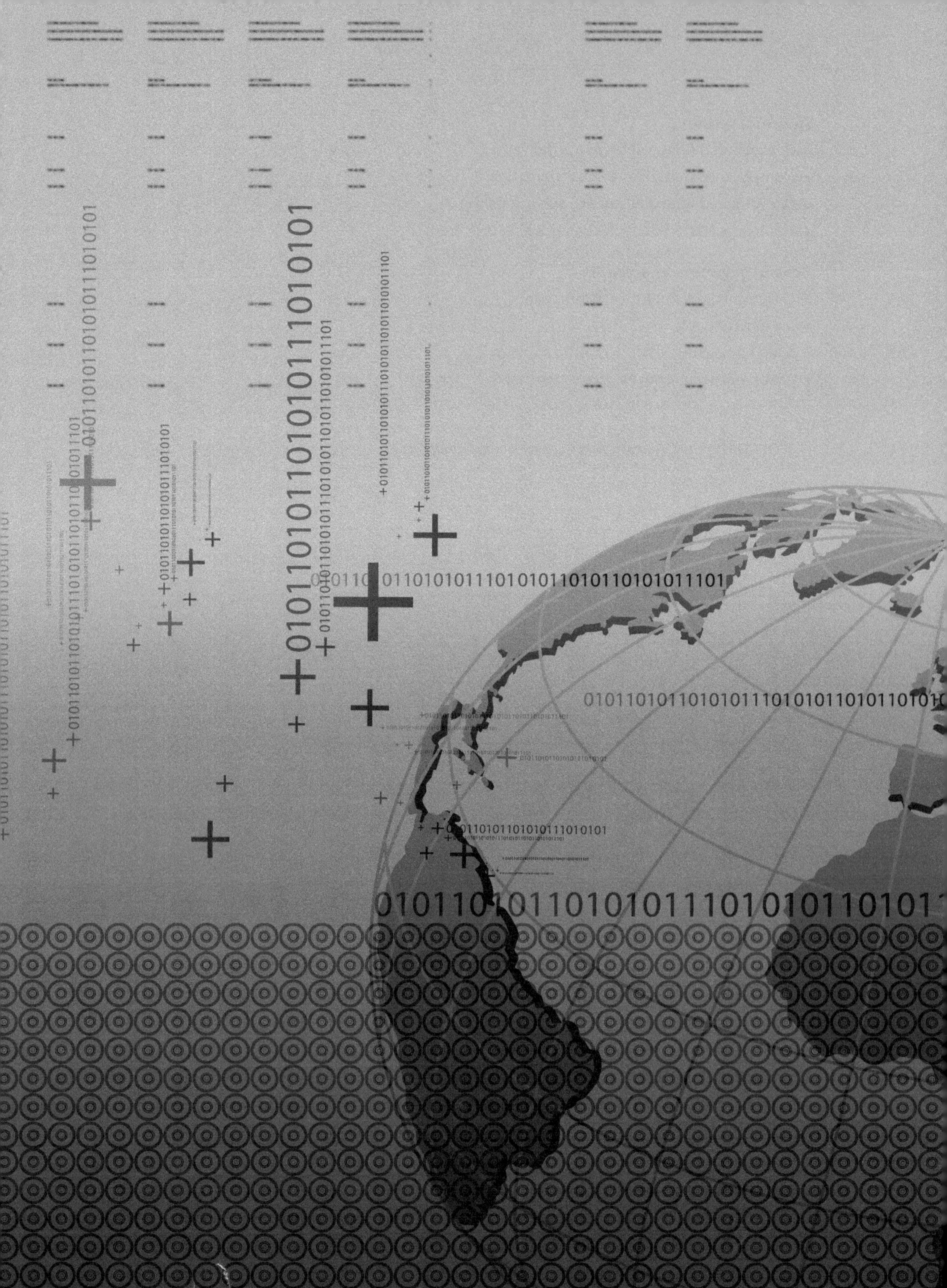

GROSS DOMESTIC PRODUCT (GDP)

1. Size of GDP
2. GDP growth
3. GDP per capita

Table 1.1. **Gross domestic product, current PPPs**

Billion US dollars

	2000	2001	2002	2003	2004	2005	2006	2007	2008	2009	2010	2011	2012	2013
Australia	538	568	599	635	675	719	774	825	851	898	936	985	999	1 040
Austria	237	240	253	262	276	285	311	326	342	339	350	369	378	383
Belgium	290	300	318	322	333	346	370	389	405	406	427	451	460	462
Canada	895	930	961	1 014	1 075	1 162	1 232	1 290	1 333	1 302	1 362	1 428	1 469	1 513
Chile	147	155	162	171	188	206	255	277	274	273	311	349	368	386
Czech Republic	167	180	187	200	214	228	250	275	282	282	283	300	301	304
Denmark	158	162	170	169	179	185	202	211	224	219	232	241	244	246
Estonia	14	15	16	18	20	22	26	29	30	27	28	32	33	35
Finland	137	143	148	150	163	168	182	198	211	200	205	217	218	218
France	1 582	1 682	1 762	1 748	1 821	1 919	2 054	2 179	2 262	2 252	2 332	2 439	2 445	2 478
Germany	2 190	2 283	2 346	2 423	2 534	2 654	2 859	3 026	3 156	3 041	3 239	3 447	3 507	3 554
Greece	209	227	248	260	279	279	312	324	345	341	322	296	278	280
Hungary	123	139	152	158	166	175	188	194	209	209	216	225	224	233
Iceland	8	9	9	9	10	11	11	12	13	13	12	13	13	14
Ireland	113	123	135	144	155	168	188	206	197	190	197	209	210	216
Israel[1]	157	161	166	159	172	172	182	198	201	206	221	237	253	264
Italy	1 518	1 610	1 593	1 632	1 661	1 720	1 860	1 971	2 070	2 019	2 058	2 132	2 115	2 109
Japan	3 290	3 377	3 472	3 569	3 753	3 890	4 065	4 264	4 289	4 079	4 321	4 386	4 541	4 613
Korea	850	909	990	1 024	1 103	1 166	1 251	1 355	1 406	1 396	1 505	1 559	1 601	1 662
Luxembourg	25	25	27	28	30	31	37	40	42	40	43	47	49	51
Mexico	1 006 e	1 029 e	1 067 e	1 132	1 212	1 322	1 464	1 551	1 641	1 624	1 730	1 893	1 967	2 000
Netherlands	502	526	548	547	577	609	668	715	759	734	743	774	777	785
New Zealand	83	87	92	97	103	106	116	123	126	131	135	142	145	156
Norway	165	171	171	178	198	224	255	268	298	271	287	311	333	333
Poland	406	419	443	460	498	527	578	644	688	730	794	857	888	909
Portugal	184	193	201	207	213	232	251	266	276	277	285	284	284	289
Slovak Republic	60	66	71	75	81	89	101	115	128	125	132	136	140	144
Slovenia	36	37	40	42	45	48	52	56	60	56	57	59	58	59
Spain	881	946	1 022	1 069	1 135	1 217	1 371	1 484	1 550	1 521	1 507	1 521	1 515	1 516
Sweden	261	265	275	287	308	310	341	371	386	369	391	413	418	428
Switzerland	248	256	265	267	279	291	325	358	386	387	402	432	447	460
Turkey	590	561	572	589	689	781	896	976	1 068	1 044	1 168	1 308	1 348	1 409
United Kingdom	1 617	1 704	1 786	1 860	1 985	2 091	2 246	2 300	2 335	2 265	2 250	2 315	2 396	2 484
United States	10 285	10 622	10 978	11 511	12 275	13 094	13 856	14 478	14 719	14 419	14 964	15 518	16 155	16 663
Euro area	8 031	8 474	8 789	8 996	9 396	9 872	10 740	11 435	11 957	11 677	12 042	12 539	12 612	12 738
OECD-Total	28 971 e	30 120 e	31 242 e	32 416	34 405	36 448	39 127	41 295	42 561	41 688	43 447	45 325	46 577	47 695
Brazil	1 555	1 598	1 663	1 720	1 863	1 988	2 142	2 343	2 521	2 538	2 772	2 974	..	..
China	3 616	4 006	4 437	4 980	5 632	6 470	7 514	8 806	9 843	10 833	12 110	13 496	14 783	16 158
India	..	..	..	..	2 964	3 343	3 765	4 244	4 458	4 969	..	..	..	..
Indonesia	1 007 e	1 068 e	1 133 e	1 211 e	1 307 e	1 425 e	1 550 e	1 692 e	1 829	1 890	2 017	2 172	2 329	2 504
Russian Federation	1 000 e	1 074 e	1 167	1 339	1 474	1 697	2 134	2 378	2 878	2 768	2 928	3 227	3 446	3 592
South Africa	341	358	382	402	433	470	510	556	589	580	598	634	666	692

Note: Detailed metadata:
http://stats.oecd.org/OECDStat_Metadata/ShowMetadata.ashx?Dataset=NAAG_2015_NOV15&Lang=en&Coords=[INDICATOR].[GDPCPC]

1. Information on data for Israel: http://dx.doi.org/10.1787/888932315602

2. GDP growth

Table 2.1. **Gross domestic product, volume**

Annual growth rates in percentage

	2000	2001	2002	2003	2004	2005	2006	2007	2008	2009	2010	2011	2012	2013
Australia	1.9	3.9	3.1	4.2	3.2	3.0	3.8	3.7	1.7	2.0	2.3	3.7	2.5	2.5
Austria	3.4	1.4	1.7	0.8	2.7	2.1	3.4	3.6	1.5	-3.8	1.9	2.8	0.8	0.3
Belgium	3.6	0.8	1.8	0.8	3.6	2.1	2.5	3.4	0.7	-2.3	2.7	1.8	0.2	0.0
Canada	5.1	1.7	2.8	1.9	3.1	3.2	2.6	2.0	1.2	-2.7	3.4	3.0	1.9	2.0
Chile	5.1	3.3	2.7	3.8	7.0	6.2	5.7	5.2	3.3	-1.0	5.8	5.8	5.5	4.2
Czech Republic	4.3	3.1	1.6	3.6	4.9	6.4	6.9	5.5	2.7	-4.8	2.3	2.0	-0.9	-0.5
Denmark	3.7	0.8	0.5	0.4	2.6	2.4	3.8	0.8	-0.7	-5.1	1.6	1.2	-0.7	-0.5
Estonia	10.6	6.3	6.1	7.4	6.3	9.4	10.3	7.7	-5.4	-14.7	2.5	7.6	5.2	1.6
Finland	5.6	2.6	1.7	2.0	3.9	2.8	4.1	5.2	0.7	-8.3	3.0	2.6	-1.4	-1.1
France	3.9	2.0	1.1	0.8	2.8	1.6	2.4	2.4	0.2	-2.9	2.0	2.1	0.2	0.7
Germany	3.0	1.7	0.0	-0.7	1.2	0.7	3.7	3.3	1.1	-5.6	4.1	3.7	0.4	0.3
Greece	4.2	3.8	3.9	5.8	5.1	0.6	5.7	3.3	-0.3	-4.3	-5.5	-9.1	-7.3	-3.2
Hungary	4.2	3.8	4.5	3.8	4.9	4.4	3.8	0.4	0.8	-6.6	0.7	1.8	-1.7	1.9
Iceland	4.7	3.8	0.5	2.7	8.2	6.0	4.2	9.5	1.5	-4.7	-3.6	2.0	1.2	3.9
Ireland	10.2	5.8	5.9	3.8	4.4	6.3	6.3	5.5	-2.2	-5.6	0.4	2.6	0.2	1.4
Israel[1]	8.9	0.2	-0.1	1.2	5.1	4.4	5.8	6.1	3.1	1.3	5.5	5.0	2.9	3.3
Italy	3.7	1.8	0.3	0.2	1.6	0.9	2.0	1.5	-1.0	-5.5	1.7	0.6	-2.8	-1.7
Japan	2.3	0.4	0.3	1.7	2.4	1.3	1.7	2.2	-1.0	-5.5	4.7	-0.5	1.8	1.6
Korea	8.9	4.5	7.4	2.9	4.9	3.9	5.2	5.5	2.8	0.7	6.5	3.7	2.3	2.9
Luxembourg	8.4 e	2.2	3.6	1.4	4.4	3.2	5.1	8.4	-0.8	-5.4	5.7	2.6	-0.8	4.3
Mexico	6.6 e	0.0 e	0.8 e	1.4 e	4.2	3.1	5.0	3.2	1.4	-4.7	5.2	3.9	4.0	1.4
Netherlands	4.2	2.1	0.1	0.3	2.0	2.2	3.5	3.7	1.7	-3.8	1.4	1.7	-1.1	-0.5
New Zealand	2.8	3.4	4.9	4.6	3.8	3.4	2.8	3.0	-1.6	-0.3	1.4	2.2	2.2	2.5
Norway	3.2	2.1	1.4	0.9	4.0	2.6	2.4	2.9	0.4	-1.6	0.6	1.0	2.7	0.7
Poland	4.6	1.2	2.0	3.6	5.1	3.5	6.2	7.2	3.9	2.6	3.7	5.0	1.6	1.3
Portugal	3.8	1.9	0.8	-0.9	1.8	0.8	1.6	2.5	0.2	-3.0	1.9	-1.8	-4.0	-1.1
Slovak Republic	1.2	3.3	4.5	5.4	5.3	6.4	8.5	10.8	5.7	-5.5	5.1	2.8	1.5	1.4
Slovenia	4.2	2.9	3.8	2.8	4.4	4.0	5.7	6.9	3.3	-7.8	1.2	0.6	-2.7	-1.1
Spain	5.3	4.0	2.9	3.2	3.2	3.7	4.2	3.8	1.1	-3.6	0.0	-1.0	-2.6	-1.7
Sweden	4.7	1.6	2.1	2.4	4.3	2.8	4.7	3.4	-0.6	-5.2	6.0	2.7	-0.3	1.2
Switzerland	3.9	1.4	0.1	0.0	2.8	3.0	4.0	4.1	2.3	-2.1	3.0	1.8	1.1	1.8
Turkey	6.8	-5.7	6.2	5.3	9.4	8.4	6.9	4.7	0.7	-4.8	9.2	8.8	2.1	4.2
United Kingdom	3.8	2.8	2.5	3.3	2.5	3.0	2.7	2.6	-0.5	-4.2	1.5	2.0	1.2	2.2
United States	4.1	1.0	1.8	2.8	3.8	3.3	2.7	1.8	-0.3	-2.8	2.5	1.6	2.2	1.5
Euro area	3.8	2.1	0.9	0.7	2.3	1.7	3.2	3.0	0.5	-4.6	2.0	1.6	-0.8	-0.3
OECD-Total	4.1 e	1.4 e	1.7 e	2.1 e	3.3	2.8	3.1	2.7	0.3	-3.5	3.0	1.9	1.3	1.2
Brazil	..	1.3	3.1	1.2	5.7	3.1	4.0	6.0	5.0	-0.2	7.6	3.9	..	..
China	8.4 e	8.3 e	9.1 e	10.0 e	10.1 e	11.3 e	12.7 e	14.2 e	9.6 e	9.2 e	10.4 e	9.3	7.7	..
India	..	..	..	..	..	9.3	9.3	9.8	4.9	9.1	..	..	..	..
Indonesia	4.9	3.6	4.5	4.8	5.0	5.7	5.5	6.3	6.0	4.7	6.4	6.2	6.0	5.6
Russian Federation	10.0 e	5.1 e	4.7 e	7.3	7.2	6.4	8.2	8.5	5.2	-7.8	4.5	4.3	3.4	1.3
South Africa	4.2	2.7	3.7	2.9	4.6	5.3	5.6	5.4	3.2	-1.5	3.0	3.2	2.2	2.2

Note: Detailed metadata:
http://stats.oecd.org/OECDStat_Metadata/ShowMetadata.ashx?Dataset=NAAG_2015_NOV15&Lang=en&Coords=[INDICATOR].[GDPG]

1. Information on data for Israel: http://dx.doi.org/10.1787/888932315602

Table 3.1. Gross domestic product per capita, current prices and current PPPs

US dollars

	2000	2001	2002	2003	2004	2005	2006	2007	2008	2009	2010	2011	2012	2013
Australia	28 155	29 337	30 603	32 088	33 699	35 440	37 583	39 343	39 704	41 138	42 253	43 802	43 676	44 706
Austria	29 574	29 849	31 261	32 212	33 820	34 702	37 653	39 240	41 151	40 642	41 876	44 039	44 870	45 133
Belgium	28 300	29 207	30 776	31 059	31 997	33 057	35 110	36 596	37 857	37 664	39 276	41 118	41 595	41 595
Canada	29 156	29 996	30 634	32 054	33 654	36 051	37 822	39 226	40 108	38 709	40 055	41 567	42 283	43 038
Chile	9 544	9 968	10 279	10 760	11 704	12 690	15 496	16 709	16 327	16 136	18 173	20 189	21 108	21 888
Czech Republic	16 259	17 633	18 311	19 593	20 970	22 237	24 350	26 622	26 994	26 895	26 941	28 603	28 636	28 963
Denmark	29 575	30 250	31 597	31 269	33 162	34 083	37 192	38 685	40 843	39 625	41 812	43 319	43 565	43 797
Estonia	9 680	10 511	11 770	13 193	14 628	16 510	19 255	21 803	22 487	20 195	21 070	23 914	25 206	26 160
Finland	26 473	27 535	28 421	28 813	31 092	32 065	34 523	37 509	39 730	37 546	38 296	40 251	40 209	40 017
France	25 996	27 439	28 523	28 110	29 056	30 398	32 311	34 064	35 170	34 837	35 896	37 353	37 281	37 617
Germany	26 645	27 722	28 438	29 365	30 709	32 186	34 716	36 783	38 434	37 137	39 622	42 152	42 807	43 282
Greece	19 344	20 895	22 719	23 804	25 432	25 396	28 290	29 309	31 161	30 662	28 961	26 626	25 177	25 523
Hungary	12 089	13 643	14 918	15 640	16 466	17 314	18 664	19 339	20 811	20 867	21 562	22 603	22 556	23 507
Iceland	29 614	31 247	31 972	31 751	34 897	35 987	36 685	38 729	41 115	39 831	38 592	39 558	40 498	41 987
Ireland	29 627	31 786	34 441	36 016	38 183	40 446	44 030	46 727	43 839	41 845	43 223	45 670	45 757	46 858
Israel[1]	24 832	24 866	25 138	23 696	25 124	24 774	25 634	27 499	27 358	27 589	28 948	30 585	31 938	32 713
Italy	26 658	28 248	27 890	28 422	28 712	29 554	31 832	33 531	34 941	33 893	34 396	35 494	35 044	34 781
Japan	25 941	26 563	27 251	27 960	29 384	30 446	31 795	33 319	33 500	31 861	33 748	34 312	35 601	36 225
Korea	18 092	19 199	20 785	21 389	22 968	24 220	25 863	27 872	28 718	28 393	30 465	31 327	32 022	33 089
Luxembourg	56 518	56 173	59 353	60 831	65 407	67 003	77 306	82 733	84 920	80 265	84 440	90 889	91 256	93 234
Mexico	9 974 e	10 076 e	10 319 e	10 808	11 438	12 342	13 505	14 132	14 743	14 394	15 139	16 366	16 808	16 891
Netherlands	31 543	32 803	33 954	33 741	35 424	37 313	40 854	43 673	46 156	44 413	44 752	46 389	46 387	46 749
New Zealand	21 525	22 436	23 209	23 886	25 005	25 666	27 589	29 104	29 482	30 390	30 942	32 221	32 861	34 989
Norway	36 799	37 786	37 726	38 991	43 202	48 370	54 720	56 901	62 421	56 205	58 775	62 738	66 358	65 635
Poland	10 611 e	10 964 e	11 592 e	12 047 e	13 054 e	13 808 e	15 157 e	16 894 e	18 051 e	19 145 e	20 612 e	22 250 e	23 054 e	23 616 e
Portugal	17 852	18 585	19 332	19 822	20 303	22 073	23 887	25 224	26 096	26 217	26 924	26 932	27 001	27 651
Slovak Republic	11 137	12 232	13 133	13 889	14 965	16 482	18 760	21 354	23 728	23 046	24 325	25 169	25 809	26 586
Slovenia	17 878	18 793	20 123	20 938	22 693	23 884	25 873	27 670	29 589 |	27 488	27 586	28 513	28 441	28 675
Spain	21 718	23 208	24 664	25 329	26 484	27 863	30 906	32 800	33 708	32 804	32 361	32 535	32 393	32 546
Sweden	29 385	29 811	30 790	32 062	34 269	34 332	37 594	40 565	41 881	39 670	41 727	43 709	43 869	44 586
Switzerland	34 200	35 127	36 134	36 174	37 523	38 916	43 140	47 175	50 226	49 722	51 121	54 551	55 857	56 897
Turkey	9 177	8 619	8 667	8 806	10 168	11 394	12 905	13 896	15 021	14 495	16 001	17 692	18 002 e	18 599 e
United Kingdom	27 451	28 818	30 088	31 184	33 112	34 616	36 921	37 509	37 765	36 383	35 859	36 575	37 605	38 743
United States	36 419	37 240	38 122	39 606	41 857	44 237	46 369	47 987	48 330	46 930	48 302	49 710	51 368	52 592
Euro area	25 011	26 296	27 132	27 616	28 688	29 972	32 453	34 363	35 743	34 797	35 797	37 182	37 304	37 606
OECD-Total	25 090 e	25 907 e	26 678 e	27 484 e	28 972 e	30 479 e	32 492 e	34 035 e	34 809 e	33 860 e	35 053 e	36 347 e	37 135 e	37 815 e
Brazil	8 965	9 085	9 326	9 523	10 183	10 737	11 434	12 365	13 160	13 114	14 179	15 065	..	..
China	2 853	3 139	3 454	3 853	4 333	4 948	5 717	6 665	7 412	8 118	9 031	10 017	10 917	11 874
India	..	..	..	..	2 722	3 022	3 355	3 729	3 863	4 247	..	..	..	..
Indonesia	4 910 e	5 134 e	5 372 e	5 663 e	6 026 e	6 483 e	6 959 e	7 499 e	8 003	8 167	8 489	8 907 e	9 433 e	10 023 e
Russian Federation	6 818 e	7 360 e	8 029	9 254	10 231	11 822	14 916	16 649	20 164	19 387	20 498	22 570	24 069 e	25 151 e
South Africa	7 733	7 996	8 408	8 737	9 277	9 946	10 652	11 441	11 957	11 598	11 772	12 292	12 715	13 002

Note: Detailed metadata:
http://stats.oecd.org/OECDStat_Metadata/ShowMetadata.ashx?Dataset=NAAG_2015_NOV15&Lang=en&Coords=[INDICATOR].[GDPHCPC]

1. Information on data for Israel: http://dx.doi.org/10.1787/888932315602

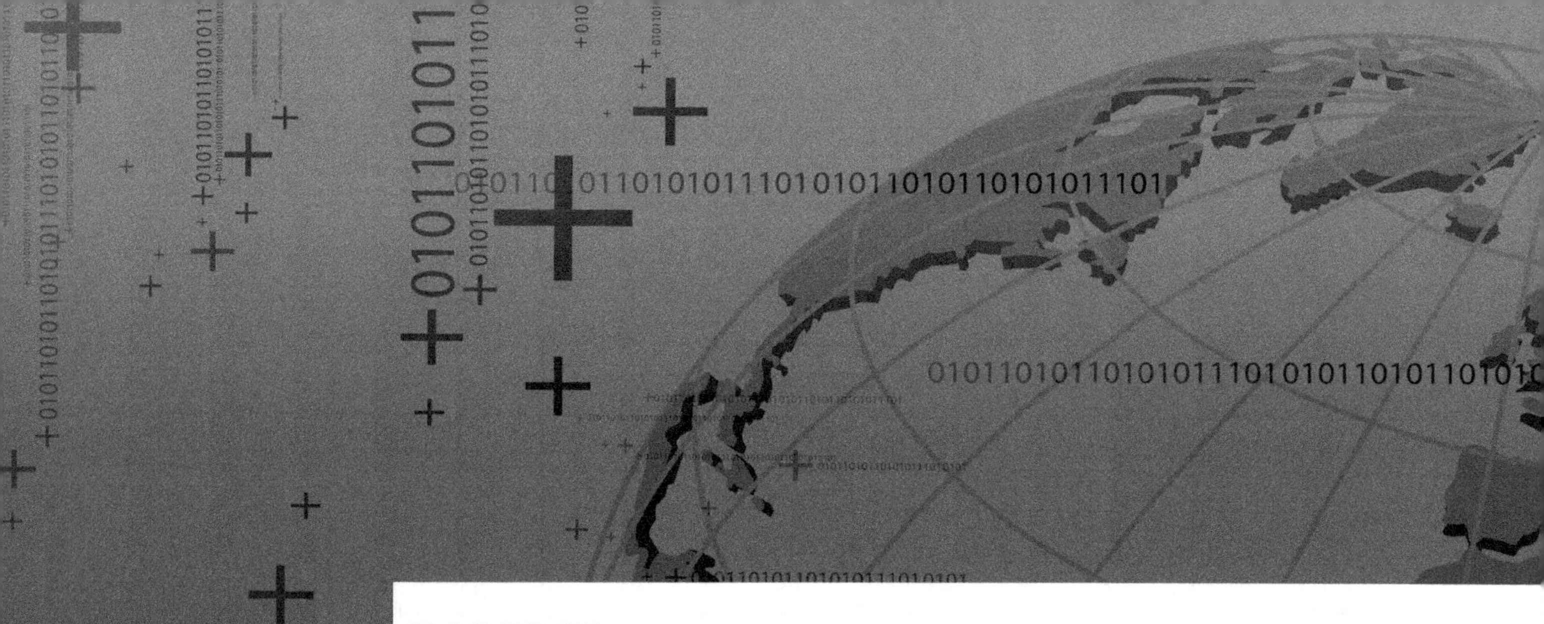

INCOME

4. National income
5. Real measures of income
6. Saving rate
7. Net lending/net borrowing

4. National income

Table 4.1. **Net national income per capita, OECD = 100**

Based on current PPPs

	2000	2001	2002	2003	2004	2005	2006	2007	2008	2009	2010	2011	2012	2013
Australia	107	109	110	113	110	110	108	110	110	117	115	116	113	114
Austria	115	112	115	115	114	111	114	114	119	119	118	119	118	116
Belgium	114	113	116	113	110	107	106	106	109	108	112	109	109	106
Canada	112	111	111	114	114	116	114	113	114	111	111	111	110	110
Chile	38 e	38 e	38 e	38 e	38 e	39 e	43 e	45 e	45 e	47 e	50 e	54 e	56 e	57 e
Czech Republic	57	60	61	63	64	64	65	68	68	68	65	66	66	65
Denmark	113	113	115	110	112	111	114	112	116	116	119	119	117	117
Estonia	38	40	43	47	49	53	57	61	62	57	56	62	65	68
Finland	102	104	105	102	106	103	104	108	112	109	107	107	104	101
France	106	108	108	104	101	101	100	101	103	104	103	103	99	98
Germany	103	104	103	104	105	104	107	108	110	111	113	117	115	114
Greece	80 e	84 e	88 e	88 e	88 e	85 e	86	85	88	89	80	69	66	65
Hungary	43	48	52	53	53	53	53	52	55	57	57	57	55	58
Iceland	118	120	123	117	119	116	107	110	90	89	86	91	94	107
Ireland	105	107	110	115	114	114	116	118	109	103	102	101	98	102
Israel[1]	94	93	91	83	84	80	78	81	79	81	83	85	85	87
Italy	106	109	105	103	99	97	98	98	99	99	96	95	91	88
Japan	98	98	98	98	97	97	94	96	93	90	93	91	93	93
Korea	70	72	76	76	77	77	77	80	80	81	85	83	83	84
Luxembourg	181	177	177	169	184	183	159	182	181	153	176	168	164	153
Mexico	41 e	40 e	40 e	41	41	42	43	43	44	44	45	46	46	45
Netherlands	128	126	127	124	123	121	127	130	130	131	127	129	126	125
New Zealand	80	82	84	84	82	79	79	80	78	87	84	85	85	90
Norway	144	146	142	143	151	163	171	169	183	168	170	174	180	175
Poland	43 e	43 e	44 e	44 e	44 e	45 e	46 e	49 e	53 e	58 e	59 e	61 e	62 e	63 e
Portugal	69	70	71	71	68	70	70	71	71	74	73	70	68	70
Slovak Republic	40	43	45	44	46	49	53	59	65	65	64	63	64	64
Slovenia	68	70	72	73	74	75	76	77	81 |	77	74	74	71	70
Spain	88	90	93	93	91	90	93	94	94	95	90	86	84	83
Sweden	117	114	115	119	119	114	118	124	126	120	122	123	121	120
Switzerland	139	133	131	133	130	132	136	132	126	142	148	143	145	144
Turkey	..	..	..	..	..	..	..	..	..	..	..	..	..	..
United Kingdom	112	114	117	117	118	118	116	113	112	112	107	105	104	104
United States	148	147	146	146	147	147	145	142	140	140	140	139	142	143
Euro area	..	..	82	81	80	79	80	81	81	80	79	79	77	76
OECD-Total	100	100	100	100	100	100	100	100	100	100	100	100	100	100
Brazil	..	..	..	..	..	..	..	..	..	..	..	..	..	..
China	..	..	..	..	..	..	..	..	..	..	..	..	..	..
India	..	..	..	..	10	10	11	12	12	13	..	..	..	..
Indonesia	..	..	..	..	..	..	..	..	..	..	..	..	..	..
Russian Federation	29 e	30 e	32	36	38	42	50	54	64	63	64	68	70 e	72 e
South Africa	31	30	32	32	32	33	33	34	34	35	34	34	34	34

Note: Detailed metadata:
http://stats.oecd.org/OECDStat_Metadata/ShowMetadata.ashx?Dataset=NAAG_2015_NOV15&Lang=en&Coords=[INDICATOR].[B5NHCPIXOE]

1. Information on data for Israel: http://dx.doi.org/10.1787/888932315602

Table 5.1. **Real net national income index**

Year 2010 = 100

	2000	2001	2002	2003	2004	2005	2006	2007	2008	2009	2010	2011	2012	2013
Australia	65	68	70	75	78	81	85	90	93	94	100	105	106	107
Austria	87	87	90	90	93	94	98	101	103	98	100	102	101	102
Belgium	90	89	91	91	93	95	96	100	99	95	100	98	99	98
Canada	80	81	82	86	91	95	98	100	102	94	100	105	106	108
Chile	55 e	57 e	58 e	61 e	68 e	75 e	83 e	89 e	89 e	90 e	100	107 e	113 e	117 e
Czech Republic	77	80	83	86	90	95	99	105	106	100	100	101	101	101
Denmark	88	89	89	90	94	98	103	102	101	96	100	101	100	102
Estonia	68	73	79	85	91	103	113	122	117	100	100	110	117	121
Finland	90	93	94	94	98	99	102	107	106	97	100	101	99	98
France	91	93	93	94	96	98	100	102	102	98	100	102	100	101
Germany	90	91	91	91	94	94	98	101	101	97	100	104	103	104
Greece	90 e	94 e	97 e	102 e	106 e	108 e	112	114	112	107	100	88	85	82
Hungary	81	85	92	96	101	104	107	106	106	100	100	101	98	103
Iceland	103	107	111	110	116	125	125	137	105	97	100	107	111	127
Ireland	84	88	91	96	98	104	109	113	109	99	100	101	99	104
Israel[1]	72	73	73	73	76	81	86	91	92	95	100	105	107	113
Italy	101	103	103	103	105	105	106	108	104	100	100	99	96	94
Japan	96	96	97	98	101	102	103	105	101	95	100	99	101	103
Korea	69	72	78	80	83	84	87	93	91	92	100	101	103	106
Luxembourg	81	81	81	80	89	95	84	101	99	81	100	96	96	95
Mexico	80 e	80 e	82 e	82	88	91	97	100	101	93	100	105	107	107
Netherlands	90	90	90	91	94	94	100	103	101	98	100	103	102	101
New Zealand	72	77	81	87	90	91	92	98	93	97	100	104	106	113
Norway	78	80	78	79	85	95	101	102	108	96	100	105	109	109
Poland	68	69	70	71	75	79	84	90	95	98	100	105	106	108
Portugal	95	97	98	98	99	99	99	102	100	98	100	98	94	95
Slovak Republic	65	67	70	70	75	82	89	99	105	97	100	100	102	103
Slovenia	79	83	86	89	92	95	100	107	109	101	100	100	95	95
Spain	82	86	89	92	94	97	100	103	103	101	100	97	95	95
Sweden	82	82	83	87	89	92	97	103	102	93	100	103	102	103
Switzerland	84	82	81	85	87	92	95	91	84	92	100	95	98	99
Turkey	..	..	..	..	..	..	..	..	..	..	..	..	..	..
United Kingdom	84	87	90	93	96	99	100	102	101	97	100	102	102	105
United States	87	88	89	91	95	98	101	101	99	97	100	102	106	107
Euro area	..	..	97	97	100	101	103	106	103	98	100	101	99	98
OECD-Total	..	..	..	..	..	..	..	..	..	..	..	..	..	..
Brazil	..	..	..	..	..	..	..	..	..	..	..	..	..	..
China	..	..	..	..	..	..	..	..	..	..	..	..	..	..
India	..	..	..	..	..	..	..	..	..	..	..	..	..	..
Indonesia	..	..	..	..	..	..	..	..	..	..	..	..	..	..
Russian Federation	59 e	59 e	61	66	74	83	92	102	109	90	100	111	114	113
South Africa	65	66	71	74	79	83	90	94	95	95	100	106	107	109

Note: Detailed metadata:
http://stats.oecd.org/OECDStat_Metadata/ShowMetadata.ashx?Dataset=NAAG_2015_NOV15&Lang=en&Coords=[INDICATOR].[B5NVIXOB]

1. Information on data for Israel: http://dx.doi.org/10.1787/888932315602

6. Saving rate

Table 6.1. **Net saving rate**

Percentage of GDP

	2000	2001	2002	2003	2004	2005	2006	2007	2008	2009	2010	2011	2012	2013
Australia	4.6	5.7	5.1	5.8	5.1	6.0	5.8	6.6	8.6	6.4	8.4	9.8	8.7	8.0
Austria	8.5	7.9	9.4	8.7	9.2	8.6	10.1	11.7	11.9	7.1	8.3	8.7	8.1	7.8
Belgium	11.0	9.7	9.6	8.9	9.7	9.4	9.6	10.5	8.4	3.2	7.0	4.7	4.9	3.4
Canada	8.7	7.0	6.0	6.8	9.0	9.8	9.6	9.0	8.3	0.9	2.8	4.7	4.4	4.3
Chile	8.4 e	8.6 e	8.8 e	8.6 e	10.9 e	11.6 e	13.9 e	13.2 e	10.3 e	10.2 e	11.9 e	10.2 e	9.5 e	8.1 e
Czech Republic	5.0	5.2	3.5	3.0	4.5	6.0	6.2	7.5	6.0	1.2	0.5	1.0	2.3	1.4
Denmark	8.4	8.9	7.9	7.5	8.0	9.4	11.0	9.6	8.5	4.0	6.5	7.6	6.7	8.0
Estonia	11.6	11.8	10.5	10.2	9.5	11.9	11.5	11.2	8.3	6.3	7.0	11.8	13.0	12.9
Finland	13.7	14.2	13.1	10.0	11.5	10.3	10.8	12.2	9.9	3.7	4.2	3.5	1.4	0.0
France	8.5	8.1	6.8	6.1	6.4	5.9	6.1	6.5	5.6	1.9	2.4	3.1	1.7	1.6
Germany	5.5	5.2	4.9	4.1	6.6	6.4	8.7	10.8	9.2	5.6	7.5	9.7	8.6	8.1
Greece	0.0 e	0.1 e	-0.6 e	-0.1 e	-0.1 e	-1.2 e	-0.9	-2.9	-6.1	-10.4	-11.1	-12.7	-9.6	-9.5
Hungary	1.4	2.7	2.2	0.2	1.7	1.1	2.4	1.0	1.7	1.7	2.9	3.3	2.7	6.8
Iceland	..	..	..	..	..	..	..	..	..	..	..	..	..	..
Ireland	13.4	11.8	10.8	12.4	12.6	11.9	11.6	8.8	3.9	-0.1	1.8	2.5	2.5	5.6
Israel[1]	7.8	6.8	4.6	4.9	6.1	8.4	10.0	9.3	6.8	7.5	8.1	9.5	9.1	9.9
Italy	5.7	6.0	5.8	5.1	5.4	4.6	4.7	5.0	2.7	0.3	-0.4	-0.3	-0.9	-0.4
Japan	7.2	5.3	4.3	4.8	5.6	5.7	5.9	6.8	4.2	-0.5	1.7	0.8	0.8	0.6
Korea	17.0	14.7	14.8	15.9	18.0	16.1	15.3	15.9	14.5	13.5	16.5	15.7	15.0	15.0
Luxembourg	..	..	..	..	..	..	..	..	..	..	..	..	..	..
Mexico	12.5 e	9.3 e	9.9 e	10.4	12.6	12.0	13.7	13.4	12.3	9.9	10.9	11.2	9.2	6.5
Netherlands	13.9	11.9	10.3	11.0	12.4	11.9	14.5	15.1	11.7	10.3	11.1	12.7	12.6	12.3
New Zealand	5.1	7.3	6.8	7.7	6.5	3.7	2.5	4.1	0.4	3.0	2.7	3.2	3.3	6.2
Norway	21.4	21.0	17.1	16.3	19.4	25.0	26.9	25.4	27.6	19.1	20.3	22.6	23.5	22.4
Poland	5.4	3.9	2.1	2.7	0.5	2.9	4.3	5.6	5.7	5.2	4.7	6.6	6.6	6.9
Portugal	2.5	2.3	1.5	0.1	-0.8	-2.9	-3.7	-3.0	-5.7	-6.4	-6.4	-4.7	-4.4	-2.2
Slovak Republic	2.7	2.1	1.0	-2.5	-0.3	0.6	1.2	4.8	4.1	-2.4	-0.5	-0.5	1.0	1.0
Slovenia	5.2	6.1	7.1	6.8	7.1	7.7	10.1	11.1	9.9	3.1	1.8	1.6	-0.3	2.1
Spain	8.8	8.8	9.3	9.8	8.6	7.7	7.3	6.6	4.8	3.9	2.8	1.3	1.9	2.8
Sweden	12.0	11.8	11.0	12.5	12.8	13.4	16.0	18.2	16.9	10.1	12.9	13.4	12.3	11.5
Switzerland	16.5	13.2	10.0	13.9	14.0	17.4	19.0	14.5	7.6	13.0	18.4	14.3	14.5	13.7
Turkey	..	..	..	..	..	..	..	..	..	..	..	..	..	..
United Kingdom	4.0	3.4	2.9	2.7	2.2	3.1	2.1	2.4	0.9	-1.7	0.2	1.2	-0.4	-0.9
United States	5.9	4.4	3.0	2.3	2.6	2.7	3.7	1.6	-0.6	-2.1	-0.8	-0.1	2.0	2.4
Euro area	..	..	7.2	6.5	7.2	6.7	7.1	8.1	5.6	2.8	3.7	4.4	3.7	3.5
OECD-Total	..	..	..	..	..	..	..	..	..	..	..	..	..	..
Brazil	..	..	..	..	..	..	..	..	..	..	..	..	..	..
China	..	..	..	..	..	..	..	..	..	..	..	..	..	..
India	..	..	..	..	22.5	23.6	24.9	27.1	22.1	23.7	..	..	..	..
Indonesia	..	..	..	..	..	..	..	..	..	..	..	..	..	..
Russian Federation	27.4 e	23.9 e	21.0	21.0	23.9	24.6	25.6	26.4	25.3	15.4	21.2	24.8	22.4	18.5
South Africa	2.8	2.6	4.0	3.4	3.5	3.2	3.4	3.1	4.3	4.2	4.8	4.5	2.5	1.3

Note: Detailed metadata:
http://stats.oecd.org/OECDStat_Metadata/ShowMetadata.ashx?Dataset=NAAG_2015_NOV15&Lang=en&Coords=[INDICATOR].[B8NS]

1. Information on data for Israel: http://dx.doi.org/10.1787/888932315602

Table 7.1. **Net lending/net borrowing by institutional sector**

Percentage of GDP

	Total			Corporations			General government			Households		
	2003	2008	2013	2003	2008	2013	2003	2008	2013	2003	2008	2013
Australia	-5.5	-3.5	-3.0	-1.6	-2.2	-3.5	0.8	-4.0	-2.6	-4.7	2.7	3.3
Austria	1.5	4.1	2.0	-1.4	-0.1	1.3	-1.8	-1.4	-1.3	4.7	5.7	1.9
Belgium	5.6	1.0	0.9	2.8	-0.8	2.7	-1.8	-1.1	-2.9	4.5	3.0	1.2
Canada	1.4	0.2	-3.2	5.0	3.9	1.9	0.1	-0.3	-2.7	-3.7	-3.4	-2.4
Chile	..	-3.6	-3.7	..	-8.1	-7.5	..	4.8	-0.4	..	-0.3	4.1
Czech Republic	-4.6	-4.0	1.1	-0.1	-3.1	0.4	-6.4	-2.1	-1.3	1.9	1.2	1.8
Denmark	4.1	2.7	7.2	5.4	4.0	9.1	-0.1	3.2	-1.3	-1.2	-4.5	-0.8
Estonia	-11.9	-7.7	3.1	-9.6	-4.3	2.4	1.8	-2.7	-0.1	-4.1	-0.2	1.3
Finland	4.9	2.8	-1.7	3.8	1.6	2.4	2.4	4.2	-2.5	-1.4	-2.9	-1.6
France	0.3	-1.4	-2.6	0.5	-0.9	-1.9	-3.9	-3.2	-4.1	3.7	2.7	3.3
Germany	1.7	5.5	6.7	0.2	0.3	2.1	-4.2	-0.2	-0.1	5.6	5.3	4.6
Greece	..	-14.9	0.3	..	4.8	21.0	..	-10.2	-12.4	..	-9.7	-7.8
Hungary	-8.4	-5.7	7.5	0.4	-1.4	7.2	-7.1	-3.6	-2.5	-1.6	-0.7	2.9
Iceland	..	..	..	..	..	..	-3.1	-13.1	-1.9	..	..	..
Ireland	0.8	-5.7	3.2	4.1	3.8	9.5	0.7	-7.0	-5.7	-7.1	-3.8	-0.1
Israel[1]	0.5	1.7	2.7	..	..	..	-7.3	-2.9	-4.2	..	..	..
Italy	-0.7	-2.8	1.0	0.5	-2.1	2.2	-3.4	-2.7	-2.9	2.3	2.0	1.7
Japan	2.4	2.8	0.5	7.8	2.5	7.9	-7.7	-1.9	-8.5	2.3	2.2	1.1
Korea	1.0	-0.2	5.4	0.7	-8.3	-1.9	-2.0	2.3	1.3	2.3	5.8	5.9
Luxembourg	..	..	..	..	..	..	0.5	3.3	0.7	..	..	..
Mexico	-1.1	-1.7	-2.0	-4.6	-2.4	-3.4	0.4	-0.2	0.1	3.2	0.9	1.3
Netherlands	6.7	5.2	10.7	9.0	7.0	9.8	-3.0	0.2	-2.4	0.7	-2.1	3.2
New Zealand	-2.8	-6.6	..	-0.2	-4.7	..	3.4	0.4	-0.4	-6.0	-2.3	..
Norway	12.3	15.6	10.0	2.5	-2.3	-0.7	7.2	18.7	10.8	2.6	-0.8	-0.2
Poland	-1.7	-5.8	1.0	1.7	0.8	7.5	-6.1	-3.6	-4.0	2.7	-2.9	-2.4
Portugal	-5.2	-11.4	2.3	-2.4	-9.3	3.5	-4.4	-3.8	-4.8	1.7	1.6	3.6
Slovak Republic	-6.7	-5.7	2.2	-2.9	-1.8	4.2	-2.7	-2.3	-2.6	-1.1	-1.6	0.7
Slovenia	-1.9	-4.6	4.5	-2.2	-7.6	13.4	-2.6	-1.4	-15.0	2.9	4.3	6.1
Spain	-2.9	-8.7	2.2	-3.0	-1.9	5.0	-0.4	-4.4	-6.9	0.4	-2.4	4.2
Sweden	6.6	8.4	5.5	5.6	1.5	-0.4	-1.3	2.0	-1.4	2.0	4.8	7.3
Switzerland	11.7	1.9	12.1	5.0	-8.2	-2.3	-2.4	2.0	-0.3	9.3	9.9	12.3
Turkey	..	..	..	..	..	..	..	-2.3	..	..	..	..
United Kingdom	-1.7	-3.6	-4.5	1.1	2.3	1.4	-3.4	-5.1	-5.7	0.6	-0.8	-0.2
United States	-4.4	-5.3	-1.3	1.7	-0.5	1.8	-5.9	-7.0	-5.3	-0.2	2.2	2.3
Euro area	0.5	-1.5	2.0	0.7	-1.1	2.0	..	..	..	2.9	1.7	2.8
OECD-Total	..	..	..	..	..	..	..	..	..	..	..	..
Brazil	..	..	..	..	..	..	..	..	..	..	..	..
China	2.0	8.8	..	-7.4	-9.4	..	-3.8	1.8	..	13.2	16.3	..
India	..	..	..	..	..	..	..	..	..	..	..	..
Indonesia	..	..	..	..	..	..	..	..	..	..	..	..
Russian Federation	7.2	4.7	0.4	0.4	-5.9	-3.1	1.7	7.3	0.3	5.2	3.3	3.3
South Africa	..	-5.5	-5.8	..	-2.2	-1.1	..	-1.7	-3.3	..	-1.6	-1.4

Note: Detailed metadata:
http://stats.oecd.org/OECDStat_Metadata/ShowMetadata.ashx?Dataset=NAAG_2015_NOV15&Lang=en&Coords=[INDICATOR].[B9S1S]

1. Information on data for Israel: http://dx.doi.org/10.1787/888932315602

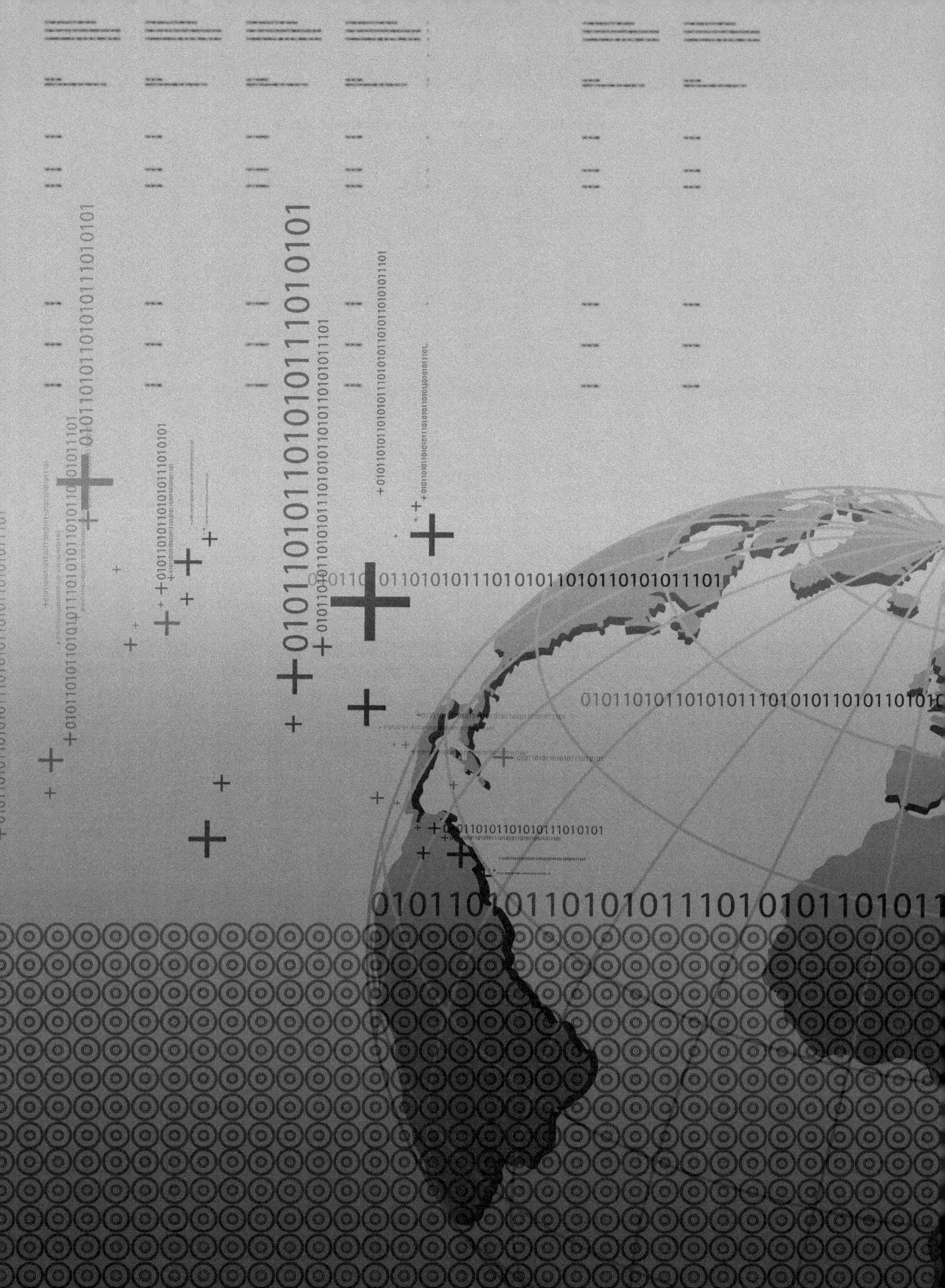

EXPENDITURE

8. Household consumption
9. General government final consumption
10. Investment
11. Exports and imports of goods and services

Table 8.1. Household final and actual individual consumption

Percentage of GDP

	Household final consumption							Actual individual consumption						
	2007	2008	2009	2010	2011	2012	2013	2007	2008	2009	2010	2011	2012	2013
Australia	56.3	54.4	55.4	53.9	53.7	55.0	55.5	66.8	65.2	66.5	64.8	64.7	65.9	66.2
Austria	52.4	52.2	53.8	53.6	53.5	53.6	53.8	64.0	64.0	66.4	66.1	65.7	65.9	66.1
Belgium	50.1	51.2	52.1	52.0	51.7	51.9	52.2	63.5	65.3	67.1	67.0	67.0	67.4	67.8
Canada	54.4	54.1	57.2	56.5	55.4	55.3	55.5	66.5 e	66.4 e	70.9 e	69.9 e	68.7 e	68.6 e	68.8 e
Chile	55.8	60.8	59.5	59.0	61.0	62.5	63.9	61.0 e	66.5	65.9	65.2	67.0	68.7	70.4
Czech Republic	46.3	47.7	48.9	49.2	49.3	49.4	49.8	55.8	57.1	59.3	59.6	59.5	59.6	60.0
Denmark	47.5	47.5	48.7	47.9	48.2	48.8	48.8	64.3	64.9	68.2	67.2	67.0	67.6	67.6
Estonia	53.4	54.1	53.4	52.2	50.6	50.6	51.2	62.3	64.5	65.4	63.6	61.0	60.7	61.4
Finland	48.8	49.6	52.6	53.2	53.7	54.6	54.9	62.5	63.9	68.6	69.1	69.6	71.1	71.5
France	54.9	55.3	56.2	56.1	55.7	55.7	55.6	69.3	69.7	71.6	71.5	71.0	71.0	71.0
Germany	55.1	55.3	57.4	56.1	55.3	55.7	55.4	66.1	66.5	69.8	68.3	67.3	67.8	67.8
Greece	64.8	67.4	68.1	69.4	69.9	69.9	70.9	75.0	77.9	79.5	80.3	80.8	80.3	80.6
Hungary	54.2	53.4	53.4	52.3	52.6	53.7	52.3	65.2	64.6	64.9	63.4	63.2	63.9	62.2
Iceland	56.4	52.7	51.2	51.2	51.7	53.4	52.5	71.7	68.3	67.4	67.0	67.3	68.7	68.0
Ireland	45.5	48.6	47.4	47.4	45.8	45.4	45.0	56.2	60.2	60.7	60.2	57.9	57.3	56.8
Israel[1]	57.2	58.0	56.6	57.2	57.1	55.5	55.5	67.6	68.6	67.4	68.1	67.9	66.5	66.9
Italy	59.3	59.6	60.7	61.0	61.5	61.6	61.0	70.5	71.0	72.8	73.0	73.0	73.0	72.4
Japan	57.3	58.3	60.1	59.3	60.3	60.7	61.1	67.4	68.7	71.4	70.6	72.2	72.8	73.3
Korea	52.4	52.4	51.7	50.3	51.0	51.4	50.9	59.2	59.6	59.2	57.4	58.3	58.9	58.6
Luxembourg	32.9	33.3	35.1	33.1	32.4	32.8	31.4	41.9	42.5	45.6	43.3	42.5	43.2	41.7
Mexico	66.2	66.9	66.8	67.1	66.4	67.4	68.7	71.3	72.2	72.5	72.8	72.0	73.1	74.8
Netherlands	45.6	45.1	45.3	44.7	44.9	44.9	44.9	60.9	60.8	62.6	62.3	62.3	62.6	62.3
New Zealand	56.7	57.6	57.9	57.6	58.1	58.6	56.9	67.7	69.6	70.1	69.9	70.4	70.9	68.7
Norway	40.5	38.4	42.2	42.0	40.3	39.7	40.2	53.0	50.7	56.9	56.5	54.6	53.9	54.7
Poland	60.5	61.9	61.7	61.6	61.5	61.6	60.9	70.5	72.4	72.4	71.8	71.3	71.3	70.8
Portugal	64.8	66.2	64.7	65.8	65.8	66.3	65.3	75.8	77.3	76.6	77.2	76.5	76.3	75.5
Slovak Republic	55.6	56.7	60.4	58.0	57.3	57.4	56.6	63.4	64.9	69.7	67.1	65.9	66.1	65.6
Slovenia	51.1	51.2	54.7	56.0	56.0	56.7	55.0	61.4	61.8	66.5	68.2	68.2	68.9	66.6
Spain	57.0	56.8	56.1	57.2	57.8	58.6	58.0	67.1	67.6	68.1	69.1	69.5	69.8	69.1
Sweden	44.3	44.6	47.1	46.4	46.3	46.5	46.7	62.0	62.5	66.1	64.6	64.4	65.1	65.5
Switzerland	54.2	53.8	55.2	54.5	53.9	54.3	54.3	59.8	59.3	61.3	60.5	60.0	60.7	60.6
Turkey	71.3	69.8	71.5	71.7	71.2	70.2	70.8	75.9 e	74.4 e	76.7 e	76.8 e	76.1 e	75.5 e	76.2 e
United Kingdom	63.5	64.2	64.7	64.7	64.5	65.0	65.0	75.7	76.9	78.6	78.3	77.6	78.0	77.6
United States	67.3	68.0	68.3	68.2	68.9	68.4	68.4	73.6	74.6	75.1	74.8	75.4	74.9	75.1
Euro area	55.2	55.5	56.6	56.3	56.1	56.3	55.9	..	..	..	..	..	..	..
OECD-Total	60.7	61.1	61.9	61.6	61.8	61.9	61.9	69.6 e	70.1 e	70.9 e	70.7 e	70.5 e	71.1 e	71.1 e
Brazil	59.9	59.8	62.0	60.2	60.3	..	..	..	..	..	67.8 e	68.0 e	..	..
China	36.2	35.6	36.3	35.1	35.7	36.7	37.3	..	..	..	..	..	..	..
India	57.0	58.4	57.7	..	..	..	..	59.9	61.5	61.5	..	..	..	..
Indonesia	59.9 e	57.2	57.2	56.2	55.4	56.4	57.3	..	..	..	59.7	58.8	59.9	60.9
Russian Federation	48.8	48.9	54.6	51.5	49.0	50.3	52.8	56.9	57.4	64.5	60.4	57.7	58.6	61.3
South Africa	61.5	60.0	59.5	59.0	59.4	60.5	60.6	69.7	68.8	68.9	68.7	68.8	69.7	70.0

Note: Detailed metadata:
http://stats.oecd.org/OECDStat_Metadata/ShowMetadata.ashx?Dataset=NAAG_2015_NOV15&Lang=en&Coords=[INDICATOR].[P31S14_S15S]

1. Information on data for Israel: http://dx.doi.org/10.1787/888932315602

Table 8.2. Household final consumption, volume

Annual growth rates in percentage

	2000	2001	2002	2003	2004	2005	2006	2007	2008	2009	2010	2011	2012	2013
Australia	3.3	3.1	4.3	5.1	4.5	3.2	4.8	4.7	0.1	2.3	3.7	2.5	1.9	2.2
Austria	3.1	1.3	0.8	1.7	2.3	2.2	2.1	1.1	0.8	0.6	1.0	1.3	0.6	0.1
Belgium	2.9	1.0	0.4	0.5	1.6	1.2	1.5	1.9	1.7	0.5	2.7	0.3	0.6	0.9
Canada	4.1	2.4	3.7	3.0	3.0	3.6	4.1	4.3	2.9	0.4	3.4	2.3	1.9	2.5
Chile	4.0	2.7	2.8	4.5	8.4	8.5	7.8	7.6	5.2	-0.8	10.8	8.9	6.1	5.9
Czech Republic	1.6	2.8	2.9	4.8	3.5	3.2	3.8	4.1	2.9	-0.7	1.0	0.3	-1.5	0.7
Denmark	0.4	0.2	1.4	1.3	4.6	3.7	2.9	1.8	0.5	-3.4	0.8	0.2	0.4	0.0
Estonia	7.2	6.5	9.4	9.1	7.7	9.3	12.7	9.0	-4.9	-15.3	-1.6	3.7	4.4	3.8
Finland	2.0	2.9	2.6	4.2	3.6	3.2	4.1	3.5	2.1	-2.7	3.1	2.9	0.3	-0.3
France	3.7	2.5	2.1	1.5	2.0	2.5	2.2	2.5	0.4	0.2	1.8	0.5	-0.2	0.4
Germany	2.1	1.6	-0.8	0.1	0.8	0.4	1.5	0.0	0.6	0.2	0.4	1.4	1.0	0.6
Greece	2.7	3.5	5.1	4.5	3.6	3.2	2.8	4.1	3.6	-1.7	-6.5	-9.7	-8.0	-2.3
Hungary	3.1	4.6	8.1	8.4	2.0	2.9	1.4	1.0	-1.2	-6.7	-2.8	0.8	-2.2	0.3
Iceland	4.2	-3.0	-0.8	6.7	7.4	10.7	2.5	6.7	-7.0	-9.2	-0.3	2.5	1.9	1.0
Ireland	10.6	4.6	3.7	2.9	3.7	7.2	6.7	6.7	0.1	-5.7	0.2	-0.5	-1.0	0.1
Israel[1]	8.4	4.0	1.6	0.2	5.3	3.4	5.0	8.3	1.4	1.0	4.8	3.4	2.2	3.9
Italy	2.3	0.6	0.0	0.8	1.0	1.3	1.4	1.2	-1.1	-1.6	1.2	0.0	-3.9	-2.7
Japan	0.4	1.6	1.2	0.5	1.2	1.5	1.1	0.9	-0.9	-0.7	2.8	0.3	2.3	2.1
Korea	9.1	5.7	8.9	-0.5	0.3	4.4	4.6	5.1	1.4	0.2	4.4	2.9	1.9	1.9
Luxembourg	5.0 e	2.4	4.4	2.0	0.7	1.9	3.3	2.4	1.4	1.0	1.7	2.2	2.7	0.9
Mexico	8.2 e	2.5 e	1.6 e	2.2 e	5.6	4.4	5.5	3.0	1.9	-6.5	5.7	4.8	4.9	2.2
Netherlands	3.7	2.1	1.1	-0.2	0.6	0.9	-0.3	1.9	0.9	-2.1	0.0	0.2	-1.2	-1.4
New Zealand	1.3	2.7	5.2	6.2	5.5	4.9	2.2	3.7	-1.5	1.7	2.0	2.7	2.5	2.9
Norway	4.2	2.1	3.1	3.2	5.4	4.4	5.0	5.3	1.7	0.0	3.8	2.3	3.5	2.1
Poland	2.9	2.0	3.9	1.6	4.2	2.4	4.7	6.4	6.1	3.4	2.7	3.1	0.7	0.2
Portugal	3.7	0.9	1.3	-0.3	2.6	1.6	1.5	2.5	1.4	-2.3	2.4	-3.6	-5.5	-1.2
Slovak Republic	1.9	5.0	5.7	2.9	5.0	5.8	6.0	7.5	6.0	-0.5	0.4	-0.6	-0.4	-0.8
Slovenia	0.8	2.4	2.5	3.4	3.0	2.2	1.2	6.4	2.4	0.9	1.3	0.0	-2.5	-4.1
Spain	4.6	3.7	3.0	2.4	4.0	4.0	3.8	3.3	-0.7	-3.6	0.3	-2.4	-3.5	-3.1
Sweden	5.2	0.7	2.6	2.3	2.8	2.8	2.7	3.8	0.2	0.4	3.9	1.9	0.8	1.9
Switzerland	1.8	2.1	0.3	0.4	1.8	1.5	1.5	2.3	1.5	1.3	1.6	0.8	2.7	2.2
Turkey	5.9	-6.6	4.7	10.2	11.0	7.9	4.6	5.5	-0.3	-2.3	6.7	7.7	-0.5	5.1
United Kingdom	5.1	3.7	4.1	3.6	3.5	3.1	1.9	3.0	-0.7	-3.1	0.0	0.1	1.8	1.9
United States	5.1	2.6	2.6	3.1	3.8	3.5	3.0	2.2	-0.3	-1.6	1.9	2.3	1.5	1.7
Euro area	3.0	2.0	0.9	1.1	1.8	1.9	2.1	1.8	0.3	-1.1	0.8	0.0	-1.2	-0.6
OECD-Total	4.1 e	2.2 e	2.4 e	2.4	3.1	3.0	2.8	2.5	0.2	-1.4	2.1	1.7	1.0	1.3
Brazil	..	0.7	1.2	-0.7	3.9	4.3	5.4	6.4	6.5	4.2	6.4	4.8	..	..
China	..	..	..	..	..	..	..	..	..	..	..	..	..	..
India	..	..	..	..	..	8.5	8.3	9.3	7.7	7.3	..	..	..	..
Indonesia	1.6	3.5	3.8	3.9	5.0	4.0	3.2	5.0	5.3	4.7	4.1	5.1	5.5	5.4
Russian Federation	7.1 e	9.3 e	8.3 e	7.5	11.9	11.7	12.0	14.2	10.4	-5.1	5.5	6.7	7.7	4.9
South Africa	4.1	3.5	3.2	2.8	6.2	6.1	8.8	6.5	1.2	-2.6	3.9	4.9	3.4	2.9

Note: Detailed metadata:
http://stats.oecd.org/OECDStat_Metadata/ShowMetadata.ashx?Dataset=NAAG_2015_NOV15&Lang=en&Coords=[INDICATOR].[P31S14_S15G]

1. Information on data for Israel: http://dx.doi.org/10.1787/888932315602

Table 8.3. Contribution to GDP growth by final demand components

Percentage

	Household consumption			General government consumption			Gross fixed capital formation			Change in inventories			Net exports of goods and services		
	2003	2008	2013	2003	2008	2013	2003	2008	2013	2003	2008	2013	2003	2008	2013
Australia	3.0	0.0	1.2	0.7	0.7	0.4	2.2	0.6	-0.4	0.5 e	-0.9 e	-0.4 e	-2.6	1.2	1.6
Austria	0.9	0.4	0.0	0.2	0.7	0.1	0.9	0.3	-0.1	0.1	-0.6	-0.6	-1.3	0.7	0.4
Belgium	0.3	0.8	0.5	0.3	0.6	0.0	-0.1	0.4	-0.4	0.1	0.1	-0.7	0.1	-1.3	0.7
Canada	1.7	1.6	1.4	0.6	0.9	0.1	1.1	0.4	0.1	0.7	-0.1	0.4	-2.2	-1.8	0.2
Chile	2.8	2.9	3.7	0.1	0.0	0.4	1.4	3.6	0.5	..	..	..	-0.7	-3.9	0.6
Czech Republic	2.4	1.3	0.4	1.3	0.2	0.5	0.5	0.8	-0.7	-0.6	-0.4	-0.6	0.0	0.8	0.0
Denmark	0.6	0.2	0.0	0.1	0.8	-0.1	0.0	-0.8	0.2	-0.5	-0.5	-0.2	0.2	-0.4	-0.3
Estonia	5.1	-2.6	1.9	0.7	0.7	0.3	5.4	-4.8	0.8	0.4	-3.2	-1.1	-3.3	5.0	0.2
Finland	2.1	1.0	-0.2	0.3	0.3	0.2	0.6	0.1	-1.2	0.0	-0.5	0.0	-1.7	-0.2	0.4
France	0.8	0.2	0.2	0.4	0.3	0.4	0.4	0.2	-0.1	-0.3	-0.2	0.2	-0.5	-0.3	0.0
Germany	0.1	0.3	0.4	0.1	0.6	0.1	-0.3	0.3	-0.3	0.4	-0.2	0.6	-1.0	0.0	-0.5
Greece	3.0	2.3	-1.6	0.6	-0.5	-1.4	3.6	-1.9	-1.2	1.0	-0.5	-0.2	-2.4	0.3	1.2
Hungary	4.5	-0.6	0.2	1.1	0.7	0.5	0.3	0.2	1.4	0.0	-0.2	-0.7	-2.1	0.7	0.5
Iceland	3.7	-4.0	0.5	0.5	1.1	0.3	1.9	-5.6	-0.2	-0.1	0.1	0.0	-3.2	9.7	3.7
Ireland	1.3	0.0	0.0	0.5	0.3	0.0	1.9	-3.3	-1.3	0.4	-0.6	0.3	0.6	2.5	3.0
Israel[1]	0.1	0.8	2.2	-0.8	0.5	0.9	-1.0	1.0	0.7	0.0	-0.6	-0.4	2.9	1.3	-0.1
Italy	0.5	-0.6	-1.7	0.2	0.2	-0.1	-0.1	-0.7	-1.2	0.1	-0.1	0.3	-0.7	0.2	0.9
Japan	0.3	-0.5	1.3	0.3	0.0	0.4	0.0	-0.9	0.7	0.3 e	0.2 e	-0.4 e	0.7	0.2	-0.3
Korea	-0.3	0.7	1.0	0.5	0.7	0.5	1.5	-0.3	1.0	0.3	0.2	-0.9	1.2	1.7	1.5
Luxembourg	0.8	0.4	0.3	0.6	0.3	0.7	1.0	1.5	-1.5	0.2	0.1	0.5	-2.3	-3.3	4.0
Mexico	1.5	1.3	1.5	0.1	0.3	0.2	0.1	1.1	-0.3	-1.0 e	0.3	-0.1	0.5	-1.7	-0.1
Netherlands	-0.1	0.4	-0.6	0.7	0.8	0.0	-0.3	0.9	-0.8	0.0	-0.3	-0.2	0.0	-0.1	1.1
New Zealand	3.6	-0.9	1.7	0.8	0.7	0.5	3.1	-1.8	2.2	0.1	-0.4	0.3	-3.0	0.2	-2.2
Norway	1.4	0.7	0.8	0.3	0.5	0.3	0.1	0.2	1.5	..	..	..	-0.4	-0.9	-2.4
Poland	1.1	3.7	0.1	0.6	0.9	0.4	0.2	1.8	-0.2	0.7	-1.3	-1.0	1.0	-1.2	1.9
Portugal	-0.1	1.0	-0.8	0.3	0.1	-0.3	-1.9	0.1	-0.8	-0.2	0.1	0.0	1.0	-1.0	0.8
Slovak Republic	1.7	3.4	-0.5	1.1	1.1	0.4	-0.9	0.4	-0.2	-1.8	1.2	0.6	5.4	-0.5	1.2
Slovenia	1.9	1.2	-2.3	0.5	0.9	-0.3	1.4	2.0	0.3	0.8	-0.9	0.2	-1.7	0.2	1.1
Spain	1.4	-0.4	-1.8	0.8	1.0	-0.6	1.9	-1.2	-0.5	-0.1	0.1	-0.2	-0.8	1.6	1.4
Sweden	1.1	0.1	0.9	0.2	0.3	0.3	0.5	0.1	0.1	0.2	-0.5	0.2	0.4	-0.6	-0.3
Switzerland	0.2	0.8	1.3	0.3	-0.2	0.2	-0.3	0.2	0.3	0.4	0.1	0.9	-0.7	-0.1	2.6
Turkey	6.9	-0.2	3.6	-0.3	0.2	1.0	2.4	-1.3	0.9	-0.5 e	0.3 e	1.4 e	-3.8	1.7	-2.9
United Kingdom	2.3	-0.4	1.2	0.8	0.4	0.1	0.3	-1.1	0.4	0.1	-0.5	0.7	-0.1	0.8	-0.5
United States	2.1	-0.2	1.2	0.3	0.4	-0.4	0.8	-1.1	0.5	0.0	-0.5	0.0	-0.4	1.1	0.2
Euro area	0.6	0.2	-0.4	0.4	0.5	0.0	0.3	-0.1	-0.5	..	..	..	-0.7	0.1	0.4
OECD-Total	1.5	0.1	0.8	0.3	0.4	0.0	0.6	-0.5	0.2	0.1	-0.2	0.0	-0.4	0.5	0.2
Brazil	..	..	..	..	..	..	..	..	..	..	..	..	..	..	..
China	..	..	..	..	..	..	..	..	..	..	..	..	..	..	..
India	..	4.4	..	..	1.1	..	..	0.5	..	..	-2.0	..	..	-2.6	..
Indonesia	2.5 e	3.2	3.1	0.8 e	0.9	0.6	0.1 e	3.4	1.7	66.3 e	3.5 e	-0.3	4.6 e	2.1	0.6
Russian Federation	3.8	5.1	2.5	0.4	0.6	0.2	2.5	2.0	0.1	0.5 e	0.9 e	-1.0 e	0.2	-3.0	0.5
South Africa	1.7	0.7	1.8	1.1	1.0	0.7	1.6	2.6	1.4	0.3	-0.7	-1.2	-2.2	-0.4	0.8

Note: Detailed metadata:
http://stats.oecd.org/OECDStat_Metadata/ShowMetadata.ashx?Dataset=NAAG_2015_NOV15&Lang=en&Coords=[INDICATOR].[P31S14_S15CG]

1. Information on data for Israel: http://dx.doi.org/10.1787/888932315602

Table 9.1. **General government final consumption expenditure**

Percentage of GDP

	Individual consumption							Collective consumption						
	2007	2008	2009	2010	2011	2012	2013	2007	2008	2009	2010	2011	2012	2013
Australia	10.5	10.8	11.1	10.9	11.0	10.9	10.8	6.6	6.7	6.9	7.0	6.9	6.9	6.9
Austria	11.6	11.9	12.6	12.4	12.2	12.3	12.3	7.1	7.3	8.0	7.9	7.6	7.5	7.4
Belgium	13.3	14.0	15.1	15.0	15.2	15.5	15.6	8.2	8.5	9.0	8.6	8.5	8.8	8.8
Canada	12.0 e	12.3 e	13.7 e	13.5 e	13.2 e	13.2 e	13.2 e	7.5 e	7.8 e	8.8 e	8.5 e	8.4 e	8.4 e	8.4 e
Chile	5.1 e	5.7	6.4	6.2	6.0	6.1	6.5	5.3 e	5.5	6.2	6.1	6.1	6.0	6.0
Czech Republic	9.4	9.4	10.4	10.3	10.2	10.2	10.2	9.6	9.7	10.3	10.2	9.5	9.2	9.4
Denmark	16.8	17.4	19.5	19.3	18.8	18.8	18.8	7.5	7.8	8.6	8.3	8.0	8.1	7.9
Estonia	8.9	10.4	12.1	11.4	10.4	10.1	10.2	7.1	8.2	9.0	8.7	8.2	8.2	8.5
Finland	13.7	14.3	16.0	15.9	15.9	16.5	16.6	7.1	7.4	8.2	8.0	7.8	7.9	8.2
France	14.3	14.5	15.4	15.4	15.2	15.4	15.4	7.9	7.9	8.5	8.4	8.4	8.5	8.6
Germany	11.0	11.2	12.4	12.2	12.0	12.1	12.4	6.5	6.6	7.2	6.9	6.7	6.9	6.8
Greece	10.2	10.5	11.4	10.9	10.9	10.4	9.7	10.4	10.2	11.9	11.3	10.9	11.3	10.7
Hungary	11.0	11.2	11.5	11.1	10.6	10.3	9.8	9.8	10.2	10.7	10.6	10.2	9.8	9.9
Iceland	15.3	15.6	16.1	15.8	15.5	15.3	15.4	7.6	7.9	8.7	8.9	9.2	9.2	8.9
Ireland	10.6	11.6	13.2	12.8	12.1	11.9	11.9	6.3	7.2	7.0	6.1	5.8	5.9	5.5
Israel[1]	10.4	10.6	10.7	10.8	10.8	11.0	11.4	12.2	12.0	11.7	11.5	11.3	11.2	11.1
Italy	11.2	11.4	12.1	12.0	11.4	11.4	11.4	7.7	8.0	8.5	8.4	8.2	8.1	8.2
Japan	10.1	10.5	11.4	11.3	11.9	12.1	12.2	8.0	8.1	8.6	8.4	8.5	8.3	8.4
Korea	6.8	7.1	7.5	7.1	7.4	7.5	7.6	7.2	7.5	7.7	7.4	7.2	7.3	7.4
Luxembourg	9.0	9.3	10.5	10.2	10.0	10.4	10.3	5.6	5.9	6.5	6.3	6.3	6.4	6.3
Mexico	5.0	5.3	5.7	5.7	5.7	5.8	6.0	5.5	5.6	6.3	6.0	5.9	6.1	6.2
Netherlands	15.2	15.6	17.4	17.6	17.4	17.7	17.4	8.0	8.3	9.1	8.9	8.6	8.6	8.7
New Zealand	11.0	12.0	12.2	12.3	12.3	12.3	11.9	7.4	7.9	7.6	7.5	7.4	7.1	7.1
Norway	12.5	12.3	14.7	14.5	14.3	14.2	14.5	6.3	6.3	7.0	6.9	6.8	6.7	6.8
Poland	10.0	10.4	10.7	10.2	9.8	9.8	9.9	8.0	8.2	8.2	8.9	8.3	8.2	8.3
Portugal	11.0	11.1	11.9	11.4	10.7	10.0	10.2	8.8	8.8	9.5	9.3	9.2	8.5	8.9
Slovak Republic	7.8	8.2	9.3	9.1	8.5	8.7	9.0	9.2	9.2	10.6	10.2	10.0	9.3	9.2
Slovenia	10.3	10.6	11.8	12.2	12.2	12.1	11.7	7.0	7.4	8.2	8.1	8.2	8.1	8.1
Spain	10.2	10.8	12.0	11.8	11.7	11.2	11.1	7.5	8.0	8.5	8.7	8.8	8.5	8.5
Sweden	17.6	17.9	18.9	18.2	18.1	18.6	18.8	6.4	6.7	7.3	7.0	7.0	7.4	7.5
Switzerland	5.6	5.5	6.1	6.0	6.1	6.3	6.3	4.8	4.7	4.8	4.7	4.7	4.7	4.7
Turkey	4.5 e	4.6 e	5.2 e	5.1 e	5.0 e	5.3 e	5.4 e	8.2 e	8.2 e	9.5 e	9.2 e	9.0 e	9.6 e	9.7 e
United Kingdom	12.2	12.8	13.9	13.6	13.2	13.0	12.6	7.8	8.1	8.4	8.1	7.8	7.8	7.5
United States	6.3	6.5	6.8	6.7	6.5	6.3	6.2	9.0	9.6	10.1	10.2	9.8	9.5	9.1
Euro area	..	..	..	..	..	..	..	..	..	..	..	..	..	..
OECD-Total	9.1 e	9.4 e	10.0 e	9.9 e	9.7 e	9.7 e	9.6 e	8.0 e	8.3 e	8.9 e	8.8 e	8.5 e	8.4 e	8.3 e
Brazil	..	..	..	7.5 e	7.7 e	..	..	..	..	..	11.5 e	11.0 e	..	..
China	..	..	..	..	..	..	..	..	..	..	..	..	..	..
India	2.9	3.2	3.8	..	..	..	..	7.4	7.9	8.2	..	..	..	..
Indonesia	..	..	..	3.5	3.4	3.5	3.6	..	..	..	5.6	5.7	5.7	5.9
Russian Federation	8.2	8.5	9.9	8.9	8.7	8.3	8.5	9.1	9.4	10.9	9.8	9.4	10.5	11.2
South Africa	8.2	8.8	9.4	9.7	9.4	9.2	9.4	9.6	9.9	10.4	10.5	10.5	10.7	10.9

Note: Detailed metadata:
http://stats.oecd.org/OECDStat_Metadata/ShowMetadata.ashx?Dataset=NAAG_2015_NOV15&Lang=en&Coords=[INDICATOR].[P3S13S]

1. Information on data for Israel: http://dx.doi.org/10.1787/888932315602

Table 10.1. **Gross fixed capital formation, volume**

Annual growth rates in percentage

	2000	2001	2002	2003	2004	2005	2006	2007	2008	2009	2010	2011	2012	2013
Australia	-7.9	9.0	12.6	8.5	6.3	9.3	5.1	9.5	2.1	2.1	3.8	11.5	2.0	-1.5
Austria	5.9	-1.3	-2.9	3.8	0.9	0.2	1.1	4.6	1.4	-7.3	-2.1	6.7	1.3	-0.3
Belgium	4.4	1.6	-4.3	-0.4	8.9	6.1	2.0	6.8	1.9	-6.6	-0.8	4.2	0.2	-1.7
Canada	5.1	4.8	1.0	5.2	8.4	9.2	6.3	3.2	1.6	-11.5	11.5	4.8	4.8	0.4
Chile	9.1	3.5	2.2	6.5	11.3	23.5	4.3	10.8	17.9	-12.1	11.6	15.0	11.6	2.1
Czech Republic	8.4	5.6	2.2	1.8	3.9	6.4	5.9	13.5	2.5	-10.1	1.3	1.1	-3.2	-2.7
Denmark	8.2	-0.5	-0.7	0.0	4.2	4.8	15.1	0.7	-3.3	-14.3	-4.0	0.3	0.6	0.9
Estonia	13.6	12.3	23.9	17.8	5.5	15.3	22.9	10.3	-13.1	-36.7	-2.6	34.4	6.7	3.2
Finland	6.2	1.8	-3.0	2.8	4.7	3.2	1.3	10.0	0.3	-12.5	1.1	4.1	-2.2	-5.2
France	6.6	2.3	-0.9	1.9	3.5	2.9	3.6	5.5	0.9	-9.1	2.1	2.1	0.2	-0.6
Germany	2.3	-2.5	-5.8	-1.3	0.0	0.7	7.5	4.1	1.5	-10.1	5.4	7.2	-0.4	-1.3
Greece	3.0	5.2	-0.3	15.1	3.0	-11.9	19.4	15.9	-7.2	-13.9	-19.3	-20.5	-23.5	-9.4
Hungary	5.2	2.7	7.8	1.3	7.6	3.6	0.7	4.2	1.0	-8.3	-9.5	-1.3	-4.4	7.3
Iceland	11.0	-3.2	-12.8	9.8	26.7	32.0	23.4	-11.2	-19.0	-47.8	-8.6	11.6	5.3	-1.0
Ireland	4.9	5.8	5.6	7.9	9.8	16.7	7.5	-0.2	-11.5	-16.9	-15.5	3.2	8.6	-6.6
Israel[1]	3.0	-2.4	-5.4	-5.3	2.0	3.2	6.5	10.1	5.1	-2.9	10.0	14.6	3.6	3.6
Italy	6.7	2.9	4.2	-0.3	2.1	1.7	3.2	1.6	-3.1	-9.9	-0.5	-1.9	-9.3	-6.6
Japan	0.7	-2.1	-4.9	0.2	0.4	0.8	1.5	0.3	-4.1	-10.6	-0.2	1.4	3.4	3.2
Korea	12.9	1.5	6.9	4.8	2.9	2.0	3.6	5.0	-0.9	0.3	5.5	0.8	-0.5	3.3
Luxembourg	-4.7 e	8.2	0.2	4.4	6.4	-3.3	4.7	14.9	7.3	-13.2	0.0	17.2	-0.3	-7.2
Mexico	11.4 e	-5.6 e	-0.6 e	0.4 e	7.5	5.9	8.7	6.0	5.0	-9.3	1.3	7.8	4.8	-1.6
Netherlands	1.9	0.6	-4.5	-1.6	0.2	3.1	7.2	6.5	4.1	-9.2	-6.5	5.6	-6.3	-4.4
New Zealand	-3.0	8.5	7.9	14.2	8.1	5.7	-2.0	7.8	-7.4	-9.3	3.3	5.5	7.2	10.4
Norway	-3.3	-0.6	-0.3	0.4	10.0	12.0	9.1	11.7	0.9	-6.8	-6.6	7.4	7.6	6.8
Poland	2.2	-10.6	-6.1	1.2	6.7	8.7	13.3	19.2	8.4	-1.9	-0.4	8.8	-1.8	-1.1
Portugal	4.1	1.0	-3.4	-7.3	0.1	0.1	-0.8	3.1	0.4	-7.6	-0.9	-12.5	-16.6	-5.1
Slovak Republic	-8.8	12.9	0.0	-3.2	4.7	16.5	9.1	8.9	1.6	-18.7	7.2	12.7	-9.2	-1.1
Slovenia	2.4	2.0	0.5	5.8	5.4	3.5	10.2	12.0	7.0	-22.0	-13.3	-4.9	-8.8	1.7
Spain	7.4	4.9	4.6	7.0	5.1	7.5	7.4	4.4	-3.9	-16.9	-4.9	-6.9	-7.1	-2.5
Sweden	6.5	2.5	-2.3	2.5	5.8	5.1	9.3	8.1	0.6	-13.4	6.0	5.7	-0.2	0.6
Switzerland	4.9	-2.0	0.2	-1.0	5.1	3.2	4.7	4.9	0.7	-7.5	4.4	4.3	2.9	1.2
Turkey	17.5	-30.0	14.7	14.2	28.4	17.4	13.3	3.1	-6.2	-19.0	30.5	18.0	-2.7	4.4
United Kingdom	3.2	-1.1	2.8	2.3	2.8	3.4	3.0	5.7	-5.9	-14.4	5.0	2.0	1.5	2.6
United States	6.3	-0.5	-1.8	3.9	5.8	5.6	2.2	-1.2	-4.8	-13.1	1.1	3.7	6.3	2.4
Euro area	4.7	1.0	-1.2	1.3	2.7	2.8	5.5	4.9	-0.6	-11.3	-0.4	1.6	-3.6	-2.6
OECD-Total	5.1 e	-0.6 e	-0.6 e	2.8 e	4.5	4.6	4.1	2.6	-2.2	-10.9	2.0	3.6	1.8	0.8
Brazil	..	..	..	..	..	..	..	..	..	..	..	..	..	..
China	..	..	..	..	..	..	..	..	..	..	..	..	..	..
India	..	..	..	..	..	16.2	13.8	16.2	1.5	7.3	..	..	..	..
Indonesia	16.7	6.5	4.7	0.6	14.7	10.9	2.6	9.3	11.9	3.9	6.7	8.9	9.1	5.3
Russian Federation	16.6 e	10.9 e	3.1 e	13.9	12.0	10.2	17.9	21.1	9.7	-14.7	6.4	9.2	7.0	0.6
South Africa	3.9	2.8	3.5	10.2	12.9	11.0	12.1	13.8	12.8	-6.7	-3.9	5.7	3.6	7.6

Note: Detailed metadata:
http://stats.oecd.org/OECDStat_Metadata/ShowMetadata.ashx?Dataset=NAAG_2015_NOV15&Lang=en&Coords=[INDICATOR].[P51G]

1. Information on data for Israel: http://dx.doi.org/10.1787/888932315602

Table 10.2. **Gross fixed capital formation by asset**

Percentage of total GFCF

	Dwellings		Other buildings and structures		Transport equipment		Machinery and equipment and weapon system		Cultivated biological resources		Intellectual property products	
	2002	2012	2002	2012	2002	2012	2002	2012	2002	2012	2002	2012
Australia	23.6	16.7	25.1	44.9	8.5	7.1	23.1	15.0	1.2	1.0	10.9	10.8
Austria	19.2	19.1	29.8	28.6	9.8	8.9	25.2	24.0	0.2	0.1	15.7	19.2
Belgium	22.9	26.1	19.3	24.3	10.0	7.7	32.7	24.7	0.2	0.2	14.9	17.0
Canada	27.7	28.8	27.2	39.5	6.3	3.7	23.9	15.4	..	..	14.9	12.6
Chile	..	13.7	..	39.5	34.0	38.5	..	..	..	0.9	..	7.3
Czech Republic	10.7	14.2	32.0	28.9	12.5	9.2	35.4	33.4	0.6	0.2	8.8	14.0
Denmark	20.6	21.6	24.5	21.9	11.4	7.9	25.0	21.0	0.0	0.0	18.6	27.6
Estonia	8.3	10.8	40.9	37.4	16.2	12.0	30.6	32.0	0.5	0.3	3.4	7.5
Finland	23.5	28.2	29.0	27.4	5.4	5.2	21.1	17.8	0.2	0.1	20.9	21.3
France	25.8	27.8	25.9	28.2	7.4	6.2	18.9	15.6	0.2	0.2	21.8	22.0
Germany	28.0	28.8	20.8	20.3	8.0	9.2	..	..	0.0	0.1	16.1	17.6
Greece	34.3	24.5	22.3	33.0	15.3	8.7	21.0	21.5	0.2	0.4	6.9	11.9
Hungary	19.3	10.5	31.3	33.7	7.8	9.0	30.9	32.6	1.4	0.9	9.2	13.3
Iceland	23.8	15.8	37.5	28.1	9.7	15.6	17.7	26.9	1.3	1.4	10.1	12.2
Ireland	36.0	9.6	26.8	18.3	10.9	27.0	12.0	9.6	-0.1	0.2	14.4	35.2
Israel[1]	24.9	30.0	20.4	19.6	7.7	7.3	23.2	21.3	0.2	0.3	23.6	21.6
Italy	23.0	27.4	27.6	25.3	7.6	4.8	29.3	28.2	0.3	0.2	12.3	14.1
Japan	16.7	14.2	35.1	32.3	8.1	10.0	31.9	33.7	..	..	8.2	9.7
Korea	15.6	11.0	37.1	38.6	8.9	8.7	24.3	22.8	..	..	14.1	19.0
Luxembourg	11.0	15.0	46.6	33.2	16.2	26.1	..	..	0.1	0.3	10.1	9.8
Mexico	..	27.4	..	37.4	..	9.0	..	24.2	..	0.1	..	1.8
Netherlands	26.3	18.5	28.3	29.6	5.6	6.7	22.0	21.9	0.3	0.2	17.4	23.0
New Zealand	25.1	24.1	23.2	30.2	12.2	7.1	27.1	24.0	..	..	12.4	14.5
Norway	..	..	..	..	..	..	..	..	..	..	..	..
Poland	14.8	13.4	36.8	44.2	9.1	8.0	32.6	27.7	0.3	0.2	6.5	6.5
Portugal	28.6	18.6	34.2	37.9	8.8	4.5	..	20.3	1.3	1.6	6.8	17.1
Slovak Republic	12.0	11.0	29.3	31.2	12.2	10.4	35.5	37.4	4.1	1.9	6.9	8.1
Slovenia	12.3	13.2	37.3	33.1	8.1	6.6	30.3	30.7	0.6	0.4	11.4	16.0
Spain	36.1	25.8	29.9	30.8	8.1	7.4	18.2	21.3	0.4	0.5	7.2	14.2
Sweden	13.4	15.2	21.3	24.6	6.3	6.6	29.2	26.7	0.3	0.3	29.4	26.6
Switzerland	14.6	19.8	20.9	18.3	6.0	7.6	35.3	28.1	0.1	0.1	23.1	26.1
Turkey	48.6	44.3	..	..	..	..	51.4	55.7	..	..	..	..
United Kingdom	18.5	20.2	30.3	31.7	7.2	3.6	23.0	21.0	0.3	0.5	20.6	23.0
United States	23.8	14.4	21.1	23.6	7.5	8.6	25.0	27.0	..	..	22.7	26.5
Euro area	27.1	26.1	25.8	26.0	8.0	7.4	23.8	22.1	0.2	0.2	15.0	18.2
OECD-Total	..	..	..	..	..	..	..	..	..	..	..	..
Brazil	..	..	..	..	..	..	..	..	..	..	..	..
China	..	..	..	..	..	..	..	..	..	..	..	..
India	..	..	..	..	..	..	..	..	..	..	..	..
Indonesia	..	72.9	..	..	..	6.4	..	13.0	..	5.6	..	2.1
Russian Federation	..	12.9	..	43.1	..	9.2	..	26.8	..	0.1	..	2.7
South Africa	13.1	10.2	21.6	35.9	11.1	10.7	48.3	37.9	1.4	0.8	4.6	4.4

Note: Detailed metadata:
http://stats.oecd.org/OECDStat_Metadata/ShowMetadata.ashx?Dataset=NAAG_2015_NOV15&Lang=en&Coords=[INDICATOR].[P51N1111SP51]

1. Information on data for Israel: http://dx.doi.org/10.1787/888932315602

Table 10.3. **Gross fixed capital formation by institutional sector**

Percentage of total GFCF

	Corporations				General government				Households			
	2000	2004	2008	2012	2000	2004	2008	2012	2000	2004	2008	2012
Australia	48.7	50.2	55.6	60.3	13.0	10.5	12.4	11.8	38.2	39.2	32.0	27.9
Austria	63.9	66.7	63.7	63.5	10.2	10.0	13.8	12.8	25.9	23.3	22.5	23.8
Belgium	63.1	64.5	62.9	63.0	10.8	9.7	8.7	11.0	26.1	25.8	28.3	26.0
Canada	55.7	48.3	48.1	50.9	14.9	15.5	16.7	16.5	29.4	36.2	35.2	32.7
Chile	..	..	66.9	75.4	..	..	9.7	8.8	..	..	23.3	15.8
Czech Republic	68.2	66.2	64.7	67.8	13.6	16.6	17.1	14.8	18.2	17.2	18.2	17.4
Denmark	59.2	58.2	57.1	56.4	12.9	13.6	13.1	21.1	27.9	28.2	29.9	22.5
Estonia	71.7	69.3	62.8	62.7	16.5	13.9	19.9	23.5	11.8	16.9	17.3	13.7
Finland	56.8	52.8	58.9	52.9	15.3	17.5	14.7	17.9	27.9	29.6	26.3	29.3
France	55.1	52.5	54.3	55.2	18.3	18.6	16.7	18.0	26.6	28.9	28.9	26.8
Germany	58.3	59.4	61.2	57.6	10.0	10.2	10.1	11.2	31.7	30.4	28.7	31.2
Greece	..	..	31.0	34.9	..	..	20.6	20.7	..	..	48.3	44.4
Hungary	65.2	57.6	63.9	65.7	14.0	15.8	13.8	19.3	20.8	26.6	22.3	15.0
Iceland	..	..	..	..	..	..	..	..	..	..	..	..
Ireland	47.6	42.7	42.1	73.8	14.6	12.9	20.9	10.8	37.8	44.5	37.0	15.4
Israel[1]	..	..	..	..	9.0	8.7	7.9	7.3	..	..	..	..
Italy	52.6	51.3	50.2	51.1	14.0	14.5	14.0	13.9	33.5	34.2	35.8	34.9
Japan	59.7	62.5	69.7	68.3	20.2	17.5	13.4	15.0	20.2	20.0	16.9	16.7
Korea	62.6	60.9	67.5	68.2	17.2	18.3	16.9	16.1	20.1	20.8	15.6	15.7
Luxembourg	..	..	..	..	..	..	..	..	..	..	..	..
Mexico	..	58.6	54.6	57.0	..	7.7	11.5	11.0	..	33.7	33.9	32.0
Netherlands	53.6	46.4	48.2	55.9	16.4	18.9	17.9	19.8	30.0	34.7	34.0	24.3
New Zealand	67.6	62.7	64.4	66.2	14.8	16.3	18.9	16.7	17.5	21.0	16.7	17.1
Norway	61.6	55.7	62.1	58.6	17.2	19.3	17.0	17.4	21.1	25.0	20.9	24.0
Poland	71.2	56.5	55.9	52.2	7.9	15.9	21.3	24.3	20.9	27.6	22.8	23.5
Portugal	51.2	51.5	60.4	60.8	16.5	19.0	16.3	15.6	32.4	29.5	23.3	23.6
Slovak Republic	62.3	68.4	67.0	64.1	13.4	11.8	12.8	14.2	24.3	19.8	20.1	21.7
Slovenia	64.3	64.0	62.4	59.8	13.5	15.1	15.9	21.1	22.2	20.9	21.6	19.1
Spain	58.2	55.0	56.1	67.7	14.0	13.9	15.8	12.4	27.7	31.1	28.1	19.9
Sweden	72.8	68.2	69.9	69.1	17.8	19.0	17.5	20.1	9.4	12.8	12.6	10.8
Switzerland	67.5	66.9	69.7	70.3	12.4	12.6	11.8	12.8	20.1	20.5	18.5	16.9
Turkey	..	..	..	..	..	..	..	..	..	..	..	..
United Kingdom	65.3	51.7	54.2	56.0	9.3	14.1	17.1	17.2	25.4	34.2	28.7	26.8
United States	53.4	44.5	51.7	54.0	15.6	17.1	19.2	18.9	31.0	38.4	29.1	27.1
Euro area	..	55.0	56.0	58.1	..	14.2	14.3	14.2	..	30.7	29.7	27.6
OECD-Total	..	..	..	..	..	..	..	..	..	..	..	..
Brazil	..	..	..	..	..	..	..	..	..	..	..	..
China	69.0	62.2	69.1	64.5	8.8	11.6	11.5	10.6	22.1	26.1	19.5	24.8
India	..	..	..	..	..	..	..	..	..	..	..	..
Indonesia	..	..	..	..	..	..	..	..	..	..	..	..
Russian Federation	..	64.1	66.3	68.5	..	16.2	9.7	13.3	..	19.7	24.0	18.2
South Africa	..	..	70.1	74.2	..	..	15.5	15.2	..	..	14.3	10.6

Note: Detailed metadata:
http://stats.oecd.org/OECDStat_Metadata/ShowMetadata.ashx?Dataset=NAAG_2015_NOV15&Lang=en&Coords=[INDICATOR].[P51S11_S12SP51]

1. Information on data for Israel: http://dx.doi.org/10.1787/888932315602

Table 11.1. **Exports of goods and services, volume**

Annual growth rates in percentage

	2000	2001	2002	2003	2004	2005	2006	2007	2008	2009	2010	2011	2012	2013
Australia	8.3	-0.8	0.2	1.2	3.3	2.6	3.9	3.6	1.8	5.1	0.9	5.0	6.0	5.8
Austria	13.5	5.7	4.1	0.4	8.8	6.5	7.5	7.4	2.3	-15.0	13.8	6.0	1.7	0.8
Belgium	12.4	0.3	3.7	1.6	6.2	5.0	5.3	5.7	1.7	-9.4	10.3	6.7	1.8	1.6
Canada	9.1	-3.0	1.2	-1.7	5.5	2.2	0.9	1.1	-4.5	-13.1	6.9	4.6	2.6	2.0
Chile	5.1	6.9	2.0	6.7	14.0	2.8	5.1	7.2	-0.7	-4.5	2.3	5.5	0.1	3.4
Czech Republic	14.8	9.5	0.9	8.8	29.7	18.2	14.3	11.0	4.2	-9.8	14.8	9.3	4.3	0.0
Denmark	12.6	3.4	3.6	-0.4	2.6	8.1	9.8	3.6	3.2	-9.5	1.9	7.3	0.1	0.8
Estonia	-7.0	6.3	2.8	10.2	17.3	19.9	9.5	12.6	0.9	-20.3	24.0	24.2	6.2	4.7
Finland	16.1	1.3	3.7	-1.2	8.7	6.9	10.1	9.1	6.6	-20.1	6.2	2.0	1.2	1.1
France	12.7	2.9	1.9	-1.1	5.1	3.5	5.6	2.8	0.4	-11.3	9.0	6.9	2.5	1.7
Germany	13.8	5.7	4.3	1.9	11.4	6.7	12.3	9.3	1.9	-14.3	14.5	8.3	2.8	1.6
Greece	22.2	0.1	-7.3	-0.7	18.6	3.3	5.2	10.6	3.5	-18.5	4.9	0.0	1.2	2.2
Hungary	25.0	8.8	5.8	6.3	18.0	12.9	19.5	16.1	6.9	-11.4	11.3	6.6	-1.8	6.4
Iceland	3.9	6.7	3.4	0.9	8.2	7.1	-4.7	23.3	3.3	8.3	1.0	3.4	3.6	6.7
Ireland	19.8	8.9	5.7	0.8	7.7	6.3	7.0	9.6	-0.1	-1.1	6.4	2.1	2.1	2.5
Israel[1]	23.4	-11.7	-2.1	8.1	17.6	4.7	5.0	10.4	5.8	-11.9	15.0	8.9	0.9	0.1
Italy	11.9	2.7	-2.8	-1.3	6.2	3.4	8.2	6.2	-3.1	-18.1	11.8	5.2	2.3	0.8
Japan	12.6	-7.0	7.9	9.5	14.0	6.2	9.9	8.7	1.4	-24.2	24.4	-0.4	-0.2	1.5
Korea	17.2	-2.3	13.0	13.9	20.6	7.8	12.1	12.7	7.5	-0.3	12.7	15.1	5.1	4.3
Luxembourg	12.6 e	5.5	2.1	2.8	10.9	5.5	13.0	8.9	6.0	-12.0	8.3	5.4	0.2	6.9
Mexico	16.3 e	-3.6 e	1.4 e	2.7 e	9.1	5.7	7.7	3.6	-1.3	-11.8	20.5	8.2	5.8	2.2
Netherlands	12.7	1.4	0.5	1.6	8.9	5.6	7.0	5.6	1.8	-8.9	10.5	4.4	3.8	2.1
New Zealand	6.1	3.3	7.5	2.7	3.2	-0.4	3.5	3.9	-2.7	4.0	2.8	2.3	3.0	0.3
Norway	3.2	4.3	-0.3	-0.1	1.0	0.5	-0.8	1.4	0.1	-4.1	0.7	-0.8	1.4	-3.0
Poland	23.6	3.1	4.8	14.1	4.9	9.7	15.6	10.2	7.0	-6.3	12.9	7.9	4.6	6.1
Portugal	8.4	2.3	3.1	3.3	4.5	0.5	12.4	7.3	-0.3	-10.2	9.5	7.0	3.4	7.0
Slovak Republic	7.5	10.6	7.0	18.4	20.9	12.9	22.9	14.6	3.0	-16.8	15.7	12.0	9.3	6.2
Slovenia	12.6	7.2	7.8	3.2	13.0	11.4	14.1	13.6	4.2	-16.6	10.2	6.9	0.6	3.1
Spain	10.5	3.7	1.4	3.4	4.3	1.8	4.9	8.3	-0.8	-11.0	9.4	7.4	1.1	4.3
Sweden	11.7	0.7	1.3	4.2	10.7	6.6	8.7	4.5	2.0	-14.5	11.9	6.1	1.0	-0.8
Switzerland	12.2	0.0	-2.0	-1.0	9.5	6.5	6.3	11.4	3.9	-10.0	12.8	4.9	1.1	15.2
Turkey	16.0	3.9	6.9	6.9	11.2	7.9	6.6	7.3	2.7	-5.0	3.4	7.9	16.3	-0.2
United Kingdom	9.6	2.1	2.4	2.8	5.1	8.1	12.4	-1.6	1.3	-8.8	5.8	5.8	0.7	1.2
United States	8.6	-5.8	-1.7	1.8	9.8	6.3	9.0	9.3	5.7	-8.8	11.9	6.9	3.4	2.8
Euro area	13.1	3.7	2.1	1.0	8.2	5.0	8.5	7.1	1.0	-12.8	11.3	6.7	2.7	2.1
OECD-Total	12.2 e	0.3 e	2.2 e	2.9 e	9.5	6.0	8.8	7.1	2.2	-10.9	11.6	6.7	3.1	2.6
Brazil	..	..	..	..	..	..	..	..	..	..	..	..	..	..
China	..	..	..	..	..	..	..	..	..	..	..	..	..	..
India	..	..	..	..	..	25.8	20.0	5.9	14.4	-5.5	..	..	..	..
Indonesia	26.5	0.6	-1.2	5.9	13.5	16.6	9.4	8.5	9.5	-2.0	15.3	14.8	1.6	4.2
Russian Federation	9.5 e	4.2 e	10.3 e	12.6	11.8	6.5	7.3	6.3	0.6	-4.7	7.0	0.3	1.1	4.6
South Africa	8.3	2.4	1.0	0.1	2.8	8.6	7.5	7.8	1.5	-17.0	7.7	4.3	0.1	4.6

Note: Detailed metadata:
http://stats.oecd.org/OECDStat_Metadata/ShowMetadata.ashx?Dataset=NAAG_2015_NOV15&Lang=en&Coords=[INDICATOR].[P6G]

1. Information on data for Israel: http://dx.doi.org/10.1787/888932315602

Table 11.2. **Imports of goods and services, volume**

Annual growth rates in percentage

	2000	2001	2002	2003	2004	2005	2006	2007	2008	2009	2010	2011	2012	2013
Australia	-1.1	1.4	13.2	13.3	12.4	7.9	10.2	14.5	-3.7	6.4	10.3	11.6	0.7	-2.1
Austria	10.2	5.2	0.3	3.5	8.0	5.4	5.9	5.6	0.9	-12.0	12.0	6.2	1.1	0.0
Belgium	13.1	-0.7	0.9	1.5	6.3	6.2	4.6	5.9	3.6	-9.1	9.6	7.3	1.4	0.8
Canada	8.5	-4.9	1.8	4.2	8.5	7.3	5.3	5.8	0.8	-12.4	13.6	5.7	3.7	1.3
Chile	9.9	4.5	2.0	9.6	18.3	17.3	11.4	14.3	11.2	-16.2	25.5	16.0	4.8	1.7
Czech Republic	14.5	11.2	4.8	8.6	26.1	12.8	11.5	12.8	3.2	-11.0	14.9	6.7	2.7	0.1
Denmark	13.7	2.4	6.4	-1.0	7.1	11.0	14.2	5.7	4.3	-12.4	0.9	7.1	0.9	1.5
Estonia	-5.4	12.4	13.3	14.0	16.1	16.7	20.7	13.0	-6.2	-30.6	21.2	27.2	11.7	4.5
Finland	14.9	1.4	4.3	4.1	8.1	11.2	6.7	7.4	7.9	-16.9	6.5	6.0	1.6	0.0
France	15.4	2.4	1.9	0.9	6.2	6.3	5.6	5.7	1.3	-9.4	8.9	6.3	0.7	1.7
Germany	10.9	0.8	-2.5	5.7	7.9	5.8	11.1	6.2	2.2	-9.6	12.9	7.0	-0.3	3.1
Greece	20.2	1.0	-3.4	7.4	4.4	0.9	13.3	15.5	1.3	-20.4	-3.4	-9.4	-9.1	-1.9
Hungary	23.1	5.8	8.7	9.5	17.3	7.8	15.5	13.9	6.0	-14.7	10.1	4.5	-3.5	6.3
Iceland	7.8	-10.0	-2.7	10.3	13.7	28.8	9.8	-2.3	-20.3	-22.4	4.4	6.8	4.6	0.2
Ireland	19.6	7.5	3.3	0.2	8.3	10.5	10.6	7.3	-2.7	-3.3	3.5	-1.5	2.9	0.0
Israel[1]	12.0	-5.5	-1.2	-0.7	11.9	3.5	3.3	11.0	2.4	-14.0	15.0	10.4	2.3	0.5
Italy	10.3	2.1	0.7	1.5	4.7	3.0	7.8	5.4	-3.7	-12.9	12.4	0.5	-8.1	-2.5
Japan	10.7	0.9	0.3	3.9	7.9	4.2	4.5	2.3	0.3	-15.7	11.1	5.9	5.3	3.1
Korea	21.8	-3.6	15.0	10.6	12.3	7.8	12.4	11.6	3.2	-6.8	17.3	14.3	2.4	1.7
Luxembourg	10.5 e	6.4	0.4	5.4	11.2	5.8	12.6	7.1	9.4	-13.3	8.6	7.5	1.5	5.7
Mexico	21.5 e	-1.6 e	1.5 e	0.7 e	9.7	7.7	10.2	5.9	4.4	-17.6	20.5	8.0	5.5	2.5
Netherlands	11.4	2.0	0.4	1.7	7.1	5.3	7.8	5.6	2.2	-7.7	9.3	3.5	2.7	0.9
New Zealand	-1.1	4.3	7.3	13.2	13.4	4.9	-1.7	10.9	-3.5	-9.3	11.5	6.6	1.3	8.0
Norway	2.0	1.7	1.0	1.2	9.0	7.9	9.1	10.0	3.2	-10.0	8.3	4.0	3.1	4.3
Poland	15.5	-5.3	2.8	9.6	8.1	6.3	18.1	15.8	9.4	-12.4	14.0	5.8	-0.3	1.7
Portugal	5.5	1.1	-0.2	-0.4	7.6	2.2	7.5	5.4	2.5	-9.9	7.8	-5.8	-6.3	4.7
Slovak Republic	6.6	18.9	5.8	8.0	21.6	15.3	19.5	9.4	3.6	-18.8	14.7	9.6	2.5	5.1
Slovenia	6.6	3.6	5.6	6.5	14.0	7.3	12.4	16.8	3.8	-18.8	6.8	5.0	-3.7	1.7
Spain	9.5	3.5	3.6	5.9	10.1	7.0	8.2	8.6	-5.6	-18.3	6.9	-0.8	-6.2	-0.3
Sweden	11.7	-1.7	-1.3	3.8	6.6	7.0	8.2	7.6	3.8	-14.1	12.8	7.3	0.5	-0.1
Switzerland	7.9	1.0	-2.3	0.4	3.9	9.8	3.2	5.8	4.9	-3.8	8.1	9.2	-2.6	13.4
Turkey	21.8	-24.8	20.9	23.5	20.8	12.2	6.9	10.7	-4.1	-14.3	20.7	10.7	-0.4	9.0
United Kingdom	9.6	4.8	5.5	2.7	6.7	6.6	10.2	-1.3	-1.7	-9.2	8.3	0.6	2.9	2.8
United States	13.0	-2.8	3.7	4.5	11.4	6.3	6.3	2.5	-2.6	-13.7	12.7	5.5	2.2	1.1
Euro area	12.0	2.2	0.4	3.2	7.5	5.8	8.4	6.6	0.7	-11.5	9.9	4.3	-0.8	1.3
OECD-Total	12.5 e	-0.1 e	3.0 e	4.6 e	9.5	6.7	8.3	5.9	0.4	-11.9	12.0	5.8	1.0	2.0
Brazil	..	..	..	..	..	..	..	..	..	..	..	..	..	..
China	..	..	..	..	..	..	..	..	..	..	..	..	..	..
India	..	..	..	..	..	32.5	21.3	10.2	22.7	-1.8	..	..	..	..
Indonesia	25.9	4.2	-4.2	1.6	26.7	17.8	8.6	9.1	10.0	-9.3	16.6	15.0	8.0	1.9
Russian Federation	32.4 e	18.7 e	14.6 e	17.3	23.3	16.6	21.3	26.2	14.8	-30.4	25.8	20.3	8.7	3.8
South Africa	5.3	0.2	5.3	8.1	15.5	10.9	18.3	9.4	2.8	-17.7	10.8	10.5	6.0	1.8

Note: Detailed metadata:

http://stats.oecd.org/OECDStat_Metadata/ShowMetadata.ashx?Dataset=NAAG_2015_NOV15&Lang=en&Coords=[INDICATOR].[P7G]

1. Information on data for Israel: http://dx.doi.org/10.1787/888932315602

Table 11.3. Exports of goods and services

Percentage of GDP

	2000	2001	2002	2003	2004	2005	2006	2007	2008	2009	2010	2011	2012	2013
Australia	22.1	20.7	18.9	17.0	18.1	19.6	19.9	19.8	22.5	19.5	21.2	21.3	19.9	20.9
Austria	43.4	44.7	45.3	44.6	46.9	48.6	50.8	52.5	53.2	44.9	51.0	53.7	53.8	53.2
Belgium	71.9	71.0	70.3	68.6	70.4	73.5	75.7	77.5	79.7	69.3	76.4	81.6	82.3	82.2
Canada	44.4	42.2	40.3	37.0	37.5	37.0	35.5	34.3	34.5	28.4	29.1	30.6	30.2	30.2
Chile	30.5	32.2	32.6	35.5	39.8	40.3	43.9	45.2	41.5	37.2	38.1	38.1	34.3	32.4
Czech Republic	48.3	49.1	45.2	47.1	57.4	62.3	65.3	66.6	63.4	58.8	66.2	71.6	76.6	77.3
Denmark	44.9	45.6	45.4	43.9	43.8	47.4	50.5	51.3	53.8	46.7	49.7	52.9	54.0	54.3
Estonia	61.6	61.3	58.3	57.4	61.5	65.9	63.5	63.2	66.8	60.8	75.1	86.5	86.6	86.8
Finland	42.1	39.7	39.1	37.3	38.6	40.3	43.2	44.0	45.1	36.3	38.7	39.2	39.5	39.0
France	28.2	27.8	27.0	25.6	25.9	26.4	27.2	27.1	27.4	24.1	26.0	27.8	28.5	28.5
Germany	30.8	31.9	32.6	32.6	35.4	37.7	41.2	43.0	43.5	37.8	42.3	44.8	46.0	45.5
Greece	23.7	22.8	20.1	18.5	20.7	21.3	21.2	22.5	23.4	19.0	22.1	25.5	28.7	30.6
Hungary	66.8	64.9	58.1	56.4	59.7	62.8	74.3	78.3	79.7	74.8	82.3	87.2	86.8	88.0
Iceland	32.5	37.4	36.0	33.0	32.7	30.5	31.1	33.4	41.5	49.8	53.7	56.6	57.0	55.7
Ireland	94.5	95.4	90.5	80.7	80.5	79.7	79.0	80.8	84.2	93.6	103.1	101.2	107.2	106.7
Israel[1]	35.6	31.3	32.9	34.7	39.2	40.8	40.7	40.4	38.5	33.3	35.0	36.1	36.9	33.2
Italy	25.6	25.7	24.5	23.4	24.1	24.6	26.2	27.4	27.0	22.5	25.2	27.0	28.6	28.9
Japan	10.9	10.4	11.3	11.9	13.2	14.3	16.2	17.7	17.7	12.7	15.2	15.1	14.7	16.2
Korea	35.0	32.7	30.8	32.7	38.3	36.8	37.2	39.2	50.0	47.5	49.4	55.7	56.3	53.9
Luxembourg	147.5	148.7	142.2	139.6	152.7	161.1	175.6	184.2	189.0	166.5	179.0	185.6	189.2	195.6
Mexico	27.7 e	24.7 e	24.0 e	24.9	26.2	26.6	27.6	27.7	27.9	27.3	29.9	31.3	32.7	31.8
Netherlands	66.5	63.8	60.8	59.7	63.5	66.6	69.3	70.3	71.6	63.2	72.0	77.4	81.9	82.6
New Zealand	35.7	35.4	32.8	29.8	29.5	28.2	29.6	29.4	32.4	29.0	30.5	30.8	29.2	29.3
Norway	45.7	45.0	40.4	39.6	41.1	43.4	44.7	43.3	45.9	39.2	39.8	41.3	40.6	38.8
Poland	27.2	27.2	28.8	33.4	34.6	34.9	38.2	38.8	38.3	37.6	40.0	42.5	44.4	46.3
Portugal	28.2	27.4	26.9	26.8	27.3	26.7	29.9	31.0	31.1	27.1	29.9	34.3	37.7	39.5
Slovak Republic	54.1	57.8	57.5	62.2	68.7	72.3	81.3	83.5	80.2	67.8	76.6	85.3	91.8	93.8
Slovenia	50.0	51.7	52.2	50.9	55.0	59.6	64.7	67.6	66.1	57.2	64.3	70.4	73.3	75.2
Spain	28.6	27.9	26.5	25.4	25.2	24.7	24.9	25.7	25.3	22.7	25.5	28.9	30.6	32.0
Sweden	44.1	43.8	42.1	41.2	43.4	45.9	48.2	48.3	49.8	44.5	46.2	46.7	46.3	43.8
Switzerland	52.2	50.9	49.0	48.2	51.6	53.9	56.7	61.6	63.0	57.4	64.2	65.8	67.3	72.3
Turkey	20.1	27.4	25.2	23.0	23.6	21.9	22.7	22.3	23.9	23.3	21.2	24.0	26.3	25.6
United Kingdom	26.3	26.1	25.0	24.6	24.4	25.7	27.7	25.6	27.7	26.8	28.6	30.7	30.1	30.0
United States	10.7	9.7	9.1	9.0	9.6	10.0	10.7	11.5	12.5	11.0	12.4	13.6	13.6	13.6
Euro area	35.0	35.1	34.4	33.4	34.9	36.2	38.2	39.4	39.8	34.8	38.9	41.8	43.6	43.9
OECD-Total	23.0 e	22.5 e	21.9 e	21.5	22.7	23.4	24.9	25.9	27.0	24.0	26.3	28.3	28.7	28.7
Brazil	10.2	12.4	14.2	15.2	16.5	15.2	14.4	13.3	13.5	10.9	10.7	11.5	..	..
China	23.3	22.6	25.1	29.6	34.1	37.1	39.1	38.4	35.0	26.7	29.4	28.5	27.3	26.2
India	..	..	..	..	17.6	19.3	21.1	20.4	23.8	19.8	..	..	..	..
Indonesia	39.1 e	37.2 e	31.2 e	29.0 e	30.7 e	32.5 e	29.6 e	28.1 e	28.4	23.6	24.3	26.3	24.6	24.0
Russian Federation	44.1 e	36.9 e	35.2	35.2	34.4	35.2	33.7	30.2	31.3	27.9	29.2	30.3	29.5	28.6
South Africa	27.2	29.4	31.8	26.9	25.5	26.4	29.3	31.2	35.6	27.9	28.6	30.4	29.7	31.0

Note: Detailed metadata:
http://stats.oecd.org/OECDStat_Metadata/ShowMetadata.ashx?Dataset=NAAG_2015_NOV15&Lang=en&Coords=[INDICATOR].[P6S]

1. Information on data for Israel: http://dx.doi.org/10.1787/888932315602

Table 11.4. **Imports of goods and services**

Percentage of GDP

	2000	2001	2002	2003	2004	2005	2006	2007	2008	2009	2010	2011	2012	2013
Australia	22.0	20.6	21.0	19.7	20.8	21.4	21.5	22.4	22.4	20.4	20.1	21.5	21.1	21.3
Austria	42.0	42.9	41.7	41.9	44.0	45.5	47.4	48.3	49.0	41.9	47.7	51.2	51.2	50.2
Belgium	69.2	67.7	64.8	63.4	65.7	69.9	72.0	73.7	79.2	67.0	74.7	81.1	81.7	80.9
Canada	38.8	36.6	36.0	33.2	33.0	33.1	32.8	32.2	32.7	29.9	31.0	31.8	32.1	31.8
Chile	28.7	30.5	30.3	31.5	30.5	31.8	29.6	31.9	39.5	29.6	31.7	34.9	34.5	33.1
Czech Republic	50.2	50.4	46.5	48.3	56.6	60.0	62.5	64.1	61.2	54.9	63.1	67.7	71.7	71.5
Denmark	38.2	38.5	38.9	37.1	38.3	41.8	46.6	48.5	50.6	42.4	43.6	47.4	48.6	48.5
Estonia	64.9	65.3	65.8	65.9	69.4	71.0	73.6	72.1	70.7	55.8	68.7	80.8	85.6	84.6
Finland	32.9	30.6	30.2	30.8	32.4	36.4	39.0	39.2	41.4	34.3	37.4	40.0	40.9	39.8
France	27.1	26.5	25.4	24.5	25.3	26.8	28.0	28.4	29.1	25.5	27.9	30.4	30.7	30.4
Germany	30.6	30.1	28.2	28.9	30.4	32.7	35.9	36.4	37.5	32.9	37.1	39.9	39.9	39.5
Greece	34.6	33.4	30.2	29.6	29.2	29.6	31.7	35.0	36.0	28.8	30.7	32.3	33.1	33.4
Hungary	70.5	66.1	60.1	60.4	63.7	65.1	75.4	77.7	79.3	70.8	77.0	81.1	80.1	80.7
Iceland	39.5	38.3	34.5	36.0	38.1	42.4	48.3	42.5	43.7	40.8	43.5	48.6	50.9	47.7
Ireland	80.7	79.7	73.3	65.6	66.1	68.8	71.0	72.6	75.6	80.1	87.1	83.3	90.0	87.4
Israel[1]	35.6	33.6	35.7	35.4	39.0	40.7	40.4	41.1	38.8	30.4	32.8	35.4	35.6	31.4
Italy	24.8	24.5	23.7	22.9	23.5	24.8	27.1	27.8	27.7	23.1	27.1	28.6	27.6	26.5
Japan	9.4	9.8	9.9	10.2	11.3	12.9	14.9	16.1	17.5	12.3	14.0	16.0	16.7	19.0
Korea	32.9	31.2	29.3	30.7	34.5	34.4	36.4	38.1	50.0	42.9	46.2	54.3	53.5	48.9
Luxembourg	121.7	125.8	117.8	116.8	128.9	136.5	145.3	152.1	159.4	136.5	147.1	154.8	158.9	161.9
Mexico	29.5 e	26.6 e	25.6 e	26.3	28.0	28.1	28.9	29.3	30.2	28.8	31.1	32.6	33.8	32.7
Netherlands	60.0	57.2	54.0	52.9	55.6	57.9	60.5	61.4	63.0	55.8	63.6	68.8	72.3	71.6
New Zealand	32.8	31.8	29.8	28.0	29.2	29.6	30.0	29.2	32.6	26.6	28.2	29.2	28.5	27.6
Norway	28.9	28.3	27.3	26.9	27.9	27.4	27.7	29.9	29.0	27.9	28.6	28.5	27.7	28.6
Poland	33.6	30.8	32.2	36.0	37.2	35.9	40.1	42.1	43.2	38.3	42.1	44.5	44.9	44.4
Portugal	39.2	37.6	35.2	33.7	35.5	35.8	38.2	38.6	40.8	34.0	37.4	38.6	38.2	38.5
Slovak Republic	56.6	65.8	64.7	64.1	71.4	76.9	85.3	84.6	83.1	69.3	78.0	86.2	88.1	89.6
Slovenia	53.7	52.8	51.2	51.2	56.4	60.2	64.7	68.9	68.0	55.4	62.9	68.5	69.1	69.3
Spain	31.6	30.2	28.5	27.7	29.0	29.7	30.8	31.7	30.4	23.8	26.8	29.2	29.1	28.7
Sweden	38.2	37.5	35.8	34.9	35.8	38.7	40.6	41.3	43.5	38.7	40.7	42.0	41.4	39.3
Switzerland	46.1	45.3	42.3	41.5	42.6	46.7	48.2	50.3	52.4	49.9	53.5	57.3	56.9	60.2
Turkey	23.1	23.3	23.6	24.0	26.2	25.4	27.6	27.5	28.3	24.4	26.8	32.6	31.5	32.2
United Kingdom	28.2	28.5	27.9	27.2	27.2	28.4	30.3	28.3	30.7	29.2	31.3	32.3	32.2	32.0
United States	14.3	13.1	13.0	13.4	14.7	15.5	16.2	16.5	17.4	13.8	15.8	17.3	17.1	16.6
Euro area	34.3	33.6	32.0	31.5	32.9	34.8	37.1	38.0	38.9	33.4	37.5	40.4	40.9	40.5
OECD-Total	23.8 e	23.0 e	22.4 e	22.4	23.7	24.8	26.4	27.0	28.6	24.3	27.0	29.4	29.3	29.0
Brazil	12.4	14.6	13.4	12.9	13.1	11.8	11.7	12.0	13.7	11.3	11.8	12.2	..	..
China	20.9	20.5	22.6	27.4	31.4	31.5	31.4	29.6	27.3	22.3	25.6	25.9	24.5	23.8
India	..	..	..	..	19.3	22.0	24.2	24.4	28.9	25.0	..	..	..	..
Indonesia	29.7 e	30.0 e	25.7 e	22.6 e	26.9 e	29.2 e	25.0 e	24.8 e	28.0	21.1	22.4	23.9	25.0	24.8
Russian Federation	24.1 e	24.2 e	24.5	23.9	22.2	21.5	21.0	21.5	22.1	20.5	21.1	21.7	22.3	22.7
South Africa	24.3	25.4	28.0	24.5	25.6	26.7	31.0	32.5	37.2	27.5	27.4	29.6	31.0	33.2

Note: Detailed metadata:
http://stats.oecd.org/OECDStat_Metadata/ShowMetadata.ashx?Dataset=NAAG_2015_NOV15&Lang=en&Coords=[INDICATOR].[P7S]

1. Information on data for Israel: http://dx.doi.org/10.1787/888932315602

Table 11.5. **Terms of trade**

Ratio of export prices to import prices

	2000	2001	2002	2003	2004	2005	2006	2007	2008	2009	2010	2011	2012	2013
Australia	52.8	53.6	54.3	58.4	64.0	70.9	76.0	80.3	86.4	82.9	100.0	100.4	90.4	87.0
Austria	102.1	102.3	103.1	103.9	103.4	102.5	101.4	101.0	99.6	101.8	100.0	98.3	97.9	98.0
Belgium	103.0	103.1	103.7	103.4	102.5	101.7	101.0	101.2	98.5	101.6	100.0	98.8	98.5	98.6
Canada	87.5	86.5	84.5	89.1	93.1	96.4	97.4	100.3	104.6	95.3	100.0	103.5	102.5	102.5
Chile	54.7	53.1	54.0	58.0	69.9	77.2	95.9	97.6	81.1	85.2	100.0	99.7	95.2	92.3
Czech Republic	97.0	99.8	103.3	103.4	104.6	102.2	100.2	101.3	100.0	102.0	100.0	98.5	97.9	99.0
Denmark	92.6	92.5	93.5	94.2	95.0	96.7	96.3	95.9	97.5	97.7	100.0	97.9	98.0	99.4
Estonia	85.6	89.5	93.0	94.6	95.3	97.1	99.4	101.4	101.6	102.0	100.0	100.4	99.8	101.0
Finland	111.8	113.7	113.8	112.3	109.9	106.2	102.9	102.8	100.8	102.1	100.0	98.4	97.4	97.8
France	100.1	100.4	102.1	102.1	101.2	99.8	98.3	99.5	98.8	101.4	100.0	97.6	97.3	98.3
Germany	99.3	99.4	101.4	102.6	102.8	101.0	99.4	99.5	97.9	102.4	100.0	97.3	96.9	98.3
Greece	98.1	98.9	100.3	102.1	102.0	101.0	101.0	101.5	100.3	99.6	100.0	99.5	97.9	99.5
Hungary	101.2	101.8	103.1	102.7	102.6	100.8	99.4	99.9	98.6	99.9	100.0	98.6	97.6	98.2
Iceland	116.5	116.6	117.3	112.4	110.7	111.8	115.2	111.1	103.7	95.7	100.0	97.3	94.4	92.6
Ireland	105.4	106.3	107.1	106.1	105.5	104.4	103.7	101.6	98.9	101.5	100.0	99.1	97.7	97.8
Israel[1]	107.3	107.1	106.8	104.5	101.8	100.2	99.3	97.5	95.0	102.6	100.0	96.7	99.6	102.1
Italy	101.9	103.1	104.8	106.5	105.5	102.2	99.1	100.1	98.0	104.2	100.0	97.4	95.9	97.4
Japan	135.9	136.0	134.8	131.0	125.4	116.2	108.0	103.6	93.8	106.2	100.0	92.4	91.0	89.2
Korea	118.1	115.0	117.2	115.3	112.0	107.9	103.2	103.1	96.1	99.8	100.0	95.5	95.3	97.3
Luxembourg	97.4	95.8	96.3	97.7	97.1	97.0	99.0	97.6	98.7	100.0	100.0	100.5	101.1	101.4
Mexico	92.4 e	92.9 e	94.0 e	92.9	92.6	95.5	98.6	99.6	103.0	98.8	100.0	99.9	100.1	100.9
Netherlands	98.2	99.4	100.1	100.4	100.0	100.4	100.6	100.5	100.3	101.1	100.0	98.5	98.2	98.8
New Zealand	82.4	85.0	83.9	89.2	93.2	92.5	91.2	99.0	97.1	92.7	100.0	101.5	97.0	108.3
Norway	78.8	77.1	72.9	73.4	79.2	91.5	102.4	99.9	112.6	93.7	100.0	109.1	112.2	111.5
Poland	95.2	95.2	94.5	94.1	97.6	98.7	98.7	100.3	98.7	102.0	100.0	98.5	97.2	98.3
Portugal	97.6	97.9	99.5	99.5	99.1	97.9	98.5	99.0	96.7	101.4	100.0	98.0	98.6	100.3
Slovak Republic	108.2	107.0	106.9	106.5	106.2	106.1	104.6	103.4	101.7	100.6	100.0	98.7	97.5	97.0
Slovenia	100.7	102.4	104.4	105.0	103.8	101.6	101.0	102.0	100.7	104.2	100.0	98.6	97.6	98.4
Spain	92.9	94.5	97.3	98.6	98.2	99.0	99.2	99.8	97.4	102.4	100.0	96.3	94.6	95.7
Sweden	105.0	103.6	101.9	102.0	100.7	98.9	98.6	100.0	99.6	100.5	100.0	99.2	99.3	99.6
Switzerland	99.1	99.3	102.1	103.7	102.6	100.9	99.7	98.7	97.8	100.1	100.0	99.5	98.9	98.9
Turkey	101.0	98.9	101.6	105.1	107.4	107.0	102.3	104.3	101.0	103.2	100.0	95.1	92.7	96.5
United Kingdom	99.1	100.0	100.9	102.2	102.6	101.9	101.1	100.4	96.9	98.6	100.0	99.0	99.7	101.4
United States	104.3	106.3	106.9	105.4	104.2	102.5	101.8	101.6	96.2	101.5	100.0	98.8	99.1	100.0
Euro area	100.3	100.9	102.4	103.0	102.5	101.3	100.0	100.3	98.7	102.0	100.0	97.7	97.2	98.2
OECD-Total	100.4 e	101.2 e	102.0 e	102.2	102.0	101.0	100.3	100.5	97.7	100.6	100.0	97.9	97.4	98.1
Brazil	..	..	..	..	..	..	..	..	..	..	..	..	..	..
China	..	..	..	..	..	..	..	..	..	..	..	..	..	..
India	..	..	..	..	..	..	..	..	..	..	..	..	..	..
Indonesia	119.2	116.4	110.1	112.3	111.2	109.4	115.5	111.1	99.7	101.8	100.0	102.0	96.7	93.0
Russian Federation	67.8 e	64.2 e	63.1	67.3	78.0	90.1	99.9	103.4	119.6	83.9	100.0	120.8	123.6	116.8
South Africa	73.3	74.2	76.1	79.3	80.8	82.1	86.2	88.8	89.6	94.4	100.0	104.3	102.9	97.4

Note: Detailed metadata:
http://stats.oecd.org/OECDStat_Metadata/ShowMetadata.ashx?Dataset=NAAG_2015_NOV15&Lang=en&Coords=[INDICATOR].[TOT]

1. Information on data for Israel: http://dx.doi.org/10.1787/888932315602

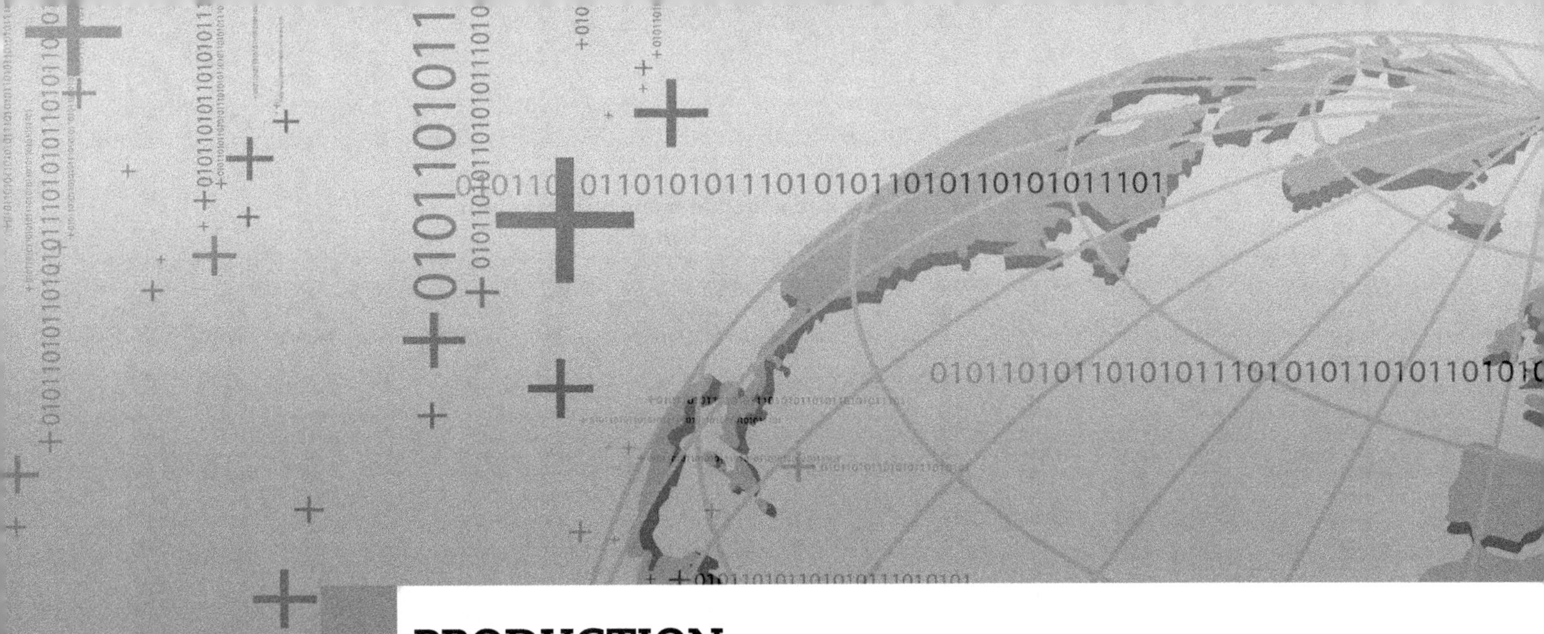

PRODUCTION

12. Value added

Table 12.1. Gross value added at basic prices, volume

Annual growth rates in percentage

	2000	2001	2002	2003	2004	2005	2006	2007	2008	2009	2010	2011	2012	2013
Australia	2.3	3.8	2.9	4.2	3.3	3.1	3.8	3.9	2.0	2.1	2.3	3.9	2.6	2.6
Austria	3.9	1.5	1.6	0.9	2.9	2.2	3.7	3.7	1.7	-4.2	2.0	3.1	0.6	0.5
Belgium	3.5	1.3	1.7	0.9	3.2	2.2	2.4	3.4	1.2	-2.3	2.5	2.1	0.1	0.0
Canada	5.4	1.4	2.6	2.1	3.1	3.0	2.8	2.2	1.0	-3.0	3.5	2.7	1.8	..
Chile	5.0	3.3	2.7	3.6	6.7	5.9	5.6	4.7	3.0	-0.8	5.1	5.6	5.3	4.2
Czech Republic	4.5	3.1	2.1	3.0	4.9	6.6	7.5	5.2	3.6	-5.5	2.9	2.0	-0.9	-0.5
Denmark	4.7	0.8	0.3	0.4	1.9	1.7	3.7	0.4	-0.2	-4.6	1.6	1.3	-0.6	-0.6
Estonia	9.8	6.0	5.6	7.5	5.7	9.4	9.9	7.3	-3.3	-15.3	3.8	7.8	4.9	1.7
Finland	6.3	2.7	1.3	1.2	3.8	2.6	3.9	5.9	0.9	-8.8	3.0	2.0	-1.9	-1.3
France	3.8	2.0	1.1	0.7	3.0	1.4	2.4	2.5	0.4	-2.7	1.8	2.1	0.4	0.7
Germany	3.3	2.0	0.3	-0.6	1.6	0.7	3.7	3.9	1.2	-6.1	4.3	3.6	0.5	0.3
Greece	3.3	3.8	3.9	6.2	5.8	0.4	4.4	2.7	-0.2	-3.4	-5.7	-9.0	-6.4	-2.6
Hungary	4.1	3.9	4.5	3.9	4.9	4.3	3.8	0.3	0.7	-6.6	0.8	1.9	-1.8	2.5
Iceland	4.5	3.7	-0.2	3.3	7.4	6.3	5.9	9.7	1.6	-4.4	-2.5	2.8	1.5	3.3
Ireland	9.5	5.9	5.4	2.9	4.0	5.0	6.8	5.0	-1.7	-3.9	1.0	0.9	-0.7	0.5
Israel[1]	8.1	0.3	0.2	0.9	4.7	4.2	5.5	5.9	2.7	1.4	5.2	4.8	2.9	3.3
Italy	3.8	1.7	0.3	0.1	1.6	0.8	1.9	1.6	-0.8	-5.5	1.8	0.6	-2.4	-1.5
Japan	2.1	0.0	0.2	1.4	2.1	1.7	1.9	2.2	-1.1	-6.4	4.5	-0.3	1.4	1.2
Korea	8.8	4.5	7.6	3.1	4.9	4.1	5.1	5.8	3.1	1.1	6.4	3.5	2.3	3.0
Luxembourg	7.5 e	2.7	3.5	1.1	4.1	2.8	5.6	8.5	-1.1	-5.7	6.0	2.0	-1.2	4.2
Mexico	6.6 e	0.1 e	1.0 e	1.6 e	4.2	3.1	5.0	3.2	1.4	-4.7	5.2	3.9	4.0	1.4
Netherlands	4.3	2.1	0.1	0.3	2.1	2.2	3.5	3.8	1.9	-3.4	1.7	2.0	-0.8	-0.2
New Zealand	2.9	3.4	4.7	4.4	3.7	3.4	2.6	2.8	-1.5	-0.3	1.4	2.3	2.1	2.4
Norway	3.2	1.9	1.1	0.8	3.7	2.5	1.9	2.4	0.6	-1.8	0.3	0.7	2.7	0.5
Poland	4.3	1.3	2.0	3.4	5.5	3.4	6.2	7.3	3.8	2.9	3.8	5.0	1.6	1.3
Portugal	3.7	2.2	0.7	-0.8	1.7	0.5	1.6	2.8	0.6	-2.5	1.8	-1.1	-3.2	-0.8
Slovak Republic	0.4	4.7	4.1	4.5	4.7	5.6	10.1	11.0	6.3	-5.4	5.2	2.2	2.5	1.1
Slovenia	4.6	3.6	4.2	3.0	4.3	3.9	5.9	7.1	2.9	-7.3	1.3	0.3	-2.4	-0.7
Spain	5.4	4.1	2.8	2.8	2.9	3.5	4.3	4.2	1.3	-3.4	0.0	-0.6	-2.5	-1.6
Sweden	5.3	1.4	1.9	2.4	4.6	2.7	4.8	3.4	-0.3	-5.8	6.2	2.9	-0.1	1.3
Switzerland	3.7	1.6	0.3	0.0	2.7	2.9	3.9	4.1	2.4	-2.2	2.9	2.0	1.2	1.8
Turkey	6.5	-4.5	5.2	4.5	9.6	8.5	7.5	4.8	1.3	-3.6	9.1	8.9	2.3	4.9
United Kingdom	3.9	2.5	2.2	3.4	2.3	3.3	2.6	2.6	-0.2	-4.3	1.7	1.9	1.0	2.2
United States	3.9	0.9	1.9	2.6	3.5	3.2	2.7	1.5	-0.5	-2.6	2.2	1.4	2.1	1.9
Euro area	3.8 e	2.2	1.0	0.6	2.4	1.5	3.2	3.3	0.7	-4.6	2.1	1.7	-0.6	-0.2
OECD-Total	4.1	1.3	1.7	2.0	3.2	2.8	3.2	2.6	0.3	-3.5	2.9	1.9	..	..
Brazil	..	1.4	3.6	1.3	5.5	3.0	3.7	5.7	4.6	-0.2	7.0	3.7	..	..
China	8.4 e	8.3 e	9.1 e	10.0 e	10.1 e	11.3 e	12.7 e	14.2 e	9.6 e	9.2 e	10.4 e	9.3	7.7	..
India	..	..	..	..	..	..	..	..	..	..	..	..	..	..
Indonesia	4.9 e	3.6 e	4.5 e	4.8 e	5.0 e	5.7 e	5.5 e	6.3 e	6.0 e	4.6 e	6.2 e	6.9	5.8	5.2
Russian Federation	9.3 e	4.9 e	4.7 e	7.5 e	6.6	6.0	7.9	8.4	5.2	-6.7	4.1	3.8	3.5	1.4
South Africa	4.4	2.9	3.8	3.0	4.5	5.3	5.5	5.4	3.3	-1.4	2.9	3.0	2.2	2.3

Note: Detailed metadata:
http://stats.oecd.org/OECDStat_Metadata/ShowMetadata.ashx?Dataset=NAAG_2015_NOV15&Lang=en&Coords=[INDICATOR].[B1GG]

1. Information on data for Israel: http://dx.doi.org/10.1787/888932315602

Table 12.2. Gross value added by activity

Percentage of total activity

	Agriculture, forestry and fishing	Industry, including energy	Construction	Distributive trade, repairs, transport; accommodation and food service activities	Information and communication	Financial and insurance activities	Real estate activities	Professional, scientific, technical, administration and support services activities	Public administration, defence, education, human health and social work activities	Other services
	2012	2012	2012	2012	2012	2012	2012	2012	2012	2012
Australia	2.4	18.4	8.4	17.0	3.0	8.8	11.8	10.1	17.3	2.7
Austria	1.5	22.4	6.4	23.3	3.3	4.3	9.3	9.2	17.4	2.8
Belgium	0.9	16.8	5.7	20.0	4.3	6.3	8.7	12.9	22.3	2.2
Canada	..	..	..	..	..	..	..	..	..	..
Chile	3.2	28.5	8.1	15.3	2.1	5.7	..	14.7	13.8	8.5
Czech Republic	2.6	31.1	5.9	18.3	5.1	4.4	8.8	6.5	15.0	2.3
Denmark	1.8	18.6	4.5	18.9	4.5	6.4	10.2	8.2	23.5	3.6
Estonia	4.0	21.6	7.2	23.2	5.0	3.8	9.8	8.8	14.2	2.3
Finland	2.7	20.5	6.6	17.0	5.2	2.7	11.6	8.4	22.1	3.1
France	1.8	13.8	5.9	17.8	5.0	4.2	12.8	12.8	22.8	3.0
Germany	0.8	26.3	4.5	15.6	4.7	4.2	11.2	10.7	17.9	4.0
Greece	3.7	12.8	3.4	22.3	3.3	5.0	19.1	5.1	21.3	4.1
Hungary	4.6	26.4	3.9	17.9	5.3	4.3	8.5	9.1	17.2	2.9
Iceland	7.8	19.0	4.6	17.2	4.2	8.7	9.2	7.1	19.1	3.1
Ireland	1.2	24.5	2.4	15.6	11.0	9.4	6.4	9.8	17.2	2.3
Israel[1]	1.3	16.5	5.5	13.7	9.2	5.2	14.8	12.4	18.4	3.1
Italy	2.2	18.5	5.4	20.1	4.0	5.4	13.9	9.4	17.2	4.0
Japan	1.2	20.4	5.7	19.4	5.5	4.6	12.0	..	11.6	19.7
Korea	2.5	33.3	4.8	15.2	3.9	6.1	7.9	7.1	16.6	2.7
Luxembourg	0.4	6.9	5.3	17.5	6.8	26.6	8.1	10.5	15.8	2.0
Mexico	3.3	28.4	8.0	24.3	2.4	3.4	11.3	6.2	10.6	2.1
Netherlands	1.8	17.4	4.8	19.7	4.8	8.5	5.0	13.5	22.0	2.6
New Zealand	..	..	..	..	..	..	..	..	..	..
Norway	1.3	35.3	5.8	13.8	3.7	4.4	6.7	7.0	20.2	1.8
Poland	3.0	25.7	7.9	26.1	3.8	4.0	5.1	7.1	14.8	2.4
Portugal	2.2	17.0	4.9	24.4	3.7	6.3	11.8	6.8	20.0	2.9
Slovak Republic	3.5	26.3	9.0	21.1	4.7	4.1	6.8	7.2	13.8	3.4
Slovenia	2.1	25.9	5.8	20.0	4.3	4.3	7.5	9.5	17.9	2.8
Spain	2.5	17.2	6.3	23.6	4.4	4.3	11.6	7.4	18.6	4.2
Sweden	1.5	21.3	5.6	17.3	5.6	4.3	8.5	9.1	24.0	2.9
Switzerland	0.7	21.0	5.2	20.9	4.0	10.4	1.0	9.4	18.7	8.8
Turkey	8.8	21.7	4.9	29.5	2.3	3.7	11.3	5.6	10.5	1.7
United Kingdom	0.7	14.9	5.9	17.8	6.3	7.6	11.7	11.8	19.2	4.2
United States	1.3	16.7	3.8	15.8	6.1	7.1	11.3	11.7	22.9	3.2
Euro area	1.7	19.6	5.3	18.9	4.6	5.0	11.5	10.5	19.4	3.5
OECD-Total	..	..	..	..	..	..	..	..	..	..
Brazil	..	..	..	..	..	..	..	..	..	..
China	10.1	38.4	6.8	16.3	..	5.5	5.7	..	..	17.2
India	..	..	..	..	..	..	..	..	..	..
Indonesia	13.7	35.0	9.6	20.2	3.7	3.8	2.8	1.5	8.3	1.5
Russian Federation	..	..	..	..	..	..	..	..	..	..

Note: Detailed metadata: http://stats.oecd.org/OECDStat_Metadata/ShowMetadata.ashx?Dataset=NAAG_2015_NOV15&Lang=en&Coords=[INDICATOR].[B1GVASB1G]

1. Information on data for Israel: http://dx.doi.org/10.1787/888932315602

Table 12.3. **Contribution to gross value added growth by activity**

Percentage

	Agriculture, forestry and fishing	Industry, including energy	Construction	Distributive trade, repairs, transport; accommodation and food service activities	Information and communication	Financial and insurance activities	Real estate activities	Professional, scientific, technical, administration and support services activities	Public administration, defence, education, human health and social work activities	Other services
	2012	2012	2012	2012	2012	2012	2012	2012	2012	2012
Australia	0.0	0.7	0.2	0.4	0.0	0.3	0.4	0.3	0.4	-0.1
Austria	-0.1	0.7	0.0	-0.1	-0.1	0.0	0.1	0.2	0.1	0.0
Belgium	0.0	-0.3	0.0	-0.2	0.1	0.3	0.0	-0.4	0.4	0.0
Canada	..	..	..	..	..	..	..	..	..	..
Chile	0.0	1.3	0.5	1.2	0.2	0.6	..	0.6	0.7	0.2
Czech Republic	0.1	-0.7	-0.2	0.0	-0.1	0.0	0.2	0.1	0.0	0.0
Denmark	0.2	0.2	-0.1	-0.6	0.1	-0.1	-0.4	0.2	-0.3	0.0
Estonia	0.6	0.1	0.5	2.1	0.5	0.3	0.0	0.4	0.2	0.3
Finland	-0.1	-1.9	-0.3	0.3	0.3	-0.1	0.0	0.1	-0.1	-0.1
France	-0.2	0.1	-0.3	0.1	0.2	0.1	0.2	0.0	0.3	0.0
Germany	0.0	0.1	-0.1	0.4	0.2	-0.1	-0.3	0.1	0.1	0.0
Greece	0.4	-0.8	-0.2	-3.8	-0.4	-0.2	0.9	-0.4	-2.0	0.1
Hungary	-1.0	-0.6	-0.3	0.0	0.1	-0.1	-0.2	0.1	0.3	-0.1
Iceland	0.3	0.5	0.0	1.0	0.3	-0.1	-0.1	0.0	-0.3	0.0
Ireland	-0.1	-0.6	-0.1	-0.5	0.4	-0.4	0.4	0.3	-0.3	0.2
Israel[1]	-0.1	-0.6	0.4	0.4	0.7	0.0	0.4	1.5	0.0	0.2
Italy	-0.1	-0.5	-0.4	-0.7	-0.1	0.1	-0.1	-0.4	-0.2	-0.1
Japan	0.0	0.0	0.1	0.5	0.1	0.1	0.1	..	0.1	0.4
Korea	0.0	0.8	-0.1	0.4	0.2	0.2	0.0	0.2	0.5	0.0
Luxembourg	0.1	0.4	-0.6	-1.4	0.5	-1.1	0.3	0.0	0.7	0.0
Mexico	0.3	0.8	0.2	1.1	0.4	0.3	0.3	0.2	0.3	0.1
Netherlands	0.0	-0.2	-0.4	-0.1	0.0	-0.2	0.1	0.1	-0.1	0.0
New Zealand	0.2	0.2	0.6	0.4	0.1	0.1	0.1	0.2	0.3	0.0
Norway	0.1	0.3	0.4	0.5	0.1	0.1	0.2	0.5	0.4	0.0
Poland	-0.3	0.7	-0.3	1.0	0.4	-0.5	0.0	0.3	0.0	0.3
Portugal	0.0	-0.5	-0.8	-0.2	-0.1	-0.7	-0.2	-0.3	-0.3	0.0
Slovak Republic	0.1	-0.1	0.5	0.5	0.6	0.0	0.3	0.4	0.0	0.3
Slovenia	-0.2	-0.7	-0.5	-0.8	0.0	-0.2	0.0	-0.1	0.2	-0.1
Spain	-0.3	-0.9	-1.1	-0.1	0.1	-0.1	0.2	-0.1	-0.1	-0.1
Sweden	0.0	-0.9	-0.3	0.3	0.2	0.0	0.3	0.1	0.2	0.0
Switzerland	0.0	-0.1	0.1	0.2	0.0	0.3	0.0	0.4	0.4	-0.1
Turkey	0.3	0.4	0.0	0.3	0.2	0.1	0.2	0.3	0.4	0.0
United Kingdom	-0.1	-0.4	-0.5	0.2	0.3	0.0	0.4	0.7	0.4	0.0
United States	0.0	0.4	0.2	0.3	0.2	0.3	0.2	0.5	0.1	0.1
Euro area	-0.1	-0.2	-0.3	0.0	0.1	0.0	0.0	-0.1	0.0	0.0
OECD-Total	..	..	..	..	..	..	..	..	..	..
Brazil	..	..	..	..	..	..	..	..	..	..
China	0.5	3.1	0.6	1.4	..	0.5	0.2	..	..	1.3
India	..	..	..	..	..	..	..	..	..	..
Indonesia	0.6	1.8	0.6	1.2	0.5	0.3	0.2	0.1	0.4	0.1
Russian Federation	..	..	..	..	..	..	..	..	..	..
South Africa	..	..	..	..	..	..	..	..	..	..

Note: Detailed metadata:
http://stats.oecd.org/OECDStat_Metadata/ShowMetadata.ashx?Dataset=NAAG_2015_NOV15&Lang=en&Coords=[INDICATOR].[B1GVACG]

1. Information on data for Israel: http://dx.doi.org/10.1787/888932315602

Table 13.1. **Compensation of employees**

Percentage of gross value added

	2000	2001	2002	2003	2004	2005	2006	2007	2008	2009	2010	2011	2012	2013
Australia	53.8	52.9	53.0	52.5	52.5	51.9	52.0	52.2	50.3	50.9	50.8	51.2	51.5	51.0
Austria	54.3	53.7	53.3	53.3	52.4	51.8	51.3	50.9	51.8	53.5	53.0	52.5	53.3	53.7
Belgium	55.8	56.9	57.1	56.6	55.3	54.9	54.9	54.8	56.3	57.5	56.1	56.4	57.2	57.5
Canada	53.5	53.8	54.1	53.5	53.1	52.7	53.4	53.4	52.6	55.2	53.7	..	..	..
Chile	43.8 e	43.8 e	43.6 e	42.5 e	39.9 e	38.3 e	34.8 e	35.2 e	39.7	41.1	39.3	40.6	42.3	43.6
Czech Republic	42.2	42.2	43.3	43.6	43.7	44.0	43.7	43.6	44.3	44.1	44.4	44.7	45.7	45.8
Denmark	57.9	59.0	59.6	60.0	59.1	59.4	59.4	61.2	61.6	64.0	61.5	61.2	60.9	61.0
Estonia	50.6	49.9	49.8	49.7	49.8	49.5	49.8	51.6	56.0	58.2	54.0	51.0	51.3	51.7
Finland	53.3	52.8	53.3	53.7	53.3	54.2	54.3	52.7	54.0	57.4	56.5	56.8	58.2	58.0
France	56.4	56.5	56.9	57.0	56.6	56.7	56.8	56.1	56.2	57.8	57.8	57.8	58.3	58.3
Germany	58.7	57.8	57.3	57.2	55.8	55.0	53.8	52.9	53.9	56.4	55.2	55.1	56.1	56.3
Greece	34.6	34.6	37.1	37.0	36.7	38.2	37.8	38.2	38.8	40.0	41.1	40.3	39.1	37.1
Hungary	50.9	50.8	49.8	51.9	51.6	51.9	51.0	51.8	51.8	51.9	50.4	49.9	50.7	49.9
Iceland	63.8	61.0	61.7	63.7	63.6	66.0	69.0	67.7	62.0	53.7	54.9	56.9	58.7	59.1
Ireland	43.2	42.9	41.5	42.1	43.1	44.3	44.7	45.5	48.7	48.8	45.2	42.7	42.4	41.7
Israel[1]	53.9 e	55.4 e	54.0 e	52.8 e	51.7 e	51.7 e	52.3	52.5	53.1	51.0	51.1	51.3	50.5	..
Italy	41.2	41.2	41.6	41.8	41.7	42.3	42.9	42.7	43.4	44.6	44.5	44.3	44.4	44.1
Japan	52.9	53.3	52.4	51.5	50.6	50.7	50.8	50.0	51.5	52.0	50.9	52.3	52.0	52.0
Korea	45.7	46.4	46.4	47.4	47.1	48.4	48.9	48.6	48.5	48.0	46.8	47.1	47.9	48.3
Luxembourg	50.7	54.5	55.6	54.9	55.0	54.7	52.4	52.0	54.6	58.3	55.4	54.5	55.2	54.6
Mexico	31.2 e	32.3 e	32.1 e	31.7	30.1	29.8	29.0	28.8	28.6	30.0	28.8	28.0	28.0	28.6
Netherlands	56.2	56.1	56.6	56.7	55.8	54.4	53.1	53.1	53.8	56.3	54.7	54.9	55.3	55.2
New Zealand	43.1	43.1	43.8	44.2	44.8	46.0	46.9	46.9	48.9	48.0	47.9	47.9	..	..
Norway	48.0	49.1	51.6	50.9	48.4	45.9	45.0	47.4	46.4	51.6	49.9	49.1	49.3	50.4
Poland	46.5	47.4	45.6	44.5	41.8	41.9	41.6	41.7	44.1	42.3	43.0	42.1	42.0	42.1
Portugal	54.9	54.9	54.8	54.9	54.3	55.0	54.2	53.2	53.6	53.8	53.6	52.9	51.1	50.9
Slovak Republic	45.0	43.3	43.3	42.4	40.3	41.0	39.7	39.2	38.9	41.3	40.6	40.8	40.5	40.7
Slovenia	57.8	58.0	57.3	56.8	56.9	56.9	56.4	55.9	57.0	59.4	60.2	58.9	59.2	58.3
Spain	53.4	53.0	52.9	53.1	53.0	53.2	53.5	53.7	54.6	54.6	54.7	54.0	52.1	51.7
Sweden	50.9	52.3	52.3	51.9	51.1	51.2	50.2	50.9	51.9	53.8	51.7	52.5	54.1	54.4
Switzerland	58.2	59.9	61.4	61.1	59.5	59.1	58.1	57.4	57.8	60.1	58.7	59.7	60.5	60.9
Turkey	..	..	..	..	..	..	..	..	..	..	..	..	..	..
United Kingdom	58.7	60.1	59.1	58.3	58.6	57.8	58.3	58.7	57.8	59.0	58.6	57.6	57.2	56.4
United States	60.9	60.8	60.0	59.3	58.9	58.1	58.2	58.6	58.9	58.0	57.1	57.2	57.1	56.5
Euro area	53.2	52.9	52.9	52.8	52.1	52.0	51.7	51.3	52.1	53.7	53.2	53.0	53.3	53.2
OECD-Total	..	..	..	..	..	..	..	..	..	..	..	..	..	..
Brazil	45.5	46.5	45.6	44.8	45.0	45.8	46.5	46.8	47.5	49.1	49.0	49.7	..	..
China	52.7	52.5	53.6	52.8	50.6	50.3	49.1	48.0	47.8	48.8	47.3	46.8	49.2	..
India	..	..	..	..	30.3	29.1	27.8	27.7	29.6	30.0	..	..	..	..
Indonesia	..	..	..	..	..	..	..	..	..	..	..	..	..	..
Russian Federation	45.9 e	49.2 e	52.9	53.6	52.8	51.2	52.2	54.5	55.6	60.3	57.4	58.2	58.9	60.2
South Africa	51.8	50.2	47.9	48.4	48.3	48.2	48.0	47.6	47.8	48.6	49.5	49.8	50.1	50.8

Note: Detailed metadata:
http://stats.oecd.org/OECDStat_Metadata/ShowMetadata.ashx?Dataset=NAAG_2015_NOV15&Lang=en&Coords=[INDICATOR].[D1SB1G]

1. Information on data for Israel: http://dx.doi.org/10.1787/888932315602

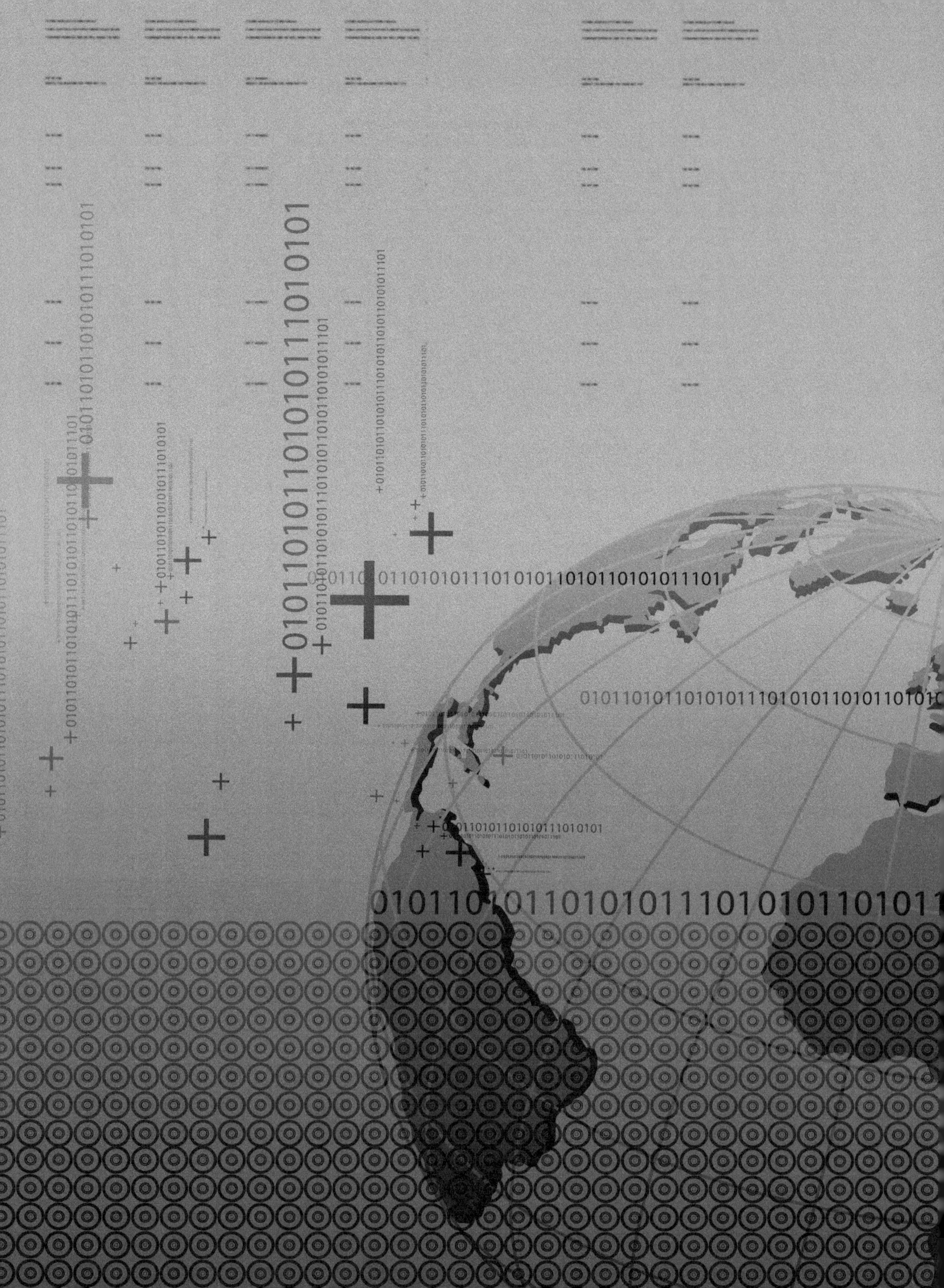

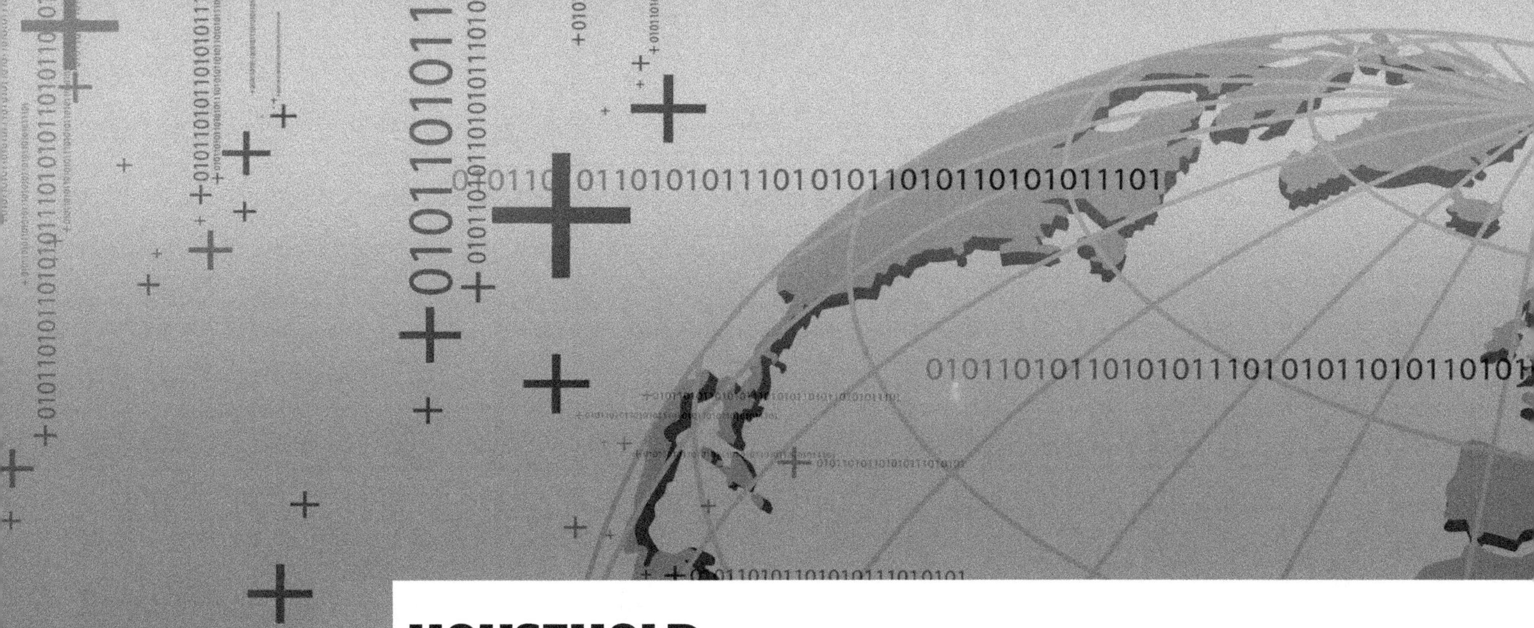

HOUSEHOLD

14. Disposable income

Table 14.1. **Household gross adjusted disposable income per capita**

US dollars at current PPPs

	2000	2001	2002	2003	2004	2005	2006	2007	2008	2009	2010	2011	2012	2013
Australia	21 450	22 530	23 421	24 323	26 054	26 440	27 474	29 464	30 817	30 753	32 200	33 715	34 151	34 843
Austria	22 973	22 900	24 455	25 161	26 174	26 794	28 597	29 288	30 404	30 362	31 061	31 553	32 785	32 421
Belgium	21 872	22 787	24 272	23 783	24 445	24 332	25 257	25 951	27 509	27 899	28 285	29 156	29 970	29 903
Canada	20 924 e	21 668 e	22 231 e	22 885 e	24 066 e	25 071 e	26 164 e	27 528 e	28 412 e	28 305 e	29 233 e	29 987 e	30 551 e	31 175 e
Chile	..	..	..	..	..	..	..	..	10 583	11 161	11 920	13 696	14 912	15 923
Czech Republic	11 994	12 942	13 745	14 335	15 014	15 437	16 393	17 371	17 182	17 983	18 301	18 930	19 296	19 452
Denmark	18 300	18 858	20 748	20 226	21 038	20 956	22 456	23 298	24 272	25 044	26 368	27 149	28 025	27 796
Estonia	7 548	7 833	8 606	9 202	10 015	10 622	11 906	13 301	14 956	14 166	14 269	15 234	15 799	16 880
Finland	17 051	17 503	19 074	19 451	20 826	21 232	22 485	24 249	26 123	26 568	27 498	28 489	29 586	29 939
France	21 295	22 708	24 620	23 770	24 626	24 931	25 881	27 180	28 112	28 305	29 211	29 785	30 235	30 259
Germany	21 547	22 497	23 499	24 384	25 098	26 304	27 330	28 229	29 488	29 207	30 946	32 140	33 391	33 586
Greece	..	..	..	..	..	..	21 636	22 799	24 632	24 645	22 971	21 298	20 213	19 359
Hungary	9 730	10 615	11 801	12 201	12 850	13 290	13 841	13 732	14 171	14 325	14 832	15 801	15 941	16 390
Iceland	..	..	..	..	..	..	..	..	..	..	..	..	..	..
Ireland	16 819	18 349	19 560	20 486	21 664	22 903	23 722	24 889	25 390	24 971	25 019	24 234	24 305	24 199
Israel[1]	..	..	..	..	..	..	..	..	..	..	..	..	..	..
Italy	20 948	22 607	22 595	22 847	23 191	23 536	24 796	25 893	27 223	26 490	27 251	27 354	26 684	26 813
Japan	18 596	18 750	19 827	20 509	21 269	22 382	23 044	23 868	24 275	24 593	25 609	26 568	27 603	28 005
Korea	12 278	12 658	13 454	13 967	14 882	15 494	16 364	17 200	17 924	18 157	19 039	19 859	20 593	21 450
Luxembourg	..	..	..	..	..	..	..	..	..	..	..	..	..	..
Mexico	..	..	..	9 320	9 816	10 339	11 347	11 780	12 441	11 492	12 230	12 843	13 277	13 622
Netherlands	22 048	23 541	25 356	24 362	25 118	25 311	27 161	28 563	29 619	29 506	28 894	29 321	29 540	29 186
New Zealand	15 007	15 815	15 899	16 656	17 692	17 914	19 374	20 670	21 493	21 650	22 559	23 182	24 162	..
Norway	20 350	20 696	23 159	24 518	25 821	27 098	26 587	28 698	29 967	30 826	31 685	32 525	34 325	34 989
Poland	9 271 e	9 726 e	10 373 e	10 418 e	10 669 e	10 818 e	11 566 e	12 909 e	13 784 e	14 738 e	15 887 e	16 485 e	17 551 e	18 251 e
Portugal	14 491	15 096	15 987	16 148	16 862	18 154	18 957	19 524	20 432	20 676	21 264	20 917	21 353	21 723
Slovak Republic	8 814	9 665	10 684	10 549	11 075	11 935	12 806	14 695	16 271	16 661	17 883	17 981	18 418	19 192
Slovenia	14 064	14 809	16 116	16 046	16 892	17 558	18 509	19 359	20 630 |	19 924	20 273	20 794	20 830	20 740
Spain	17 135	18 297	20 065	20 175	20 830	21 239	22 246	22 427	23 535	23 857	23 332	23 396	23 328	23 555
Sweden	18 786	19 890	21 502	21 708	22 288	22 275	23 631	25 447	26 980	27 194	27 414	28 683	29 930	30 124
Switzerland	24 013	25 046	26 382	25 805	26 603	26 871	28 329	30 585	32 243	32 649	32 811	34 130	35 867	36 620
Turkey	..	..	..	..	..	..	..	..	..	..	..	..	..	..
United Kingdom	21 807	23 230	24 804	25 050	26 599	27 057	28 284	28 595	28 534	29 003	28 098	27 661	28 948	28 669
United States	28 728	29 894	31 030	32 295	33 984	35 238	37 240	38 573	40 044	39 588	40 313	41 888	43 502	43 689
Euro area	19 728	20 940	22 174	22 302	22 993	23 622	24 758	25 713	26 887	26 773	27 432	27 928	28 302	28 397
OECD-Total	..	..	..	..	..	..	..	..	..	..	..	..	..	..
Brazil	..	..	..	..	..	..	..	..	..	..	..	..	..	..
China	..	..	..	..	..	..	..	..	..	..	..	..	..	..
India	..	..	..	..	..	..	..	..	..	..	..	..	..	..
Indonesia	..	..	..	..	..	..	..	..	..	..	..	..	..	..
Russian Federation	..	..	6 615	7 086	7 907	8 818	10 687	12 340	14 365	14 522	15 808	17 351	19 204 e	20 865 e
South Africa	..	..	..	..	..	..	..	..	7 613	7 734	7 837	8 357	8 647	8 913

Note: Detailed metadata:
http://stats.oecd.org/OECDStat_Metadata/ShowMetadata.ashx?Dataset=NAAG_2015_NOV15&Lang=en&Coords=[INDICATOR].[B7GS14_S15HCPC]

1. Information on data for Israel: http://dx.doi.org/10.1787/888932315602

Table 14.2. **Real household net (adjusted) disposable income**

Annual growth rates in percentage

	Net							Net adjusted						
	2007	2008	2009	2010	2011	2012	2013	2007	2008	2009	2010	2011	2012	2013
Australia	7.1	6.8	1.3	4.9	3.7	0.9	1.5	6.5	6.5	1.4	4.4	3.8	0.8	1.6
Austria	2.1	0.7	-0.3	-1.1	-0.3	2.0	-2.0	2.3	1.1	0.0	-1.0	0.0	1.8	-1.5
Belgium	2.0	2.2	2.1	-1.2	-1.1	0.4	-0.7	2.0	2.2	1.9	-0.6	-0.5	0.6	-0.5
Canada	3.7	4.0	1.6	2.4	2.3	2.7	2.4	3.4 e	3.8 e	1.6 e	2.6 e	1.9 e	2.4 e	1.9 e
Chile	..	..	6.4	6.3	9.2	7.4	5.8	..	..	..	..	..	..	..
Czech Republic	3.1	2.3	2.1	0.1	-1.6	-1.1	-0.9	2.8	2.0	2.3	0.1	-1.6	-1.0	-0.5
Denmark	-0.8	-0.9	2.7	3.6	1.0	-0.5	-1.4	-0.2	0.5	2.9	3.2	0.4	-0.5	-1.0
Estonia	11.0	5.3	-9.2	-4.3	3.8	0.3	6.3	10.2	5.1	-7.8	-3.7	3.2	0.6	5.2
Finland	3.5	2.3	1.1	2.9	1.0	-0.2	0.3	3.0	2.2	1.0	2.4	1.0	0.0	0.2
France	2.9	0.1	1.7	1.3	0.1	-0.9	0.0	2.8	0.3	1.8	1.4	0.4	-0.3	0.3
Germany	0.0	0.6	-0.6	0.4	0.9	0.5	0.5	0.4	1.1	-0.1	0.7	1.0	0.6	0.6
Greece	3.2	0.9	0.0	-11.0	-9.8	-7.6	-8.4	3.7	0.8	-0.3	-9.5	-9.2	-7.9	-8.4
Hungary	-3.2	-2.4	-4.4	-2.5	3.9	-3.2	1.6	-4.1	-1.5	-3.7	-2.6	3.3	-3.1	1.6
Iceland	..	..	..	..	..	..	..	..	..	..	..	..	..	..
Ireland	6.3	6.7	0.3	-2.7	-3.5	-1.0	-2.3	6.4	5.3	1.0	-2.5	-3.3	-1.2	-1.4
Israel[1]	..	..	..	..	..	..	..	..	..	..	..	..	..	..
Italy	1.3	-1.4	-2.3	-1.8	-0.5	-5.7	-0.6	1.2	-1.1	-1.9	-1.4	-0.6	-4.9	-0.5
Japan	0.8	-1.2	1.3	2.6	0.7	1.0	0.7	1.0	-0.8	1.4	2.5	1.1	1.3	0.8
Korea	2.9	1.4	1.1	3.5	2.0	1.5	4.0	3.1	1.7	1.8	3.6	2.4	1.8	4.0
Luxembourg	..	..	..	..	..	..	..	..	..	..	..	..	..	..
Mexico	2.5	2.0	-7.5	6.3	3.3	2.6	3.2	2.4	2.1	-6.9	6.0	3.3	2.6	3.2
Netherlands	1.9	-0.9	0.7	-0.7	0.6	-1.2	-0.9	1.9	0.2	1.7	0.0	0.8	-1.1	-0.8
New Zealand	5.0	-1.9	2.8	3.5	1.4	3.9	..	4.9	-0.8	2.4	3.5	1.5	3.2	..
Norway	6.0	3.4	3.2	2.3	4.1	4.4	3.0	5.2	3.0	4.0	2.3	3.2	3.8	2.7
Poland	5.2	4.3	6.0	1.8	0.0	1.1	2.8	5.0	4.5	5.8	2.7	-0.6	1.1	3.6
Portugal	1.4	1.0	1.5	1.0	-5.6	-5.1	-0.9	1.2	1.1	1.7	0.7	-5.6	-4.8	-0.7
Slovak Republic	9.6	5.0	1.4	2.9	-2.3	-1.8	1.7	10.3	5.4	1.4	2.8	-2.7	-1.4	2.0
Slovenia	4.6	2.8	-1.3	-0.5	0.1	-4.2	-2.1	4.1	2.9	-0.7	-0.4	0.3	-3.7	-1.8
Spain	0.4	1.8	3.0	-3.5	-1.3	-5.3	-1.5	1.2	2.4	3.4	-2.9	-1.2	-5.2	-1.8
Sweden	5.6	2.0	2.6	1.7	4.1	3.8	1.7	4.1	1.7	2.5	1.5	3.1	2.8	1.4
Switzerland	3.9	1.1	2.1	1.2	1.7	4.0	3.2	3.5	0.7	2.6	1.1	1.7	4.0	3.0
Turkey	..	..	..	..	..	..	..	..	..	..	..	..	..	..
United Kingdom	2.6	0.9	3.3	0.7	-2.1	2.6	-1.1	2.4	1.1	3.1	0.8	-1.5	2.5	-0.6
United States	1.9	1.8	-0.3	1.3	2.7	3.3	-1.5	1.9	1.7	-0.1	1.0	2.3	2.9	-0.3
Euro area	1.5	0.3	0.3	-0.8	-0.1	-1.9	-0.5	..	..	..	..	..	..	..
OECD-Total	..	..	..	..	..	..	..	..	..	..	..	..	..	..
Brazil	..	..	..	..	5.0	..	..	..	..	..	..	..	..	..
China	..	..	..	..	..	..	..	..	..	..	..	..	..	..
India	..	..	..	..	..	..	..	..	..	..	..	..	..	..
Indonesia	..	..	..	..	..	..	..	..	..	..	..	..	..	..
Russian Federation	14.1	8.0	-2.0	8.6	4.7	6.1	3.1	12.3	7.2	-1.9	7.0	4.0	4.9	2.4
South Africa	..	..	0.8	5.1	5.3	2.7	3.3	..	..	0.9	5.0	4.7	2.5	3.2

Note: Detailed metadata:
http://stats.oecd.org/OECDStat_Metadata/ShowMetadata.ashx?Dataset=NAAG_2015_NOV15&Lang=en&Coords=[INDICATOR].[B7NS14_S15DEFG]

1. Information on data for Israel: http://dx.doi.org/10.1787/888932315602

15. Household final expenditure on housing

Table 15.1. **Household housing consumption**

Percentage of net adjusted disposable income

	2000	2001	2002	2003	2004	2005	2006	2007	2008	2009	2010	2011	2012	2013
Australia	16.3	16.2	16.7	16.7	16.6	16.8	16.8	16.7	16.6	17.2	17.3	17.4	18.1	18.4
Austria	14.8	15.1	15.1	15.1	15.4	15.9	15.9	15.4	15.7	15.8	16.2	16.5	16.5	17.0
Belgium	16.8	16.8	16.7	16.8	16.8	16.8	16.8	16.3	16.9	16.3	16.9	17.1	17.5	17.6
Canada	18.2 e	18.1 e	18.1 e	18.3 e	18.2 e	18.2 e	17.7 e	17.9 e	17.9 e	17.9 e	17.9 e	18.0 e	18.0 e	18.3 e
Chile	..	..	..	..	..	..	..	..	..	..	..	..	..	..
Czech Republic	18.9	19.0	19.5	19.7	19.9	20.0	20.0	20.3	20.7	21.6	22.1	22.2	22.2	22.4
Denmark	20.8	20.7	20.4	20.5	20.5	20.5	20.4	20.5	20.9	20.5	21.1	21.4	21.8	22.4
Estonia	19.9	19.6	19.9	19.2	19.0	18.0	18.0	17.8	15.9	16.2	16.3	16.2	16.4	16.1
Finland	18.4	18.4	18.4	18.4	18.1	18.2	18.2	18.0	17.9	18.3	18.7	18.7	19.1	19.5
France	16.7	16.6	16.4	16.7	16.8	17.3	17.5	17.4	17.6	17.7	17.8	17.8	18.4	18.8
Germany	17.5	17.5	17.5	17.6	17.7	17.9	18.1	17.9	18.3	18.2	18.2	17.9	18.0	18.1
Greece	..	..	..	..	..	..	19.0	18.9	19.2	18.7	19.3	21.1	23.1	24.1
Hungary	15.6	15.2	15.0	15.1	14.9	14.8	15.2	15.9	16.8	18.0	18.7	18.1	18.3	17.2
Iceland	..	..	..	..	..	..	..	..	..	..	..	..	..	..
Ireland	15.3	15.2	15.8	16.2	15.9	15.7	16.0	16.6	17.0	15.4	15.8	16.5	17.1	18.0
Israel[1]	..	..	..	..	..	..	..	..	..	..	..	..	..	..
Italy	15.1	15.0	15.1	15.5	15.9	16.3	16.4	16.5	17.1	17.9	18.4	18.7	20.0	20.2
Japan	18.2	18.8	19.0	19.4	19.5	19.8	20.1	20.1	20.4	20.3	20.2	20.0	20.1	20.1
Korea	16.4	16.3	16.1	16.1	15.7	15.6	15.4	15.2	15.0	14.7	14.6	14.5	14.7	14.6
Luxembourg	..	..	..	..	..	..	..	..	..	..	..	..	..	..
Mexico	..	..	..	19.7	20.4	19.7	19.3	19.3	19.7	19.4	18.4	18.2	18.5	17.8
Netherlands	14.0	13.6	13.6	14.2	14.6	15.2	15.1	14.8	15.1	15.3	15.7	15.6	16.1	16.8
New Zealand	22.0	21.0	21.5	21.1	21.1	21.2	20.6	20.1	20.3	19.9	19.6	19.6	19.6	..
Norway	14.6	15.5	15.1	15.2	14.9	14.3	15.8	15.1	15.1	14.8	15.6	14.8	14.2	14.4
Poland	15.0	15.9	17.1	17.3	17.7	18.7	18.6	18.5	18.2	19.1	19.2	20.0	18.9	18.2
Portugal	10.2	10.4	10.8	11.5	11.7	12.0	12.3	12.7	13.1	13.6	14.1	15.2	16.6	16.0
Slovak Republic	18.1	18.1	18.4	21.2	23.1	22.9	23.8	22.8	22.1	21.7	21.0	21.6	22.0	21.1
Slovenia	15.4	15.3	15.0	14.9	15.1	15.3	15.1	14.8	15.0	16.1	16.4	16.3	16.5	16.1
Spain	13.0	13.1	13.6	13.9	14.2	14.7	15.5	16.4	16.8	17.2	18.3	18.9	20.0	20.3
Sweden	19.9	19.0	18.7	19.2	19.0	19.0	18.5	18.1	18.0	18.0	18.4	17.9	17.2	17.2
Switzerland	19.3	19.4	19.8	19.9	20.0	20.1	19.9	19.5	20.0	19.6	20.0	20.0	19.7	19.5
Turkey	..	..	..	..	..	..	..	..	..	..	..	..	..	..
United Kingdom	15.4	15.3	15.5	15.5	16.2	16.6	17.1	17.5	17.8	18.2	19.7	20.1	20.1	20.6
United States	15.7	16.1	15.9	15.9	15.8	16.3	16.3	16.3	16.2	16.6	16.4	16.0	15.6	15.9
Euro area	..	..	..	..	..	..	..	..	..	..	..	..	..	..
OECD-Total	..	..	..	..	..	..	..	..	..	..	..	..	..	..
Brazil	..	..	..	..	..	..	..	..	..	..	..	..	..	..
China	..	..	..	..	..	..	..	..	..	..	..	..	..	..
India	..	..	..	..	..	..	..	..	..	..	..	..	..	..
Indonesia	..	..	..	..	..	..	..	..	..	..	..	..	..	..
Russian Federation	..	..	..	..	6.6	7.8	7.5	7.2	7.1	7.3	7.6	7.5	7.4	7.1
South Africa	..	..	..	..	..	..	..	..	13.6	13.8	13.8	13.7	13.7	13.4

Note: Detailed metadata: http://stats.oecd.org/OECDStat_Metadata/ShowMetadata.ashx?Dataset=NAAG_2015_NOV15&Lang=en&Coords=[INDICATOR].[P040B7NS14_S15]

1. Information on data for Israel: http://dx.doi.org/10.1787/888932315602

Table 16.1. **Household net saving rate**

Percentage of household net disposable income

	2000	2001	2002	2003	2004	2005	2006	2007	2008	2009	2010	2011	2012	2013
Australia	2.3	3.5	0.0	0.5	1.5	1.1	1.8	4.0	10.0	9.1	10.2	11.2	10.3	9.7
Austria	10.5	8.8	8.9	9.2	9.2	10.7	11.3	12.1	11.9	11.3	9.3	7.9	9.2	7.3
Belgium	10.4	11.9	11.0	10.6	8.9	8.5	9.2	9.4	10.0	11.4	8.2	6.6	6.4	5.0
Canada	3.8	3.6	2.3	1.7	2.3	1.5	3.5	2.9	3.9	5.1	4.3	4.3	5.0	4.9
Chile	..	..	..	..	..	..	..	..	7.0	12.3	8.8	8.6	9.9	9.7
Czech Republic	6.0	6.2	6.3	5.7	4.9	6.1	7.8	7.0	6.3	8.5	7.6	5.9	6.2	5.5
Denmark	-6.0	0.0	1.2	1.8	-2.2	-4.6	-1.7	-3.1	-4.2	0.8	2.1	0.9	0.0	-0.4
Estonia	0.3	-1.9	-9.5	-9.3	-11.0	-10.7	-11.2	-7.3	1.6	6.9	3.3	4.1	1.4	3.9
Finland	3.0	2.7	2.7	2.3	3.0	1.0	-0.4	-0.4	-0.2	3.4	3.2	1.3	0.7	1.3
France	10.0	10.7	11.6	10.9	11.0	9.4	9.4	9.8	9.5	10.8	10.4	10.0	9.5	9.1
Germany	9.0	9.6	9.6	10.1	10.1	10.1	10.1	10.2	10.5	10.0	10.0	9.6	9.3	9.1
Greece	..	..	..	..	..	..	-3.4	-3.5	-5.6	-4.5	-9.0	-8.2	-8.3	-16.4
Hungary	5.3	6.0	3.1	1.7	4.5	5.7	6.3	2.2	1.5	3.6	3.6	4.1	2.6	3.9
Iceland	..	..	..	..	..	..	..	..	..	..	..	..	..	..
Ireland	-3.8	1.1	-0.7	-0.5	0.3	0.7	-2.0	-2.1	3.9	9.4	6.4	3.6	3.5	1.0
Israel[1]	..	..	..	..	..	..	..	..	..	..	..	..	..	..
Italy	7.4	8.9	9.6	9.1	9.5	9.0	8.4	8.0	7.7	7.0	4.1	3.6	1.8	3.9
Japan	7.0	3.8	3.3	2.7	2.3	1.6	1.3	1.1	0.6	2.3	2.1	2.6	1.4	0.0
Korea	..	..	..	..	..	6.7	5.5	3.5	3.8	4.8	4.7	3.9	3.9	5.6
Luxembourg	..	..	..	..	..	..	..	..	..	..	..	..	..	..
Mexico	..	..	..	10.1	8.6	8.2	9.1	8.4	8.1	8.4	8.8	6.9	6.1	5.4
Netherlands	6.2	8.1	7.9	7.4	6.8	5.7	3.8	3.9	3.7	7.1	4.9	5.8	6.8	7.3
New Zealand	-2.6	-1.4	-6.6	-4.1	-3.8	-5.9	-3.3	-1.0	-1.1	1.1	3.0	1.7	2.2	..
Norway	4.3	3.1	8.2	8.8	6.9	9.7	-0.5	0.9	3.6	5.1	4.0	5.8	7.1	7.6
Poland	11.0	12.4	9.0	7.9	4.0	3.0	2.7	2.2	0.8	3.2	3.0	-0.5	-0.5	0.7
Portugal	3.5	4.0	3.9	2.7	2.7	1.8	0.4	-0.8	-1.1	2.7	1.3	-0.9	-0.5	-0.2
Slovak Republic	5.8	3.7	3.4	1.1	0.3	1.1	0.1	1.9	0.8	2.3	4.7	2.9	1.7	2.9
Slovenia	6.7	8.4	8.5	6.1	7.1	9.4	11.1	9.4	9.7	7.7	6.1	5.5	3.2	5.7
Spain	5.8	5.5	5.2	6.7	5.0	3.2	1.4	-1.0	1.6	7.3	3.7	4.6	2.6	4.2
Sweden	4.0	8.0	7.8	6.6	5.8	5.4	6.9	9.4	12.7	12.2	11.0	12.7	15.3	15.1
Switzerland	15.3	15.5	15.3	14.8	13.7	14.0	15.8	17.4	16.7	17.1	17.0	17.8	18.5	19.0
Turkey	..	..	..	..	..	..	..	..	..	..	..	..	..	..
United Kingdom	4.6	5.3	3.8	2.4	0.5	-0.3	-1.2	-0.7	-0.8	4.0	6.1	3.4	2.9	0.0
United States	4.3	4.5	5.2	5.0	4.7	2.7	3.4	3.1	5.1	6.3	5.8	6.2	7.9	4.9
Euro area	7.7	8.5	8.9	9.0	8.7	7.8	7.1	6.9	7.1	8.5	6.9	6.5	6.0	6.1
OECD-Total	..	..	..	..	..	..	..	..	..	..	..	..	..	..
Brazil	..	..	..	..	..	..	..	..	..	..	..	..	..	..
China	31.1	31.2	31.5	33.9	33.8	35.4	37.2	39.2	39.9	40.4	42.1	40.9	40.7	..
India	..	..	..	..	..	..	..	..	..	..	..	..	..	..
Indonesia	..	..	..	..	..	..	..	..	..	..	..	..	..	..
Russian Federation	..	..	..	..	..	11.0	12.4	12.1	10.1	13.1	15.5	13.8	12.5	10.9
South Africa	..	..	..	..	..	..	..	..	-1.1	-0.5	-0.8	-1.1	-2.1	-2.5

Note: Detailed metadata:
http://stats.oecd.org/OECDStat_Metadata/ShowMetadata.ashx?Dataset=NAAG_2015_NOV15&Lang=en&Coords=[INDICATOR].[B8NS14_S15SB6NS14]

1. Information on data for Israel: http://dx.doi.org/10.1787/888932315602

17. Household financial transactions

Table 17.1. **Net financial transactions of households**

Percentage of household net disposable income

	2000	2001	2002	2003	2004	2005	2006	2007	2008	2009	2010	2011	2012	2013
Australia	-5.7	-0.5	-7.2	-7.6	-4.5	-3.2	-4.8	-5.4	-2.6	3.0	7.0	5.8	6.6	6.4
Austria	10.1	5.9	7.1	7.8	7.1	8.6	9.2	10.2	9.7	8.6	6.6	4.1	5.4	3.3
Belgium	13.6	14.7	9.8	14.3	13.7	9.1	8.6	6.7	3.1	14.9	11.2	11.4	8.3	7.2
Canada	-2.1	-3.1	-5.1	-6.3	-6.5	-7.7	-5.9	-6.7	-6.1	-2.7	-4.5	-4.4	-3.8	-4.1
Chile	..	..	..	..	..	..	..	..	-0.6	7.1	8.5	4.7	6.6	6.2
Czech Republic	2.6	4.3	4.7	3.5	2.3	3.2	4.3	3.1	2.4	5.1	3.6	3.4	7.1	3.6
Denmark	-12.3	-5.1	-2.5	-2.8	-7.7	-12.7	-12.1	-13.6	-11.0	-1.1	1.3	-1.3	1.5	-1.9
Estonia	-1.6	-1.4	-6.5	-9.5	-12.7	-8.6	-15.1	-10.4	-5.6	8.4	5.2	9.3	8.0	3.7
Finland	-2.9	-0.4	-1.1	1.2	-2.0	-4.6	-5.9	-4.5	-2.5	3.9	-0.3	-2.3	-4.5	0.1
France	6.3	6.6	7.0	6.1	5.6	3.9	4.5	4.8	4.6	7.1	6.8	6.4	5.4	5.3
Germany	5.8	7.2	7.4	8.9	9.4	10.0	9.2	9.0	8.9	9.9	9.5	8.1	8.3	8.1
Greece	..	..	..	..	..	..	10.3	2.0	8.4	5.4	-6.8	1.0	-2.7	2.3
Hungary	10.1	9.5	5.5	1.5	5.1	7.5	6.5	3.8	2.9	7.2	9.1	9.8	9.8	9.4
Iceland	..	..	..	..	..	..	..	..	..	..	..	..	..	..
Ireland	..	..	-5.0	-12.2	-11.3	-18.2	-17.2	-19.0	-1.5	11.8	11.7	8.4	6.8	5.3
Israel[1]	..	..	..	..	..	..	..	..	..	..	..	..	..	..
Italy	8.2	12.2	10.6	6.5	7.8	8.4	3.1	0.1	5.2	2.6	-1.3	2.0	3.9	2.8
Japan	4.8	5.6	3.2	1.3	3.7	6.4	7.1	6.5	7.1	4.5	4.2	7.8	7.4	5.8
Korea	..	..	..	..	..	..	..	..	..	..	..	..	13.7	11.5
Luxembourg	..	..	..	..	..	..	..	..	..	..	..	..	..	..
Mexico	..	..	..	..	..	..	..	..	..	..	..	..	..	..
Netherlands	-0.9	2.2	2.8	0.6	1.4	-0.9	-4.9	-5.7	-3.9	3.5	2.2	4.9	5.8	8.5
New Zealand	..	..	..	..	..	..	..	..	..	..	..	..	..	..
Norway	1.6	-2.3	2.7	3.2	1.1	5.3	-5.8	-5.8	-4.2	0.6	-0.6	-1.9	-0.8	-1.7
Poland	..	..	..	..	0.7	6.5	1.2	2.9	-8.9	5.8	4.4	1.6	12.7	7.9
Portugal	0.4	3.2	4.0	2.6	3.6	3.4	2.4	1.0	2.4	6.7	5.1	4.1	4.5	5.6
Slovak Republic	1.3	0.1	-1.7	-2.1	-2.3	-2.6	-3.7	-1.9	-2.9	-0.1	2.9	0.7	0.2	1.2
Slovenia	..	..	12.3	9.2	10.7	7.9	4.2	0.8	1.7	2.2	1.9	0.4	0.5	2.0
Spain	0.2	1.3	1.8	0.0	-1.1	-3.4	-5.4	-6.1	-2.3	7.2	4.0	5.6	4.9	5.5
Sweden	2.7	5.9	9.6	9.0	3.2	4.2	2.6	5.4	9.7	5.0	4.2	6.7	9.0	10.0
Switzerland	7.3	11.4	9.8	8.2	10.8	10.4	16.1	19.8	7.9	14.2	11.5	7.7	7.4	7.1
Turkey	..	..	..	..	..	..	..	..	..	..	..	..	..	..
United Kingdom	5.0	3.9	4.4	2.3	0.6	0.1	-0.5	-0.3	-0.4	6.5	8.3	4.6	4.4	0.7
United States	-3.6	-0.6	-2.4	-0.1	1.6	-3.1	-3.5	2.6	10.7	5.5	8.0	11.6	8.9	7.5
Euro area	..	..	..	..	..	..	..	..	..	..	..	..	..	..
OECD-Total	..	..	..	..	..	..	..	..	..	..	..	..	..	..
Brazil	..	..	..	..	..	..	..	..	..	..	..	..	..	..
China	..	..	..	..	..	..	..	..	..	..	..	..	..	..
India	..	..	..	..	..	..	..	..	..	..	..	..	..	..
Indonesia	..	..	..	..	..	..	..	..	..	..	..	..	..	..
Russian Federation	..	..	..	..	..	..	..	..	..	..	..	..	..	..
South Africa	..	..	..	..	..	..	..	..	..	..	..	..	..	..

Note: Detailed metadata:
http://stats.oecd.org/OECDStat_Metadata/ShowMetadata.ashx?Dataset=NAAG_2015_NOV15&Lang=en&Coords=[INDICATOR].[B9FS14_S15NDI]

1. Information on data for Israel: http://dx.doi.org/10.1787/888932315602

Table 18.1. **Non-financial assets of households per capita**

US dollars, current PPPs

	Dwellings				Land				Other			
	2009	2010	2011	2012	2009	2010	2011	2012	2009	2010	2011	2012
Australia	45 243	44 748	45 479	46 291	99 058	92 678	86 630	89 250	16 986	16 627	16 661	16 971
Austria	46 852	48 602	50 804	52 312	..	..	..	..	..	..	..	..
Belgium	48 571	49 853	51 629	53 280	..	..	..	..	..	..	..	..
Canada	37 474	38 617	39 560	41 261	34 754	35 659	37 687	39 448	1 897	1 869	1 903	1 827
Chile	13 004	12 976	13 930	13 998	..	..	..	..	..	..	..	..
Czech Republic	26 582	26 575	28 554	28 226	7 003	7 549	8 044	8 139	5 153	5 568	6 440	6 579
Denmark	35 452	37 431	41 738	42 083	..	..	..	..	..	..	..	..
Estonia	23 807	23 446	24 609	24 213	..	..	..	..	..	..	..	..
Finland	43 895	42 709	45 142	47 617	19 244	21 335	22 256	22 850	..	..	..	..
France	53 158	55 254	58 282	58 939	56 412	63 576	66 525	62 926	6 764	7 194	7 408	7 202
Germany	51 454	53 494	56 475	58 551	..	..	..	..	..	..	..	..
Greece	44 559	44 516	44 514	44 676	..	..	..	..	..	..	..	..
Hungary	23 783	24 321	24 993	24 991	..	..	..	..	..	..	..	..
Iceland	..	..	..	..	..	..	..	..	..	..	..	..
Ireland	..	..	..	..	..	..	..	..	..	..	..	..
Israel[1]	25 781	26 791	28 532	30 052	..	..	..	..	..	..	..	..
Italy	47 661	49 145	52 164	53 517	..	..	..	..	..	..	..	..
Japan	20 453	21 083	21 645	21 985	52 485	52 882	53 479	54 129	4 628	4 550	4 601	4 649
Korea	22 149	23 117	23 927	24 402	68 674	72 576	76 634	78 033	8 667	9 086	9 511	9 414
Luxembourg	47 250	46 548	48 939	49 958	..	..	..	..	..	..	..	..
Mexico	..	..	..	..	..	..	..	..	..	..	..	..
Netherlands	53 108	53 266	53 003	51 881	..	53 982	54 145	48 740	..	..	..	..
New Zealand	..	..	..	..	..	..	..	..	..	..	..	..
Norway	..	..	..	..	..	..	..	..	..	..	..	..
Poland	5 173	5 626	5 775	5 895	..	..	..	..	..	..	..	..
Portugal	..	..	..	..	..	..	..	..	..	..	..	..
Slovak Republic	31 297	31 836	32 296	32 767	..	..	..	..	..	..	..	..
Slovenia	27 571	28 367	29 519	30 440	..	..	..	..	..	..	..	..
Spain	..	..	..	..	..	..	..	..	..	..	..	..
Sweden	29 459	29 677	30 534	31 134	..	..	..	..	..	..	..	..
Switzerland	..	..	..	..	..	..	..	..	..	..	..	..
Turkey	..	..	..	..	..	..	..	..	..	..	..	..
United Kingdom	..	..	..	..	..	..	..	..	..	..	..	..
United States	50 436	50 256	50 218	51 190	33 932	33 460	33 785	39 144	..	..	..	..
Euro area	..	..	..	..	..	..	..	..	..	..	..	..
OECD-Total	..	..	..	..	..	..	..	..	..	..	..	..
Brazil	..	..	..	..	..	..	..	..	..	..	..	..
China	..	..	..	..	..	..	..	..	..	..	..	..
India	..	..	..	..	..	..	..	..	..	..	..	..
Indonesia	..	..	..	..	..	..	..	..	..	..	..	..
Russian Federation	..	..	..	..	..	..	..	..	..	..	..	..
South Africa	..	..	..	..	..	..	..	..	..	..	..	..

Note: Detailed metadata: http://stats.oecd.org/OECDStat_Metadata/ShowMetadata.ashx?Dataset=NAAG_2015_NOV15&Lang=en&Coords=[INDICATOR].[ANNS14_S15HCPC]

1. Information on data for Israel: http://dx.doi.org/10.1787/888932315602

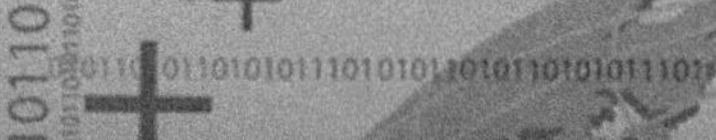

19. Composition of household portfolio

Table 19.1. **Composition of households assets portfolio**

Percentage of financial assets total

	Currency and deposits		Debt securities		Equity		Investment funds shares		Life insurance and annuities		Pension funds	
	2002	2012	2002	2012	2002	2012	2002	2012	2002	2012	2002	2012
Australia	20.8	22.6	1.1	0.2	21.1	16.9	0.0	0.0	0.0	0.0	48.3	55.7
Austria	47.0	41.8	6.5	8.6	16.4	19.4	8.2	7.5	11.5	12.7	6.8	6.0
Belgium	26.3	30.1	20.5	9.2	20.3	25.0	15.0	10.3	9.0	15.6	5.4	6.5
Canada	24.9	25.1	5.8	1.9	12.8	19.5	13.9	15.9	..	..	..	..
Chile	..	14.1	..	0.0	..	20.9	..	4.6	..	12.3	..	47.4
Czech Republic	49.7	51.3	0.4	2.9	31.4	23.4	3.7	4.0	5.1	6.4	2.8	5.7
Denmark	21.5	17.8	6.5	2.6	..	21.5	..	7.7	24.5	26.8	20.4	21.4
Estonia	27.4	27.6	0.2	0.1	61.2	54.0	0.9	0.8	1.2	1.8	0.2	7.6
Finland	33.0	35.7	1.2	2.7	34.4	33.6	5.0	7.6	7.6	6.6	12.6	9.1
France	33.1	29.5	3.3	2.2	18.9	19.8	9.0	6.7	27.5	34.2	0.0	0.0
Germany	37.3	39.6	7.4	4.9	10.4	9.5	11.9	8.7	15.9	16.8	11.3	14.1
Greece	52.7	74.0	15.8	6.3	14.7	7.3	10.7	1.0	1.8	2.4	0.2	1.0
Hungary	38.4	33.5	7.6	6.6	28.1	28.1	5.5	7.4	4.6	4.9	5.9	3.6
Iceland	..	16.0	..	3.6	..	..	..	..	..	..	..	..
Ireland	39.0	39.6	0.3	0.1	26.7	14.6	0.0	0.0	11.3	15.6	20.1	25.3
Israel[1]	34.8	23.4	9.5	12.0	14.5	8.6	0.0	7.3	7.7	10.9	27.4	30.5
Italy	24.8	31.6	20.4	19.2	25.1	19.8	13.2	7.3	7.2	11.5	5.0	6.3
Japan	54.1	53.6	3.2	2.7	5.8	8.8	2.0	4.4	16.2	14.2	13.0	12.2
Korea	..	43.0	..	5.6	..	17.1	..	4.4	..	20.1	..	2.7
Luxembourg	54.2	52.9	10.8	9.9	11.0	12.7	12.0	9.2	6.8	10.9	3.5	2.7
Mexico	..	..	..	..	..	..	..	..	..	..	..	..
Netherlands	20.7	21.3	1.5	0.9	17.0	9.0	3.2	2.6	9.4	8.1	42.6	54.5
New Zealand	..	..	..	..	..	..	..	..	..	..	..	..
Norway	34.6	28.7	1.5	0.5	17.7	22.2	3.8	3.6	6.7	3.3	23.1	26.3
Poland	..	45.2	..	0.6	..	20.3	..	4.8	..	5.2	..	19.8
Portugal	46.8	42.4	5.7	6.6	17.8	19.8	8.8	3.5	9.2	11.8	7.9	5.2
Slovak Republic	74.6	63.6	0.2	1.8	0.4	0.3	5.2	5.8	6.3	7.6	0.1	13.8
Slovenia	51.0	49.8	3.0	1.1	25.6	22.1	3.5	3.1	3.0	7.0	1.7	7.0
Spain	41.7	47.4	2.6	4.3	24.0	22.7	12.3	6.6	6.2	6.9	8.3	8.1
Sweden	15.5	16.1	2.3	1.7	23.3	34.0	8.2	7.7	15.4	9.3	31.5	29.0
Switzerland	26.6	31.9	10.2	6.6	11.5	10.8	8.1	8.5	6.8	4.9	33.7	34.2
Turkey	..	80.1	..	2.5	..	9.8	..	1.3	..	0.9	..	3.1
United Kingdom	22.3	25.0	1.4	1.5	9.3	7.1	3.8	2.5	14.9	10.6	44.4	48.6
United States	12.9	13.9	6.6	6.9	32.8	30.9	9.9	11.5	2.8	2.0	32.6	32.5
Euro area	..	..	..	..	..	..	..	..	..	..	..	..
OECD-Total	..	..	..	..	..	..	..	..	..	..	..	..
Brazil	..	..	..	..	..	..	..	..	..	..	..	..
China	..	..	..	..	..	..	..	..	..	..	..	..
India	..	..	..	..	..	..	..	..	..	..	..	..
Indonesia	..	..	..	..	..	..	..	..	..	..	..	..
Russian Federation	..	..	..	..	..	..	..	..	..	..	..	..
South Africa	..	..	..	..	..	..	..	..	..	..	..	..

Note: Detailed metadata:
http://stats.oecd.org/OECDStat_Metadata/ShowMetadata.ashx?Dataset=NAAG_2015_NOV15&Lang=en&Coords=[INDICATOR].[SAF2ASS14_S15]

1. Information on data for Israel: http://dx.doi.org/10.1787/888932315602

Table 20.1. **Household debt**

Percentage of net disposable income

	2000	2001	2002	2003	2004	2005	2006	2007	2008	2009	2010	2011	2012	2013
Australia	137.5	142.7	154.6	165.0	178.4	186.4	190.3	192.8	188.1	195.3	195.5	194.2	196.6	200.4
Austria	75.5	77.1	79.3	79.4	83.3	87.5	88.8	88.6	90.2	90.3	94.2	93.5	89.5	89.3
Belgium	68.3	66.3	68.3	70.7	74.6	79.5	83.3	87.4	89.8	90.8	96.0	102.4	104.2	107.3
Canada	110.1	110.8	114.4	119.4	124.8	132.1	135.2	143.4	148.4	157.4	160.2	161.5	163.1	163.8
Chile	..	..	..	..	..	..	..	..	58.9	57.2	57.5	57.2	56.8	57.9
Czech Republic	21.7	22.2	27.1	29.2	34.1	39.4	43.6	52.9	58.8	60.3	61.9	64.4	65.8	67.6
Denmark	232.8	237.7	242.9	248.7	261.9	282.1	299.4	324.7	339.4	338.7	325.1	319.5	314.6	313.0
Estonia	20.0	24.1	32.7	41.7	54.0	71.7	93.6	104.7	101.1	108.6	107.1	95.6	92.8	83.6
Finland	69.2	70.8	75.6	79.9	88.6	99.2	109.4	114.7	117.1	117.5	119.6	121.0	124.0	123.3
France	74.8	77.0	77.5	81.1	81.9	88.4	93.6	96.6	98.7	104.3	107.5	107.1	103.4	103.8
Germany	116.5	113.0	113.6	112.0	110.4	108.1	105.7	102.6	99.4	100.3	98.3	96.5	95.5	94.5
Greece	..	..	..	..	..	..	72.7	80.8	85.3	86.7	104.3	111.5	109.0	112.4
Hungary	16.5	20.0	27.0	35.8	41.2	47.1	53.8	62.2	76.1	76.6	81.1	74.5	63.1	57.1
Iceland	..	..	..	..	..	..	..	..	..	..	..	..	..	..
Ireland	..	110.6	125.3	146.1	168.7	199.0	223.2	233.3	227.1	235.6	231.3	230.3	221.9	214.1
Israel[1]	..	..	..	..	..	..	..	..	..	..	..	..	..	..
Italy	54.5	56.5	59.4	62.5	66.2	71.3	76.1	80.2	81.6	86.5	90.4	89.9	92.0	90.6
Japan	140.7	140.7	139.5	138.1	137.4	137.9	137.3	133.6	132.2	132.4	131.9	128.3	127.1	129.2
Korea	..	..	..	..	..	..	..	..	..	..	..	157.8	159.4	160.3
Luxembourg	..	..	..	..	..	..	..	..	..	..	..	..	..	..
Mexico	..	..	..	..	..	..	..	..	..	..	..	..	..	..
Netherlands	199.1	194.2	204.4	222.9	233.0	251.5	256.9	261.4	274.3	286.6	293.9	287.8	288.4	280.9
New Zealand	..	..	..	..	..	..	..	..	..	..	..	..	..	..
Norway	135.3	148.2	147.8	151.4	161.6	167.4	199.2	207.9	207.6	207.0	212.1	216.8	220.2	221.9
Poland	..	..	..	19.7	21.6	25.0	31.2	39.2	51.5	52.8	57.2	60.7	58.6	59.5
Portugal	106.8	118.3	121.6	123.6	126.8	135.9	140.6	145.7	148.9	151.4	154.4	144.9	150.9	141.3
Slovak Republic	18.5	20.7	24.2	27.7	25.9	29.8	32.8	38.9	42.5	42.1	43.1	49.4	54.8	57.6
Slovenia	..	33.1	33.6	35.4	36.0	40.3	44.9	52.2	53.5	56.2	58.9	57.7	59.5	58.8
Spain	84.2	87.1	94.1	102.3	113.6	128.2	144.3	154.1	150.1	145.2	148.6	142.7	141.2	134.1
Sweden	108.6	119.2	121.6	128.2	137.0	146.7	153.8	157.4	159.5	163.5	170.7	168.5	167.1	169.7
Switzerland	168.2	167.0	173.3	182.5	184.2	188.2	187.6	182.1	180.4	184.0	189.3	194.0	196.0	197.4
Turkey	..	..	..	..	..	..	..	..	..	..	..	..	..	..
United Kingdom	118.9	125.6	138.8	151.6	164.9	167.2	178.9	183.3	178.2	167.5	158.7	159.1	153.7	152.0
United States	103.5	107.2	112.4	120.3	126.9	134.6	139.7	143.1	135.3	133.7	127.2	119.0	113.6	115.1
Euro area	..	..	..	..	..	..	..	..	..	..	..	..	..	..
OECD-Total	..	..	..	..	..	..	..	..	..	..	..	..	..	..
Brazil	..	..	..	..	..	..	..	..	..	..	..	..	..	..
China	..	..	..	..	..	..	..	..	..	..	..	..	..	..
India	..	..	..	..	..	..	..	..	..	..	..	..	..	..
Indonesia	..	..	..	..	..	..	..	..	..	..	..	..	..	..
Russian Federation	..	..	..	..	..	..	..	..	..	..	..	..	..	..
South Africa	..	..	..	..	..	..	..	..	..	..	..	..	..	..

Note: Detailed metadata:
http://stats.oecd.org/OECDStat_Metadata/ShowMetadata.ashx?Dataset=NAAG_2015_NOV15&Lang=en&Coords=[INDICATOR].[DBTS14_S15NDI]

1. Information on data for Israel: http://dx.doi.org/10.1787/888932315602

21. Financial net worth of households

Table 21.1. Financial net worth of households per capita

US dollars at current PPPs

	2000	2001	2002	2003	2004	2005	2006	2007	2008	2009	2010	2011	2012	2013
Australia	26 705.4	28 448.7	24 579.4	25 249.7	31 996.7	39 541.4	44 223.7	45 854.2	29 386.8	37 315.1	37 013.1	34 175.8	44 214.5	49 892.8
Austria	31 976.7	31 884.3	32 989.0	35 585.5	37 850.3	40 299.9	44 884.0	46 725.8	44 903.8	50 228.6	52 502.7	52 809.7	55 306.6	57 233.5
Belgium	68 800.1	69 814.5	66 007.3	68 163.9	72 167.7	77 648.2	81 423.3	83 032.6	75 003.5	83 050.9	85 844.0	89 395.5	92 613.9	95 912.1
Canada	48 754.7	47 783.4	43 611.7	47 348.5	49 662.7	57 808.5	63 991.0	65 985.0	52 643.5	60 414.0	65 497.7	64 501.6	69 889.7	78 173.7
Chile	..	..	..	..	..	13 092.7	15 285.0	16 652.3	13 841.7	15 679.5	17 745.0	18 410.2	19 721.4	20 848.7
Czech Republic	11 498.7	12 407.5	12 756.4	13 892.5	13 276.3	13 663.5	14 445.9	16 071.7	16 031.7	16 627.0	17 876.0	18 845.1	20 889.2	21 978.0
Denmark	28 187.8	23 905.9	22 389.2	24 645.1	28 702.2	40 483.8	46 609.2	43 541.2	30 368.5	38 707.8	47 265.5	48 299.6	58 116.9	60 418.8
Estonia	4 733.6	4 572.1	5 675.3	6 667.0	8 226.6	9 319.8	10 745.2	10 435.1	9 646.6	11 054.7	9 127.8	12 543.3	16 415.9	17 691.5
Finland	19 793.1	18 507.4	17 173.2	19 007.2	20 257.4	22 211.0	23 972.9	23 327.4	17 577.5	21 109.7	24 275.4	20 852.7	22 558.3	26 470.0
France	35 168.5	33 919.1	33 754.7	34 874.9	36 788.2	39 925.0	45 505.1	47 640.8	42 195.3	46 587.7	49 556.2	50 242.9	53 089.8	55 756.3
Germany	25 145.4	26 389.6	25 817.5	29 266.0	32 082.9	36 423.7	37 931.1	41 848.9	40 117.1	42 877.1	46 268.1	47 382.9	50 493.3	52 758.9
Greece	27 541.9	26 142.5	22 920.8	22 305.3	24 111.6	26 617.9	28 625.6	27 873.7	18 816.0	20 763.1	14 548.9	11 744.4	12 947.3	19 929.0
Hungary	8 306.4	9 168.2	9 602.3	9 613.2	10 018.8	11 156.8	12 445.1	12 933.1	12 109.1	14 143.1	14 968.6	16 276.2	18 071.6	19 972.0
Iceland	..	..	..	26 884.6	31 621.9	34 659.4	43 310.0	43 999.2	46 080.2	45 964.5	45 703.7	48 615.5	52 567.7	55 453.9
Ireland	..	31 674.9	28 595.9	30 096.3	30 949.1	30 575.4	31 437.0	24 657.2	16 179.8	22 935.4	29 427.8	30 318.8	35 029.7	37 991.9
Israel[1]	..	36 630.0	36 536.3	42 232.5	44 961.3	48 705.9	46 490.9	51 064.1	40 570.6	49 964.6	52 451.8	53 532.9	54 560.9	57 330.2
Italy	55 975.8	55 334.7	54 027.6	54 354.5	56 280.5	63 020.2	70 196.2	65 161.9	62 203.8	60 588.6	58 059.4	56 683.5	60 783.9	63 088.2
Japan	51 512.8	54 888.4	57 036.5	62 076.7	65 341.2	73 157.4	77 243.3	75 651.4	75 051.1	77 966.9	81 775.2	85 641.0	93 453.9	97 774.6
Korea	..	..	..	..	..	..	..	..	..	..	..	29 342.6	31 545.8	33 665.5
Luxembourg	..	..	38 061.4	40 394.5	45 330.2	47 535.8	55 571.3	58 523.8	61 127.1	69 032.6	70 421.8	64 949.1	65 642.0	69 434.0
Mexico	..	..	..	..	..	..	..	..	..	..	..	..	..	..
Netherlands	48 276.4	46 731.5	46 680.7	46 826.1	47 464.0	50 557.1	52 132.7	49 620.1	57 079.0	56 122.5	61 961.7	71 892.8	78 489.7	77 446.5
New Zealand	..	..	..	..	..	..	..	..	..	..	..	..	..	..
Norway	11 653.9	10 725.1	10 242.0	11 456.6	12 926.0	15 861.9	18 609.4	19 458.1	16 285.6	18 761.8	18 687.8	17 312.0	18 491.9	19 583.4
Poland	..	..	..	6 896.2	7 641.9	8 624.1	9 635.4	10 694.8	7 791.7	9 121.6	9 907.9	9 670.1	12 059.4	13 644.4
Portugal	18 456.8	17 604.3	17 572.0	19 827.9	20 933.5	22 042.1	23 642.1	24 729.4	24 361.0	25 437.5	26 346.9	28 832.9	30 345.3	33 703.0
Slovak Republic	6 057.3	6 168.1	5 553.2	4 998.6	4 855.0	5 029.7	6 118.8	6 726.1	7 200.1	7 962.6	8 900.2	9 064.7	9 515.8	9 785.1
Slovenia	..	11 223.4	13 176.5	14 293.3	16 593.4	17 479.8	19 584.4	20 469.0	17 766.6	18 423.0	18 788.8	18 120.7	18 718.9	19 474.5
Spain	22 909.2	23 111.2	21 630.7	23 406.3	24 364.0	26 049.9	30 609.4	29 181.9	22 053.8	23 924.1	23 510.7	25 048.6	27 482.0	33 196.5
Sweden	32 233.6	31 024.8	31 019.9	36 364.8	38 675.6	47 310.6	56 007.9	57 160.4	51 342.6	57 542.8	64 316.4	62 063.4	66 621.1	74 360.1
Switzerland	83 597.4	80 117.6	77 282.8	80 754.7	83 744.5	90 976.0	103 206.0	110 429.9	99 776.8	108 363.7	108 687.7	114 492.2	122 379.3	129 704.3
Turkey	..	..	..	..	..	..	..	..	..	4 435.0	4 861.7	4 648.5	4 603.9	4 644.2
United Kingdom	70 220.9	65 620.3	61 853.0	62 119.9	65 056.5	71 321.3	72 741.6	71 051.6	63 536.8	68 801.4	71 396.7	77 356.9	81 068.2	80 001.9
United States	95 306.6	90 107.3	82 036.5	93 234.5	105 550.5	112 670.0	123 559.3	128 206.2	104 399.2	112 821.7	126 560.1	129 558.7	142 494.8	163 120.6
Euro area	..	..	..	..	..	..	..	..	..	..	..	..	..	..
OECD-Total	..	..	..	..	..	..	..	..	..	..	..	..	..	..
Brazil	..	..	..	..	..	..	..	..	..	..	..	..	..	..
China	..	..	..	..	..	..	..	..	..	..	..	..	..	..
India	..	..	..	..	..	..	..	..	..	..	..	..	..	..
Indonesia	..	..	..	..	..	..	..	..	..	..	..	..	..	..
Russian Federation	..	..	..	..	..	..	..	..	..	..	..	..	..	..
South Africa	..	..	..	..	..	..	..	..	..	..	..	..	..	..

Note: Detailed metadata:
http://stats.oecd.org/OECDStat_Metadata/ShowMetadata.ashx?Dataset=NAAG_2015_NOV15&Lang=en&Coords=[INDICATOR].[SBF90S14_S15PPC]

1. Information on data for Israel: http://dx.doi.org/10.1787/888932315602

Table 22.1. **Total net worth of households**

Percentage of net disposable income

	2000	2001	2002	2003	2004	2005	2006	2007	2008	2009	2010	2011	2012	2013
Australia	330.5	332.7	318.5	322.2	352.9	388.7	395.9	385.2	301.2	329.3	322.3	300.7	338.2	355.5
Austria	357.9	361.6	363.4	369.6	373.2	372.7	379.2	383.6	371.5	397.6	411.5	408.1	409.3	426.3
Belgium	..	..	..	..	..	..	..	..	..	..	..	..	..	..
Canada	418.3	404.7	378.9	398.4	406.0	439.3	456.9	456.1	392.7	419.5	440.7	432.4	451.4	478.6
Chile	..	..	..	..	..	..	..	..	268.4	279.2	278.9	255.0	245.1	242.5
Czech Republic	318.4	316.2	314.3	315.7	305.1	300.3	294.0	311.7	313.2	303.1	311.8	318.5	327.8	335.6
Denmark	457.9	413.7	384.9	401.5	416.7	495.2	527.0	514.0	428.0	421.6	450.9	456.4	503.8	520.4
Estonia	360.2	383.2	364.5	354.5	373.6	356.9	345.2	324.6	278.4	305.3	287.5	298.0	321.9	..
Finland	358.3	347.0	320.8	323.8	323.1	344.8	352.6	349.5	314.6	318.2	318.1	301.0	316.9	334.4
France	418.8	397.5	389.6	407.6	417.3	436.7	459.5	463.3	435.0	454.4	466.2	468.9	488.7	503.0
Germany	356.1	350.0	346.2	355.7	365.7	379.4	379.0	403.2	390.5	409.8	416.0	414.1	427.3	438.2
Greece	..	..	..	..	..	..	369.0	364.6	312.5	321.2	317.3	326.3	351.7	..
Hungary	329.5	320.7	311.7	298.7	292.2	294.9	308.9	320.9	316.0	340.3	347.9	336.4	348.1	..
Iceland	..	..	..	..	..	..	..	..	..	..	..	..	..	..
Ireland	..	..	..	..	..	..	..	..	..	..	..	..	..	..
Israel[1]	..	..	..	..	..	..	..	..	..	..	..	..	..	..
Italy	503.5	479.2	477.4	474.5	485.8	520.0	533.9	498.6	480.2	491.4	491.1	481.5	520.8	534.6
Japan	425.5	447.0	448.7	475.5	479.9	510.1	516.9	495.3	487.3	499.2	499.9	501.5	523.6	541.0
Korea	..	..	..	..	..	..	..	..	..	..	..	324.8	332.2	335.0
Luxembourg	..	..	..	..	..	..	..	..	..	..	..	..	..	..
Mexico	..	..	..	..	..	..	..	..	..	..	..	..	..	..
Netherlands	497.9	465.8	469.7	491.2	497.0	519.1	519.4	494.4	535.4	546.5	583.3	604.3	631.3	613.9
New Zealand	..	..	..	..	..	..	..	..	..	..	..	..	..	..
Norway	..	..	..	..	..	..	..	..	..	..	..	..	..	..
Poland	..	..	..	118.4	127.5	138.0	142.8	148.0	117.0	121.2	123.5	117.5	131.2	..
Portugal	..	..	..	..	..	..	..	..	..	..	..	..	..	..
Slovak Republic	347.1	341.2	325.6	319.0	302.7	296.0	295.1	280.1	273.3	281.8	281.4	284.5	287.1	284.7
Slovenia	..	283.1	285.8	292.8	306.3	303.5	309.1	304.4	275.1	285.3	289.3	282.5	293.5	..
Spain	..	..	..	..	..	..	..	..	..	..	..	..	..	..
Sweden	376.9	353.8	343.8	377.3	390.5	447.3	478.5	460.3	418.0	441.6	470.3	434.0	441.0	..
Switzerland	..	..	..	..	..	..	..	..	..	..	..	..	..	..
Turkey	..	..	..	..	..	..	..	..	..	..	..	..	..	..
United Kingdom	..	..	..	..	..	..	..	..	..	..	..	..	..	..
United States	515.3	485.0	445.4	478.2	511.7	534.5	549.0	545.3	451.7	477.1	505.7	492.3	507.7	574.7
Euro area	..	..	..	..	..	..	..	..	..	..	..	..	..	..
OECD-Total	..	..	..	..	..	..	..	..	..	..	..	..	..	..
Brazil	..	..	..	..	..	..	..	..	..	..	..	..	..	..
China	..	..	..	..	..	..	..	..	..	..	..	..	..	..
India	..	..	..	..	..	..	..	..	..	..	..	..	..	..
Indonesia	..	..	..	..	..	..	..	..	..	..	..	..	..	..
Russian Federation	..	..	..	..	..	..	..	..	..	..	..	..	..	..
South Africa	..	..	..	..	..	..	..	..	..	..	..	..	..	..

Note: Detailed metadata:
http://stats.oecd.org/OECDStat_Metadata/ShowMetadata.ashx?Dataset=NAAG_2015_NOV15&Lang=en&Coords=[INDICATOR].[TOTNETWORTHS14_S15NDI]

1. Information on data for Israel: http://dx.doi.org/10.1787/888932315602

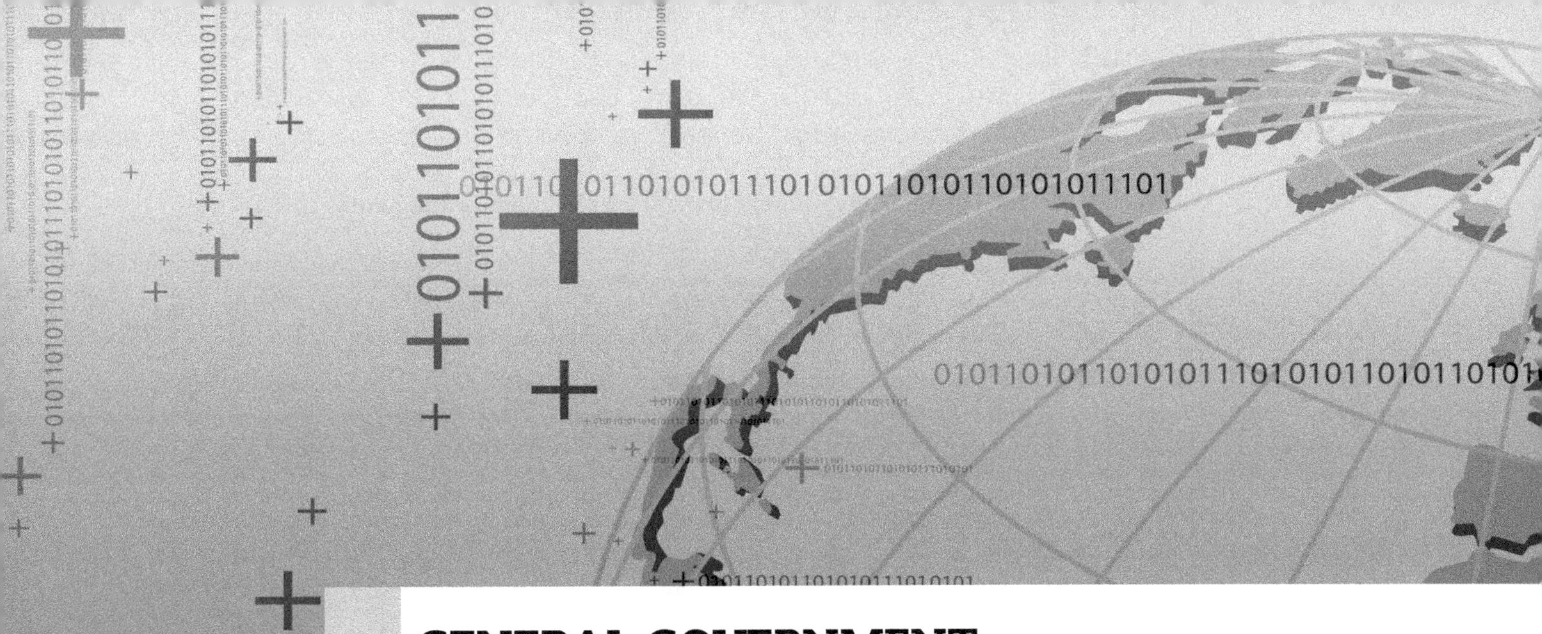

GENERAL GOVERNMENT

Table 23.1. **Total general government expenditure by main component**

Percentage of GDP

	Compensation of employees			Social benefits and social transfers in kind			Intermediate consumption			Gross fixed capital formation			Other		
	2003	2008	2013	2003	2008	2013	2003	2008	2013	2003	2008	2013	2003	2008	2013
Australia	..	..	..	10.9	11.7	10.6	..	..	..	2.7	3.5	3.4	..	..	..
Austria	10.8	10.6	10.6	22.4	21.2	23.0	5.5	6.2	6.4	2.4	3.2	3.0	9.9	8.6	8.0
Belgium	11.9	11.8	12.7	21.9	22.3	25.3	4.2	4.0	4.3	2.2	2.1	2.4	10.6	10.1	10.8
Canada	11.7	11.5	12.1	8.7	8.6	9.3	8.6	8.9	9.5	3.2	3.9	3.9	8.0	6.3	5.9
Chile	..	7.5	8.4	..	..	..	..	..	..	..	2.4	2.1	..	..	..
Czech Republic	7.6	7.0	8.9	17.8	16.8	16.6	6.6	5.5	6.5	7.3	5.0	3.7	9.2	5.9	6.8
Denmark	16.3	15.6	16.8	18.6	16.3	19.4	7.9	8.6	9.4	2.6	3.0	3.7	8.3	7.0	7.8
Estonia	10.2	11.1	10.6	10.2	12.0	12.3	7.3	6.5	6.6	5.2	6.2	5.5	2.2	4.0	3.3
Finland	13.2	12.9	14.4	18.0	16.9	21.7	8.5	9.4	11.6	3.8	3.6	4.1	5.9	5.5	5.8
France	13.1	12.4	12.9	22.5	23.0	25.7	4.7	4.7	5.2	3.9	3.9	4.0	8.5	9.0	9.2
Germany	8.2	7.4	7.8	26.0	23.1	23.6	3.8	4.0	4.8	2.1	2.1	2.2	7.7	7.0	6.1
Greece	..	11.6	12.1	..	18.9	21.5	..	6.2	4.7	..	5.6	3.4	..	8.6	19.1
Hungary	13.0	11.4	10.1	16.4	18.3	17.0	6.6	7.0	7.5	3.8	3.2	4.4	9.3	8.9	10.5
Iceland	15.3	13.5	13.6	6.9	5.8	7.1	11.0	11.3	11.8	4.3	4.9	2.9	7.3	20.1	8.8
Ireland	9.2	11.3	10.4	10.0	14.0	15.9	5.2	5.4	4.6	3.6	5.2	1.8	4.9	6.0	7.0
Israel[1]	11.7	10.3	10.3	8.5	7.3	7.5	11.9	10.5	10.2	2.9	2.2	2.2	15.2	12.0	11.3
Italy	10.4	10.4	10.3	18.7	19.6	22.6	4.9	5.1	5.6	3.0	3.0	2.4	10.2	9.7	10.2
Japan	6.5	6.2	6.0	17.0	19.0	22.8	4.2	3.7	4.3	4.2	3.0	3.5	5.9	5.0	5.8
Korea	6.5	7.0	6.8	4.6	6.8	8.2	4.0	4.7	4.6	5.7	5.3	4.7	11.7	8.2	7.5
Luxembourg	8.0	7.4	9.0	19.8	18.9	20.9	3.4	3.3	3.7	4.7	3.7	3.5	6.2	6.0	6.1
Mexico	8.8	8.2	9.2	1.5	1.6	2.3	2.5	2.6	3.0	1.7	2.7	2.2	5.5	9.7	7.8
Netherlands	9.4	8.7	9.3	18.5	18.8	22.4	6.4	6.5	6.4	4.2	4.0	3.6	6.2	5.7	4.7
New Zealand	8.5	9.8	9.4	13.2	15.2	14.8	6.2	6.7	6.4	3.9	4.3	3.6	5.0	5.7	5.8
Norway	13.8	11.9	13.6	17.4	13.3	15.2	6.6	5.4	6.0	3.9	3.8	4.3	6.3	5.8	4.9
Poland	11.6	10.9	10.4	18.8	16.0	16.3	6.8	6.3	5.9	2.8	4.8	4.1	5.7	6.5	5.6
Portugal	14.3	13.1	12.5	15.2	16.7	20.4	4.7	5.5	5.6	4.4	3.7	2.2	6.8	6.2	9.2
Slovak Republic	8.7	7.4	8.5	15.0	16.1	18.9	5.6	4.6	5.2	3.2	3.3	3.1	7.5	5.3	5.4
Slovenia	11.5	10.8	12.1	17.6	16.3	19.3	6.0	6.0	6.9	3.7	4.7	4.4	7.0	6.0	17.7
Spain	9.8	10.6	11.1	13.8	14.9	19.3	4.3	5.3	5.3	4.1	4.6	2.2	6.2	5.8	7.2
Sweden	13.1	12.4	12.6	18.3	16.4	17.8	8.2	8.1	8.5	4.2	4.3	4.5	10.5	9.2	8.9
Switzerland	7.8	7.0	7.5	11.8	10.1	11.2	4.4	4.1	4.4	3.2	2.8	3.0	8.4	7.1	7.9
Turkey	..	7.8	..	..	10.2	..	..	4.6	..	..	3.7	..	..	10.0	..
United Kingdom	10.3	10.6	9.6	12.5	12.9	14.5	9.7	11.6	11.3	2.2	3.1	2.6	6.4	8.4	6.9
United States	10.4	10.4	10.1	11.6	13.1	14.4	6.5	7.2	6.5	3.8	4.0	3.3	4.3	4.6	4.4
Euro area	..	..	..	..	..	..	..	..	..	..	..	..	..	..	..
OECD-Total	..	..	..	..	..	..	..	..	..	..	..	..	..	..	..
Brazil	..	..	..	..	..	..	..	..	..	..	..	..	..	..	..
China	8.0	7.6	..	..	..	..	..	..	..	4.6	4.7	..	..	..	..
India	..	..	..	..	..	..	..	..	..	..	..	..	..	..	..
Indonesia	..	..	..	..	..	..	..	..	..	..	..	..	..	..	..
Russian Federation	8.8	9.0	11.6	10.0	8.7	12.0	8.4	7.8	8.1	2.7	2.1	1.9	6.6	6.8	6.0
South Africa	..	11.5	13.7	..	..	..	..	8.4	8.4	..	3.7	3.1	..	..	..

Note: Detailed metadata:
http://stats.oecd.org/OECDStat_Metadata/ShowMetadata.ashx?Dataset=NAAG_2015_NOV15&Lang=en&Coords=[INDICATOR].[D1S13S]

1. Information on data for Israel: http://dx.doi.org/10.1787/888932315602

Table 24.1. **Total general government expenditure by function**

Percentage of GDP, 2012

	Total expenditure	General public services	Defence	Public order and safety	Economic affairs	Environment protection	Housing and community amenities	Health	Recreation, culture and religion	Education	Social protection
Australia	..	..	..	..	..	..	..	..	..	..	..
Austria	51.0	7.2	0.6	1.3	6.2	0.5	0.4	7.9	0.9	5.0	21.0
Belgium	54.9	8.6	0.9	1.8	7.5	0.9	0.4	8.0	1.3	6.3	19.2
Canada	..	..	..	..	..	..	..	..	..	..	..
Chile	..	..	..	..	..	..	..	..	..	..	..
Czech Republic	43.9	6.5	0.8	1.7	6.0	1.3	0.7	7.4	1.2	5.0	13.1
Denmark	58.8	9.3	1.4	1.0	3.7	0.4	0.3	8.8	1.9	7.1	24.9
Estonia	38.9	4.0	1.8	2.0	4.6	0.8	0.6	5.0	1.7	6.2	12.2
Finland	56.1	8.2	1.5	1.4	4.8	0.2	0.4	8.2	1.2	6.4	23.8
France	56.8	6.8	1.8	1.6	5.0	1.0	1.4	8.0	1.4	5.5	24.2
Germany	44.1	6.4	1.1	1.5	3.4	0.6	0.4	6.8	0.8	4.2	18.8
Greece	..	..	..	..	..	..	..	..	..	..	..
Hungary	48.6	9.6	0.7	1.9	6.2	0.7	0.9	5.2	1.9	4.7	16.7
Iceland	..	..	..	..	..	..	..	..	..	..	..
Ireland	41.7	6.7	0.4	1.6	3.4	0.7	0.8	6.9	0.7	4.4	16.1
Israel[1]	41.5	6.9	6.0	1.6	2.5	0.6	0.5	5.0	1.4	6.2	10.9
Italy	50.8	9.3	1.3	2.0	4.1	1.0	0.8	7.2	0.7	4.1	20.5
Japan	42.0	4.4	0.9	1.3	4.2	1.1	0.7	7.4	0.4	3.6	18.0
Korea	32.7	5.6	2.4	1.2	6.4	0.8	1.0	3.7	0.7	5.2	5.6
Luxembourg	44.1	5.7	0.4	1.0	4.2	1.1	0.8	5.0	1.2	5.4	19.3
Mexico	..	..	..	..	..	..	..	..	..	..	..
Netherlands	47.1	5.2	1.2	1.9	4.5	1.6	0.5	8.3	1.7	5.5	16.8
New Zealand	..	..	..	..	..	..	..	..	..	..	..
Norway	42.9	4.3	1.4	0.9	4.4	0.8	0.6	7.3	1.3	4.9	17.1
Poland	..	..	..	..	..	..	..	..	..	..	..
Portugal	48.8	9.2	1.2	2.2	2.9	0.4	0.6	6.6	0.9	6.5	18.4
Slovak Republic	40.1	4.8	1.3	3.2	3.7	0.9	0.7	7.4	1.2	4.4	12.4
Slovenia	48.1	6.2	1.1	1.8	4.0	0.7	0.8	6.9	1.8	6.4	18.5
Spain	47.9	6.6	0.9	2.0	7.9	0.9	0.5	6.2	1.2	4.2	17.5
Sweden	52.6	7.7	1.4	1.4	4.5	0.3	0.7	6.9	1.1	6.5	22.1
Switzerland	33.2	4.0	1.0	1.7	3.9	0.7	0.2	2.1	0.8	6.0	12.8
Turkey	..	..	..	..	..	..	..	..	..	..	..
United Kingdom	46.7	5.4	2.4	2.3	3.5	0.9	0.8	7.5	0.9	5.8	17.3
United States	40.1	5.8	4.2	2.2	3.7	0.0	0.7	8.7	0.3	6.4	8.1
Euro area	..	..	..	..	..	..	..	..	..	..	..
OECD-Total	..	..	..	..	..	..	..	..	..	..	..
Brazil	..	..	..	..	..	..	..	..	..	..	..
China	..	..	..	..	..	..	..	..	..	..	..
India	..	..	..	..	..	..	..	..	..	..	..
Indonesia	..	..	..	..	..	..	..	..	..	..	..
Russian Federation	37.7	..	..	..	..	..	..	..	..	..	..
South Africa	..	..	..	..	..	..	..	..	..	..	..

Note: Detailed metadata:
http://stats.oecd.org/OECDStat_Metadata/ShowMetadata.ashx?Dataset=NAAG_2015_NOV15&Lang=en&Coords=[INDICATOR].[TLYCGTGS13S]

1. Information on data for Israel: http://dx.doi.org/10.1787/888932315602

Table 25.1. **Taxes in the *System of National Accounts* (SNA)**

Percentage of GDP

	Total tax receipts			Taxes on production and imports			Current taxes on income, wealth, etc.			Capital taxes		
	2003	2008	2013	2003	2008	2013	2003	2008	2013	2003	2008	2013
Australia	30.2	26.9	27.6	12.8	10.9	11.6	17.4	16.0	16.1	0.0	0.0	0.0
Austria	28.2	27.6	27.9	14.7	13.9	14.4	13.4	13.7	13.3	0.1	0.0	0.2
Belgium	29.2	29.3	30.8	12.6	12.5	13.0	16.2	16.1	16.7	0.5	0.7	1.0
Canada	..	..	..	12.7	11.1	11.2	14.9	15.4	14.7	..	..	..
Chile	..	..	..	..	11.0	11.0	..	6.3	6.3	..	..	..
Czech Republic	19.1	18.0	19.8	10.2	10.4	12.8	8.8	7.6	7.0	0.0	0.0	0.0
Denmark	45.5	44.7	47.6	16.9	16.5	16.8	28.4	28.0	30.6	0.2	0.3	0.2
Estonia	..	..	..	12.2	12.1	13.3	8.1	7.7	7.1	..	..	..
Finland	31.0	29.6	31.0	13.7	12.4	14.5	17.1	16.8	16.2	0.3	0.3	0.3
France	26.1	26.8	28.7	14.9	14.7	15.5	10.8	11.7	12.7	0.5	0.4	0.5
Germany	21.3	22.9	22.8	10.7	10.7	10.8	10.4	12.0	11.8	0.2	0.2	0.2
Greece	..	20.9	24.7	..	12.6	14.1	..	8.1	10.5	..	0.3	0.1
Hungary	25.0	25.9	25.1	15.6	15.5	18.5	9.3	10.3	6.6	0.1	0.1	0.0
Iceland	32.7	32.6	32.3	16.3	15.0	14.2	16.3	17.5	17.9	0.1	0.1	0.1
Ireland	25.0	24.4	23.7	12.4	12.0	10.7	12.4	12.2	12.8	0.1	0.2	0.2
Israel[1]	27.7	26.5	25.6	15.5	14.6	14.7	12.0	11.6	10.6	0.2	0.3	0.4
Italy	27.8	28.3	30.1	13.7	13.6	14.9	12.8	14.7	15.0	1.3	0.0	0.3
Japan	16.0	18.4	17.6	8.2	8.5	8.6	7.5	9.6	8.7	0.3	0.3	0.3
Korea	18.6	19.9	18.2	11.5	11.3	10.2	6.9	8.2	7.7	0.2	0.3	0.3
Luxembourg	27.3	26.6	27.1	12.5	12.5	12.8	14.6	14.0	14.2	0.2	0.1	0.2
Mexico	11.3	11.3	12.5	6.1	5.4	5.7	5.1	5.9	6.8	0.0	0.0	0.0
Netherlands	21.9	22.6	21.4	11.6	11.5	11.0	10.0	10.8	10.1	0.3	0.3	0.3
New Zealand	32.2	33.4	30.9	12.4	12.3	13.3	19.8	20.9	17.6	0.1	0.1	0.1
Norway	32.0	32.8	30.4	12.8	11.0	11.4	19.1	21.7	19.0	0.1	0.1	0.1
Poland	19.9	22.9	19.6	13.6	14.5	12.8	6.3	8.4	6.8	0.0	0.0	0.0
Portugal	22.8	23.3	25.1	14.5	14.0	13.7	8.2	9.3	11.4	0.1	0.0	0.0
Slovak Republic	18.9	17.1	16.7	12.0	10.4	10.3	7.0	6.7	6.4	0.0	0.0	0.0
Slovenia	23.5	22.7	22.2	15.7	13.9	15.1	7.8	8.7	7.1	0.0	0.0	0.0
Spain	21.6	20.6	21.8	11.4	9.7	11.2	9.8	10.4	10.2	0.4	0.4	0.5
Sweden	42.0	41.1	39.9	22.8	22.3	22.2	19.1	18.7	17.8	0.1	0.0	0.0
Switzerland	20.2	20.6	20.5	6.6	6.2	6.2	13.4	14.3	14.2	0.2	0.1	0.2
Turkey	..	19.1	..	..	11.7	..	..	7.4	..	..	0.0	..
United Kingdom	27.3	29.4	27.0	12.5	11.6	12.7	14.6	16.2	14.0	0.2	1.6	0.2
United States	17.9	19.4	19.5	7.0	7.1	7.1	10.6	12.1	12.3	0.2	0.2	0.2
Euro area	..	..	..	..	..	..	..	..	..	..	..	..
OECD-Total	..	..	..	..	..	..	..	..	..	..	..	..
Brazil	..	..	..	..	..	..	..	..	..	..	..	..
China	..	..	..	12.9	12.6	..	3.1	4.7	..	..	..	..
India	..	..	..	..	..	..	..	..	..	..	..	..
Indonesia	..	..	..	..	..	..	..	..	..	..	..	..
Russian Federation	..	..	..	17.6	20.6	15.7	7.8	10.7	7.6	..	..	..
South Africa	..	..	..	..	11.8	12.4	..	15.0	14.4	..	..	..

Note: Detailed metadata:
http://stats.oecd.org/OECDStat_Metadata/ShowMetadata.ashx?Dataset=NAAG_2015_NOV15&Lang=en&Coords=[INDICATOR].[D2D5D91RS13S]

1. Information on data for Israel: http://dx.doi.org/10.1787/888932315602

Table 26.1. **Social contributions to government**

Percentage of GDP

	2000	2001	2002	2003	2004	2005	2006	2007	2008	2009	2010	2011	2012	2013
Australia	0.0	0.0	0.0	0.0	0.0	0.0	0.0	0.0	0.0	0.0	0.0	0.0	0.0	..
Austria	15.6	15.6	15.4	15.4	15.3	15.0	14.8	14.5	14.6	15.1	14.9	14.9	14.9	15.2
Belgium	15.4	15.7	16.0	15.9	15.5	15.3	15.2	15.3	15.8	16.4	16.1	16.3	16.6	16.9
Canada	4.5	4.7	4.9	4.9	4.7	4.6	4.6	4.5	4.4	4.7	4.6	4.5	4.6	4.7
Chile	..	..	..	..	..	..	..	..	1.7	1.8	1.7	1.7	1.8	1.9
Czech Republic	14.4	14.3	14.9	15.0	14.8	14.8	15.0	15.1	14.9	14.3	14.6	14.7	14.9	14.9
Denmark	2.4	2.3	1.7	1.7	1.6	1.5	1.4	1.4	1.3	1.4	1.4	1.3	1.2	1.1
Estonia	11.0	10.7	11.1	10.7	10.4	10.3	10.1	10.5	11.6	13.1	13.0	11.8	11.3	11.1
Finland	11.8	11.8	11.6	11.5	11.4	11.6	11.9	11.6	11.6	12.3	12.2	12.2	12.8	12.8
France	17.4	17.3	17.4	17.7	17.5	17.6	17.7	17.5	17.6	18.3	18.1	18.3	18.5	18.8
Germany	18.1	17.8	17.8	18.0	17.6	17.4	16.9	16.1	16.1	16.9	16.5	16.4	16.5	16.5
Greece	..	..	..	..	..	..	11.9	12.4	12.7	12.4	13.1	13.2	13.8	13.5
Hungary	13.1	12.8	12.7	12.5	12.2	12.4	12.4	13.6	13.6	13.0	12.0	13.1	13.0	13.0
Iceland	2.8	2.8	2.8	3.0	2.9	3.1	3.2	2.9	2.7	2.9	3.9	3.9	3.7	3.7
Ireland	4.9	5.0	4.9	5.0	5.1	5.1	5.2	5.4	5.9	6.0	5.7	5.7	5.5	5.7
Israel[1]	6.2	6.6	6.7	6.7	6.6	6.4	6.3	6.1	6.2	6.0	6.1	6.1	5.9	5.9
Italy	11.8	11.8	12.0	12.1	12.2	12.2	11.9	12.6	13.0	13.5	13.3	13.2	13.4	13.4
Japan	9.9	10.3	10.4	10.7	10.3	10.6	10.9	11.0	11.5	11.8	11.8	12.5	12.8	13.0
Korea	4.6	5.1	5.2	5.6	5.7	6.1	6.3	6.4	6.7	6.9	6.7	7.0	7.5	7.8
Luxembourg	10.4	11.3	11.4	11.7	11.5	11.6	10.9	10.9	11.4	12.6	12.0	12.4	12.7	12.3
Mexico	..	..	..	2.2	2.0	1.9	1.8	1.8	1.7	1.8	1.7	1.8	1.8	1.9
Netherlands	15.3	13.7	13.3	13.8	13.9	13.0	13.7	13.1	14.0	13.4	13.7	14.3	15.2	15.5
New Zealand	1.0	1.0	1.1	1.0	1.0	1.0	1.1	1.1	1.1	1.2	1.4	1.3	1.2	1.1
Norway	8.8	9.1	9.7	9.6	9.2	8.7	8.5	8.7	8.6	9.6	9.4	9.3	9.3	9.5
Poland	13.9	14.5	13.9	13.7	13.2	13.2	13.0	12.7	12.2	12.1	11.7	12.1	12.9	13.3
Portugal	10.5	10.7	11.0	11.5	11.3	11.6	11.5	11.3	11.6	12.1	11.9	12.0	11.4	12.0
Slovak Republic	14.0	14.2	14.5	13.7	13.0	12.6	11.7	11.6	11.7	12.5	12.3	12.3	12.5	13.5
Slovenia	14.2	14.4	14.2	14.1	14.2	14.2	14.0	13.7	14.0	14.9	15.2	15.0	15.2	14.9
Spain	12.6	12.7	12.7	12.7	12.7	12.6	12.6	12.6	12.7	12.9	12.8	12.9	12.6	12.4
Sweden	5.4	5.0	4.2	4.2	4.2	3.8	3.5	3.5	3.6	3.8	3.6	3.7	3.8	3.8
Switzerland	6.7	6.9	7.1	7.0	6.5	6.5	6.3	6.2	6.2	6.6	6.4	6.7	6.8	6.8
Turkey	..	..	..	..	..	..	6.7	6.8	8.6	9.6	9.4	9.2	..	..
United Kingdom	7.2	7.4	7.2	7.5	7.8	7.9	7.9	7.8	8.1	8.1	8.0	7.9	7.9	7.8
United States	6.9	6.9	6.9	6.8	6.8	6.7	6.7	6.7	6.7	6.7	6.6	5.9	5.9	6.7
Euro area	..	..	..	..	..	..	..	..	..	..	..	..	..	..
OECD-Total	..	..	..	..	..	..	..	..	..	..	..	..	..	..
Brazil	..	..	..	..	..	..	..	..	..	..	10.5	10.6	..	..
China	2.7	2.8	3.4	3.6	3.6	3.8	4.0	4.1	4.4	4.7	5.1	5.8	6.0	..
India	..	..	..	..	..	..	..	..	..	..	..	..	..	..
Indonesia	..	..	..	..	..	..	..	..	..	..	..	..	..	..
Russian Federation	..	..	8.5	8.6	7.9	6.2	5.9	6.0	6.1	6.7	6.0	7.5	7.4	7.9
South Africa	..	..	..	..	..	..	..	..	0.6	0.6	0.5	0.5	0.6	0.6

Note: Detailed metadata:
http://stats.oecd.org/OECDStat_Metadata/ShowMetadata.ashx?Dataset=NAAG_2015_NOV15&Lang=en&Coords=[INDICATOR].[D61RS13S]

1. Information on data for Israel: http://dx.doi.org/10.1787/888932315602

Table 27.1. **Social benefits to households**

Percentage of GDP

	Social benefits other than social transfers in kind							Social transfers in kind						
	2007	2008	2009	2010	2011	2012	2013	2007	2008	2009	2010	2011	2012	2013
Australia	7.4	9.0	7.7	7.6	7.9	8.1	8.0	10.5	10.8	11.1	10.9	11.0	10.9	10.8
Austria	17.6	17.8	19.2	19.4	18.7	18.8	19.2	11.6	11.9	12.6	12.4	12.2	12.3	12.3
Belgium	14.7	15.3	16.7	16.4	16.4	16.9	17.4	13.3	14.0	15.1	15.0	15.2	15.5	15.6
Canada	8.5	8.6	9.9	9.7	9.3	9.3	9.3	..	..	..	..	..	..	..
Chile	..	4.2	4.6	4.4	4.1	4.1	3.9	..	..	..	..	..	..	..
Czech Republic	11.9	11.8	13.0	13.1	13.1	13.2	13.4	9.4	9.4	10.4	10.3	10.6	10.6	10.7
Denmark	14.8	14.7	16.7	17.4	17.4	17.6	17.8	16.8	17.4	19.5	19.3	18.8	18.8	18.8
Estonia	8.4	10.4	13.8	12.7	11.2	10.7	10.6	8.9	10.4	12.1	11.4	10.4	10.1	10.2
Finland	14.5	14.7	17.3	17.5	17.2	18.1	19.0	13.7	14.3	16.0	15.9	15.9	16.5	16.6
France	17.4	17.6	19.2	19.2	19.1	19.6	19.9	14.3	14.5	15.4	15.4	15.2	15.4	15.4
Germany	16.0	15.8	17.3	16.7	15.7	15.6	15.5	11.0	11.2	12.4	12.2	12.0	12.1	12.4
Greece	14.6	16.0	17.5	17.7	19.5	20.3	19.0	10.2	10.5	11.4	10.9	10.7	10.2	9.4
Hungary	15.2	15.6	16.1	15.7	15.3	15.2	14.8	11.0	11.2	11.5	11.1	10.6	10.3	9.8
Iceland	5.5	5.8	7.7	7.5	8.1	7.6	7.1	15.3	15.6	16.1	15.8	15.5	15.3	15.4
Ireland	9.7	11.6	14.3	14.3	13.7	13.8	13.1	10.9	11.9	13.5	13.1	12.4	12.2	12.1
Israel[1]	5.4	5.5	5.7	5.7	5.7	5.6	5.5	10.4	10.6	10.7	10.8	10.8	11.0	11.4
Italy	16.4	17.0	18.5	18.6	18.6	19.3	19.9	11.2	11.4	12.1	12.0	11.4	11.4	11.4
Japan	11.6	12.1	13.7	13.8	14.4	14.3	14.4	10.1	10.5	11.4	11.3	11.9	12.1	12.2
Korea	3.4	3.8	4.0	4.1	4.3	4.5	4.7	6.8	7.1	7.5	7.1	7.4	7.5	7.6
Luxembourg	13.2	14.3	16.5	15.7	15.6	16.2	15.9	9.0	9.3	10.5	10.2	10.2	10.5	10.6
Mexico	1.6	1.6	1.9	2.0	2.1	2.2	2.3	5.0	5.3	5.7	5.7	5.7	5.8	6.0
Netherlands	9.6	9.6	10.7	11.0	11.1	11.4	11.8	15.2	15.6	17.4	17.6	17.4	17.7	17.4
New Zealand	9.8	10.5	11.1	11.1	10.8	10.8	10.3	11.0	12.0	12.2	12.3	12.3	12.3	11.9
Norway	11.9	11.5	13.4	13.3	13.1	13.0	13.2	12.5	12.3	14.2	14.0	13.8	13.7	14.0
Poland	14.1	14.0	14.5	14.5	13.8	13.9	14.4	9.7	9.9	10.1	10.2	9.8	9.8	9.9
Portugal	14.1	14.6	16.4	16.4	17.0	17.6	18.5	11.0	11.1	11.9	11.4	10.7	10.0	10.2
Slovak Republic	11.7	11.5	14.0	14.2	13.7	13.9	13.9	7.8	8.2	9.3	9.1	8.5	8.7	9.0
Slovenia	14.1	14.4	16.1	16.8	17.2	17.1	17.2	10.0	10.4	11.6	11.9	11.9	11.9	11.7
Spain	11.5	12.3	14.4	15.1	15.3	16.2	16.5	10.2	10.8	12.0	11.8	11.7	11.2	11.1
Sweden	13.6	13.6	14.8	14.0	13.4	14.0	14.3	17.6	17.9	18.9	18.2	18.1	18.6	18.8
Switzerland	9.4	9.2	10.2	10.1	10.0	10.1	10.2	5.6	5.5	6.1	6.0	6.1	6.3	6.3
Turkey	7.0	7.2	8.4	7.8	8.3	..	..	6.8	7.0	9.1	8.7	8.4	..	..
United Kingdom	12.3	12.9	14.7	14.6	14.5	14.8	14.5	12.2	12.8	13.9	13.6	13.2	13.0	12.6
United States	11.8	13.1	14.7	15.4	15.0	14.5	14.4	6.1	6.4	6.7	6.5	6.3	6.1	5.9
Euro area	..	..	..	..	..	..	..	..	..	..	..	..	..	..
OECD-Total	..	..	..	..	..	..	..	..	..	..	..	..	..	..
Brazil	..	..	..	13.7	13.6	..	..	..	..	..	..	..	..	..
China	4.2	4.8	5.4	5.5	5.9	6.3	..	..	..	..	..	..	..	..
India	..	..	..	..	..	..	..	..	..	..	..	..	..	..
Indonesia	..	..	..	..	..	..	..	..	..	..	..	..	..	..
Russian Federation	7.3	7.4	9.6	11.0	9.3	10.2	10.9	8.2	8.5	9.9	8.9	8.7	8.3	8.5
South Africa	..	12.6	13.6	13.8	13.4	13.3	13.6	..	8.8	9.4	9.7	9.4	9.2	9.4

Note: Detailed metadata:
http://stats.oecd.org/OECDStat_Metadata/ShowMetadata.ashx?Dataset=NAAG_2015_NOV15&Lang=en&Coords=[INDICATOR].[D62_D63PS13STE]

1. Information on data for Israel: http://dx.doi.org/10.1787/888932315602

Table 28.1. **Net saving and net lending/net borrowing**

Percentage of GDP

	Net saving							Net lending/net borrowing						
	2007	2008	2009	2010	2011	2012	2013	2007	2008	2009	2010	2011	2012	2013
Australia	2.2	-1.9	-2.4	-2.0	-2.1	-0.8	-0.8	0.5	-4.0	-5.7	-4.6	-4.4	-2.3	-2.6
Austria	0.3	0.2	-3.0	-2.9	-1.3	-0.8	-0.6	-1.3	-1.4	-5.3	-4.4	-2.6	-2.2	-1.3
Belgium	0.5	-0.6	-4.4	-3.2	-2.7	-2.5	-2.1	0.1	-1.1	-5.4	-4.0	-4.1	-4.1	-2.9
Canada	2.5	0.8	-3.0	-3.2	-2.4	-2.1	-1.9	1.5	-0.3	-4.5	-4.9	-3.7	-3.1	-2.7
Chile	..	..	..	..	..	..	..	..	4.8	-4.0	0.0	1.5	0.8	-0.4
Czech Republic	0.3	-0.9	-5.0	-4.6 |	-3.3	-2.7	-2.4	-0.7	-2.1	-5.5	-4.4 |	-2.7	-4.0	-1.3
Denmark	5.0	3.6	-2.6	-2.2	-1.3	-1.1	-0.2	5.0	3.2	-2.8	-2.7	-2.1	-3.6	-1.3
Estonia	6.6	2.0	0.4	0.3	1.5	2.3	1.7	2.7	-2.7	-2.2	0.2	1.2	-0.3	-0.1
Finland	5.5	4.6	-1.8	-2.3	-0.5	-1.6	-2.1	5.1	4.2	-2.5	-2.6	-1.0	-2.1	-2.5
France	-1.0	-1.5	-5.2	-5.1	-3.7	-3.4	-2.7	-2.5	-3.2	-7.2	-6.8	-5.1	-4.8	-4.1
Germany	0.9	0.9	-2.1	-2.2	0.0	0.7	0.6	0.2	-0.2	-3.2	-4.2	-1.0	-0.1	-0.1
Greece	-6.4	-8.1	-13.2	-11.8	-12.1	-8.2	-4.1	-6.7	-10.2	-15.2	-11.2	-10.2	-8.8	-12.4
Hungary	-3.2	-3.3	-4.9	-5.1	-5.1	-2.8	-2.9	-5.1	-3.6	-4.6	-4.5	-5.5	-2.3	-2.5
Iceland	8.5	3.1	-6.6	-4.1	-3.3	-1.8	-0.2	4.9	-13.1	-9.7	-9.8	-5.6	-3.7	-1.9
Ireland	2.6	-3.0	-9.1	-8.9	-7.8	-7.4	-5.9	0.3	-7.0	-13.8	-32.3	-12.5	-8.0	-5.7
Israel[1]	0.0	-1.9	-4.7	-3.3	-2.8	-4.1	-3.2	-0.9	-2.9	-5.9	-4.1	-3.4	-5.0	-4.2
Italy	0.3	-1.1	-3.7	-3.1	-3.0	-2.1	-2.7	-1.5	-2.7	-5.3	-4.2	-3.5	-3.0	-2.9
Japan	-2.1	-3.0	-8.8	-8.3	-8.3	-8.0	-7.2	-2.1	-1.9	-8.8	-8.3	-8.8	-8.7	-8.5
Korea	8.4	6.4	4.8	5.1	5.2	4.8	4.4	4.2	2.3	-1.3	1.0	1.0	1.0	1.3
Luxembourg	7.1	6.1	3.0	3.3	3.5	3.0	2.9	4.1	3.3	-0.5	-0.5	0.5	0.2	0.7
Mexico	3.1	4.7	2.1	2.6	2.9	2.1	2.3	0.2	-0.2	-0.6	-0.6	-0.1	0.0	0.1
Netherlands	0.8	1.1	-3.6	-3.6	-3.5	-3.2	-2.4	0.2	0.2	-5.4	-5.0	-4.3	-3.9	-2.4
New Zealand	5.8	2.5	-0.8	-1.2	-0.8	0.5	1.5	4.3	0.4	-2.8	-6.7	-3.5	-1.6	-0.4
Norway	18.3	20.1	12.1	12.3	14.7	14.8	12.1	17.1	18.7	10.3	11.0	13.4	13.8	10.8
Poland	0.5	-0.7	-4.1	-4.8	-2.5	-2.2	-2.9	-1.9	-3.6	-7.3	-7.5	-4.9	-3.7	-4.0
Portugal	-2.7	-3.3	-8.4	-8.0	-7.0	-7.2	-5.8	-3.0	-3.8	-9.8	-11.2	-7.4	-5.7	-4.8
Slovak Republic	-1.9	-1.6	-6.7	-7.4	-4.4	-5.0	-3.6	-1.9	-2.3	-7.9	-7.5	-4.1	-4.2	-2.6
Slovenia	2.8	1.7	-3.1	-3.3	-4.0	-3.1	-3.2	-0.1	-1.4	-5.9	-5.6	-6.6	-4.1	-15.0
Spain	5.2	-0.9	-6.9	-6.2	-7.1	-6.3	-6.7	2.0	-4.4	-11.0	-9.4	-9.5	-10.4	-6.9
Sweden	4.3	2.9	0.3	1.1	1.1	0.1	-0.4	3.3	2.0	-0.7	0.0	-0.1	-0.9	-1.4
Switzerland	1.9	3.5	1.9	1.6	2.0	1.2	1.2	0.9	2.0	0.8	0.3	0.8	0.2	-0.3
Turkey	1.7	0.9	-3.6	0.1	1.8	..	..	-1.5	-2.3	-6.5	-2.9	-0.8	..	..
United Kingdom	-1.3	-2.4	-7.2	-7.1	-5.7	-6.1	-4.3	-3.0	-5.1	-10.8	-9.7	-7.7	-8.3	-5.7
United States	-2.3	-5.4	-10.5	-10.4	-9.4	-8.0	-4.9	-3.5	-7.0	-12.7	-12.0	-10.6	-8.8	-5.3
Euro area	..	..	..	..	..	..	..	..	..	..	..	..	..	..
OECD-Total	..	..	..	..	..	..	..	..	..	..	..	..	..	..
Brazil	..	..	..	..	..	..	..	..	..	..	-2.8	-2.2	..	..
China	..	..	..	..	..	..	..	3.2	1.8	0.6	1.5	1.8	1.2	..
India	..	..	..	..	..	..	..	..	..	..	..	..	..	..
Indonesia	..	..	..	..	..	..	..	..	..	..	..	..	..	..
Russian Federation	12.3	12.8	2.6	3.8	8.4	7.1	4.4	5.6	7.3	-4.0	-1.2	3.8	2.5	0.3
South Africa	..	1.2	-1.7	-1.6	-0.9	-1.4	-1.5	..	-1.7	-3.9	-3.1	-3.0	-3.2	-3.3

Note: Detailed metadata: http://stats.oecd.org/OECDStat_Metadata/ShowMetadata.ashx?Dataset=NAAG_2015_NOV15&Lang=en&Coords=[INDICATOR].[B9S13S]

1. Information on data for Israel: http://dx.doi.org/10.1787/888932315602

29. Adjusted general government debt-to-GDP

Table 29.1. **Adjusted general government debt-to-GDP (excluding unfunded pension liabilities)**

Percentage of GDP

	2000	2001	2002	2003	2004	2005	2006	2007	2008	2009	2010	2011	2012	2013
Australia	26.4	25.1	23.9	20.9	21.4	21.0	19.7	19.5	20.7	25.4	28.5	33.1	36.6	37.0
Austria	70.5	71.6	73.4	72.0	71.3	75.8	72.4	68.7	74.0	86.3	90.3	91.3	97.5	93.6
Belgium	120.3	118.9	118.0	114.4	110.1	107.6	99.7	93.5	100.8	109.2	107.4	109.8	119.9	117.7
Canada	84.2	85.7	84.8	80.3	76.5	75.8	74.9	70.4	74.7	87.4	89.5	93.1	95.9	92.3
Chile	..	..	..	..	..	17.4	14.1	12.2	12.4	13.4	15.6	18.3	18.8	19.4
Czech Republic	24.0	28.0	30.1	32.6	32.2	31.9	31.6	30.3	34.2	41.0	45.8	48.1	57.8	57.9
Denmark	60.5	58.3	58.1	56.1	52.4	45.1	40.5	34.6	42.0	49.5	53.8	60.6	61.5	58.0
Estonia	6.8	6.7	7.6	8.4	8.6	8.2	8.0	7.2	8.4	12.6	11.9	9.4	12.9	13.4
Finland	51.0	48.4	48.2	49.2	49.4	46.5	43.1	39.1	38.3	49.2	55.1	57.5	63.4	64.4
France	71.9	71.0	74.6	78.5	80.0	81.7	76.9	75.6	81.5	93.2	96.8	100.7	110.4	110.1
Germany	59.8	58.9	61.3	64.8	67.7	70.3	68.4	64.3	68.1	75.6	84.1	83.5	86.4	81.6
Greece	110.9	112.9	111.0	105.7	107.2	111.3	115.8	113.1	117.4	134.7	128.4	110.7	167.0	181.7
Hungary	61.0	58.9	60.0	60.7	64.1	67.1	70.7	71.5	75.0	84.1	86.0	95.0	97.9	95.9
Iceland	..	..	..	39.9	34.8	26.5	32.1	30.2	70.9	85.6	90.9	97.5	95.5	87.8
Ireland	38.7	35.6	34.1	32.9	31.5	31.4	27.6	27.4	47.5	67.8	84.6	109.2	129.7	133.0
Israel[1]	..	91.2	94.9	100.2	98.0	95.7	85.4	81.3	81.0	84.0	80.3	78.6	79.0	77.0
Italy	118.9	118.1	116.9	114.2	114.6	117.4	115.0	110.6	112.9	125.9	124.8	117.8	136.0	143.2
Japan	144.5	151.4	161.8	172.3	178.8	180.2	180.0	180.0	184.2	207.3	210.6	226.5	234.8	239.3
Korea	..	..	..	..	..	..	..	..	..	..	..	..	..	..
Luxembourg	..	..	12.3	13.2	14.1	12.4	11.9	11.6	19.2	18.9	26.2	27.0	30.6	30.0
Mexico	..	..	..	42.5	38.0	35.5	34.9	37.9	41.9	44.3	40.8	46.4	49.6	48.7
Netherlands	60.1	56.2	56.9	58.0	58.0	57.1	51.0	48.2	61.0	63.7	67.6	71.6	77.4	76.4
New Zealand	..	..	..	..	..	..	..	..	..	..	..	..	..	..
Norway	32.2	31.3	38.7	48.0	49.9	46.9	57.8	55.6	54.2	48.1	48.4	33.8	34.5	34.8
Poland	..	..	..	54.8	53.7	54.4	54.5	50.9	53.9	57.1	60.7	61.1	60.7	62.6
Portugal	62.0	63.5	66.8	70.6	76.7	80.0	79.4	78.1	82.8	96.1	104.1	107.8	136.9	140.7
Slovak Republic	57.9	56.6	49.4	47.5	45.1	38.1	36.0	34.5	33.5	42.0	46.9	49.4	57.7	60.7
Slovenia	..	33.0	34.0	33.5	34.3	33.4	33.3	29.1	28.3	42.5	46.8	50.4	60.6	79.5
Spain	65.2	60.6	59.3	54.4	52.5	50.0	45.7	41.7	47.1	61.7	66.5	77.5	92.0	103.8
Sweden	56.7	57.8	57.7	56.6	56.0	56.9	51.0	45.4	44.0	47.2	44.8	45.1	45.3	47.3
Switzerland	52.5	52.3	58.9	57.4	58.1	56.1	50.1	49.9	46.1	44.9	43.5	43.3	44.5	..
Turkey	..	..	..	..	..	..	..	..	..	54.3	52.5	47.8	46.4	39.7
United Kingdom	50.5	45.9	46.0	45.6	48.9	50.8	50.0	51.0	61.7	75.5	88.0	101.5	106.6	102.6
United States	53.1	53.0	55.2	58.2	65.1	64.3	63.0	63.1	71.7	84.8	93.4	97.6	101.0	103.2
Euro area	..	..	..	..	..	..	..	..	..	..	..	..	..	..
OECD-Total	..	..	..	..	..	..	..	..	..	..	..	..	..	..
Brazil	..	..	..	..	..	..	..	..	..	..	..	..	..	..
China	..	..	..	..	..	..	..	..	..	..	..	..	..	..
India	..	..	..	..	..	..	..	..	..	..	..	..	..	..
Indonesia	..	..	..	..	..	..	..	..	..	..	..	..	..	..
Russian Federation	..	..	..	..	..	..	..	..	..	..	..	..	..	..
South Africa	..	..	..	..	..	..	..	..	..	..	..	..	..	..

Note: Detailed metadata:
http://stats.oecd.org/OECDStat_Metadata/ShowMetadata.ashx?Dataset=NAAG_2015_NOV15&Lang=en&Coords=[INDICATOR].[DBTADJS13GDP]

1. Information on data for Israel: http://dx.doi.org/10.1787/888932315602

Table 29.2. **General government debt-to-GDP (including unfunded pension liabilities)**

Percentage of GDP

	2000	2001	2002	2003	2004	2005	2006	2007	2008	2009	2010	2011	2012	2013
Australia	42.9	41.6	40.7	38.3	37.5	36.7	36.3	34.1	35.1	43.3	46.9	50.8	62.8	58.5
Canada	102.6	102.6	101.3	96.3	91.7	90.5	89.1	84.3	88.5	102.1	103.8	106.8	109.4	105.7
Iceland	..	..	..	66.1	59.6	49.7	54.9	49.8	95.7	109.4	114.6	122.1	120.2	112.2
Sweden	62.7	64.0	64.2	63.0	62.5	63.6	57.6	51.9	50.7	54.5	51.9	52.8	53.4	55.9
United States	61.5	63.9	70.5	71.4	79.2	78.5	76.2	76.5	92.3	105.7	116.0	121.6	124.7	123.8

Note: Detailed metadata:
http://stats.oecd.org/OECDStat_Metadata/ShowMetadata.ashx?Dataset=NAAG_2015_NOV15&Lang=en&Coords=[INDICATOR].[DBTS13GDP]

Table 30.1. **Financial net worth of general government**

Percentage of GDP

	2000	2001	2002	2003	2004	2005	2006	2007	2008	2009	2010	2011	2012	2013
Australia	4.3	2.2	3.8	6.5	9.9	11.0	12.1	15.6	15.7	9.3	4.0	-1.4	-11.7	-4.8
Austria	-34.9	-33.8	-37.5	-36.0	-37.8	-44.7	-42.4	-39.6	-43.7	-49.9	-51.4	-52.9	-56.2	-54.9
Belgium	-100.9	-98.5	-99.4	-96.1	-90.9	-88.8	-80.3	-74.0	-76.5	-82.9	-81.5	-83.1	-91.9	-89.9
Canada	-67.8	-64.7	-65.0	-59.1	-54.2	-48.9	-44.1	-40.9	-42.6	-49.3	-51.6	-55.7	-56.9	-53.0
Chile	..	..	..	..	..	-8.9	-0.9	6.1	18.1	7.2	1.9	4.6	1.7	1.0
Czech Republic	25.4	23.4	15.1	7.0	10.1	11.5	11.7	14.5	5.8	1.4	-6.3	-6.1	-13.6	-15.2
Denmark	-25.5	-22.0	-21.1	-18.4	-14.2	-9.5	-1.1	4.6	6.7	5.9	3.3	-1.1	-6.7	-3.4
Estonia	30.2	29.1	28.6	29.5	31.9	32.0	30.8	28.4	25.9	28.8	35.9	34.0	32.0	31.2
Finland	30.1	30.4	30.2	36.8	44.7	56.0	66.5	69.7	50.0	59.6	61.8	48.8	50.3	54.0
France	-32.5	-34.6	-39.5	-41.6	-43.0	-41.0	-35.5	-32.2	-42.6	-50.2	-54.6	-59.5	-67.4	-66.1
Germany	-33.2	-35.4	-39.6	-42.8	-46.5	-48.8	-47.0	-41.7	-43.3	-47.7	-48.2	-49.3	-49.1	-45.2
Greece	-84.6	-88.7	-90.2	-83.6	-83.1	-82.2	-87.3	-82.3	-91.1	-101.8	-92.4	-73.0	-102.8	-118.7
Hungary	-33.1	-32.4	-36.6	-37.5	-41.5	-44.5	-51.5	-52.9	-50.8	-58.7	-60.9	-62.6	-69.8	-70.4
Iceland	..	..	..	-29.9	-26.8	-13.3	-7.8	0.9	-25.1	-37.6	-45.8	-51.5	-53.7	-51.8
Ireland	-14.7	-11.3	-12.9	-10.5	-7.4	-6.0	-1.3	0.2	-12.4	-25.5	-48.2	-61.2	-79.3	-81.9
Israel[1]	..	-61.5	-66.3	-69.0	-65.4	-54.8	-45.4	-45.9	-49.4	-52.9	-50.1	-51.9	-54.2	-54.3
Italy	-96.4	-96.9	-96.4	-93.2	-94.3	-95.8	-92.3	-88.8	-92.0	-102.7	-101.2	-96.1	-112.0	-118.4
Japan	-58.3	-64.2	-72.6	-77.2	-81.3	-78.6	-77.7	-82.4	-92.0	-103.4	-110.1	-124.1	-126.0	-123.1
Korea	..	..	..	..	..	..	..	..	..	..	..	30.9	30.7	32.0
Luxembourg	..	..	57.9	57.3	54.1	52.8	52.0	56.3	53.9	57.7	52.0	46.0	48.4	48.0
Mexico	..	..	..	..	..	..	..	..	..	..	..	..	..	..
Netherlands	-27.8	-27.4	-30.9	-32.0	-32.7	-29.9	-27.2	-23.5	-22.7	-27.4	-31.9	-36.7	-39.2	-39.6
New Zealand	..	..	..	..	..	..	..	..	..	..	..	..	..	..
Norway	67.2	84.7	80.1	93.5	101.8	118.8	131.9	137.4	121.9	152.3	161.6	157.5	166.9	203.9
Poland	..	..	..	-24.8	-22.4	-22.4	-21.3	-15.8	-16.2	-21.0	-26.6	-30.5	-31.7	-35.3
Portugal	-37.8	-40.0	-44.4	-47.2	-53.9	-55.9	-54.7	-55.0	-59.6	-70.3	-71.0	-66.6	-90.6	-98.4
Slovak Republic	-13.1	-10.6	-0.9	-1.5	-4.8	-9.5	-13.9	-12.9	-14.7	-21.8	-27.4	-32.2	-30.7	-32.3
Slovenia	..	15.3	13.9	9.3	9.8	8.8	10.2	18.3	7.2	2.2	0.7	-2.2	-8.6	-13.8
Spain	-43.3	-40.5	-39.1	-35.9	-33.5	-28.5	-22.0	-17.3	-22.1	-33.2	-38.8	-47.1	-58.2	-69.9
Sweden	-8.8	-4.3	-11.2	-7.4	-5.3	-0.6	9.7	14.3	8.5	15.2	17.1	14.0	17.9	18.6
Switzerland	-7.3	-6.9	-12.5	-11.9	-13.8	-12.9	-9.6	-8.5	-11.7	-7.5	-10.3	-9.4	-7.1	..
Turkey	..	..	..	..	..	..	..	..	..	-21.0	-19.8	-18.6	-18.7	-15.6
United Kingdom	-30.8	-27.8	-30.6	-29.7	-32.0	-32.6	-32.8	-33.2	-40.2	-50.2	-55.2	-70.5	-72.1	-69.8
United States	-43.0	-44.7	-51.5	-52.6	-60.6	-59.8	-57.3	-57.0	-70.0	-81.6	-90.8	-98.6	-101.4	-99.7
Euro area	..	..	..	..	..	..	..	..	..	..	..	..	..	..
OECD-Total	..	..	..	..	..	..	..	..	..	..	..	..	..	..
Brazil	..	..	..	..	..	..	..	..	..	..	..	..	..	..
China	..	..	..	..	..	..	..	..	..	..	..	..	..	..
India	..	..	..	..	..	..	..	..	..	..	..	..	..	..
Indonesia	..	..	..	..	..	..	..	..	..	..	..	..	..	..
Russian Federation	..	..	..	..	..	..	..	..	..	..	..	..	..	..
South Africa	..	..	..	..	..	..	..	..	..	..	..	..	..	..

Note: Detailed metadata:
http://stats.oecd.org/OECDStat_Metadata/ShowMetadata.ashx?Dataset=NAAG_2015_NOV15&Lang=en&Coords=[INDICATOR].[SBF90S13GDP]

1. Information on data for Israel: http://dx.doi.org/10.1787/888932315602

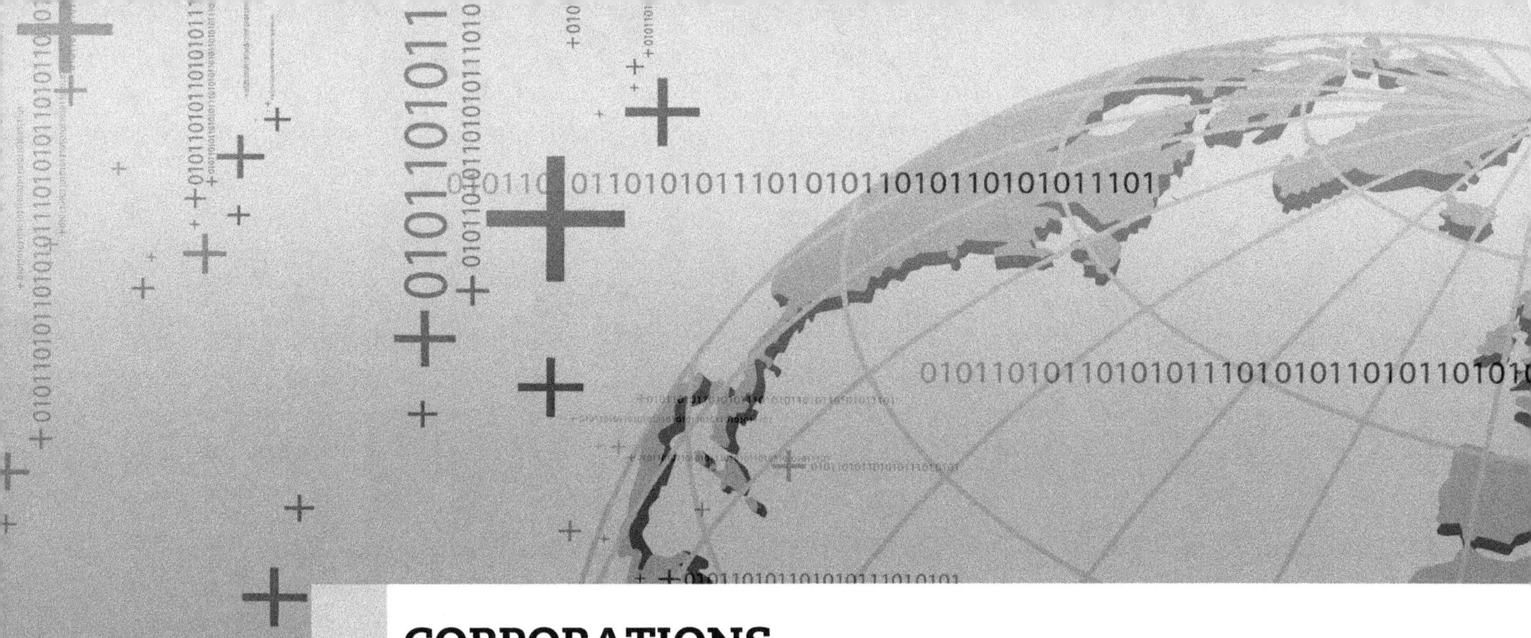

CORPORATIONS

Table 31.1. **Non-financial corporations debt**

Ratio of debt to gross operating surplus, number of times

	2000	2001	2002	2003	2004	2005	2006	2007	2008	2009	2010	2011	2012	2013
Australia	..	..	..	..	..	..	..	..	..	..	..	..	..	..
Austria	3.8	3.7	3.6	3.7	3.5	3.3	3.1	3.2	3.5	3.9	3.8	3.7	4.0	4.1
Belgium	4.4	4.5	4.3	4.3	4.2	3.9	3.9	4.2	5.4	5.8	5.4	5.9	6.6	6.3
Canada	..	..	..	..	..	..	..	..	..	..	..	..	..	..
Chile	..	..	..	..	..	..	..	..	4.1	3.8	3.3	3.6	3.9	4.3
Czech Republic	2.7	2.3	2.3	2.3	2.0	1.9	1.9	1.8	2.1	2.2	2.3	2.3	2.3	2.4
Denmark	4.6	4.7	5.0	5.1	4.7	4.8	5.4	5.7	6.3	7.1	6.2	6.3	6.5	6.3
Estonia	2.4	2.4	2.5	2.4	2.6	2.6	2.9	3.2	3.9	4.8	3.8	3.0	3.2	3.1
Finland	2.6	2.5	2.8	2.9	2.8	3.0	3.0	3.0	3.4	4.2	4.3	4.2	4.6	4.5
France	4.7	4.9	4.8	4.6	4.5	4.8	4.9	4.9	5.1	5.9	5.9	6.2	6.3	6.4
Germany	3.5	3.4	3.3	3.3	3.1	3.0	2.9	2.8	3.0	3.4	3.0	2.9	3.1	3.1
Greece	..	..	..	..	..	..	3.2	3.2	3.5	3.8	4.0	4.0	4.0	3.7
Hungary	3.5	3.3	2.6	3.0	2.9	3.2	3.0	3.4	3.6	4.2	3.9	3.9	3.6	3.3
Iceland	..	..	..	..	..	..	..	..	..	..	..	..	..	..
Ireland	..	3.8	3.1	3.1	3.2	3.8	4.4	4.3	6.3	6.6	6.1	6.5	6.8	7.2
Israel[1]	..	3.8	4.1	3.8	3.7	3.8	3.7	3.6	3.7	3.4	3.4	3.4	3.1	2.8
Italy	2.8	2.9	3.0	3.2	3.3	3.5	3.8	4.1	4.3	4.8	4.8	4.7	5.1	5.1
Japan	8.2	8.5	8.3	7.7	7.0	6.8	7.0	6.6	6.6	7.3	6.6	7.2	6.7	6.9
Korea	..	..	..	..	..	..	..	..	..	..	..	5.6	5.7	5.7
Luxembourg	..	..	..	..	..	..	..	..	..	..	..	..	..	..
Mexico	..	..	..	1.2	1.1	1.3	1.3	1.4	1.5	1.6	1.5	1.6	1.4	1.7
Netherlands	6.9	6.5	6.3	6.4	5.8	5.5	5.1	4.8	4.8	5.4	5.2	5.0	5.1	5.1
New Zealand	..	..	..	..	..	..	..	..	..	..	..	..	..	..
Norway	2.5	2.6	2.8	2.8	2.4	2.2	2.2	2.6	2.6	3.2	3.1	2.9	3.0	3.1
Poland	..	..	..	2.9	2.2	2.1	2.1	2.4	2.8	2.3	2.4	2.5	2.5	2.5
Portugal	5.8	6.8	6.7	7.2	6.9	7.3	7.5	7.4	8.7	8.1	8.1	8.5	8.2	7.8
Slovak Republic	3.7	3.6	4.0	3.6	3.1	3.1	2.9	2.9	2.7	3.3	3.0	3.2	3.0	3.1
Slovenia	..	4.1	4.0	3.9	4.1	4.8	4.8	5.0	5.5	6.5	6.8	6.4	6.2	5.7
Spain	3.7	4.0	4.2	4.5	4.7	5.3	6.2	6.3	5.9	5.8	5.8	5.8	5.2	4.8
Sweden	5.2	5.8	5.6	5.2	4.9	5.0	4.7	5.3	6.3	7.2	5.8	5.9	6.3	6.3
Switzerland	4.5	4.4	4.7	4.9	4.2	4.0	3.8	4.2	4.2	5.1	4.5	5.0	5.4	..
Turkey	..	..	..	..	..	..	..	..	..	..	..	..	..	..
United Kingdom	5.3	6.1	6.7	6.0	6.0	6.2	5.9	6.2	6.9	7.3	6.6	7.1	7.3	6.0
United States	7.5	7.9	7.6	7.1	6.8	6.7	6.5	7.1	7.4	7.6	6.8	6.7	6.6	6.6
Euro area	..	..	..	..	..	..	..	..	..	..	..	..	..	..
OECD-Total	..	..	..	..	..	..	..	..	..	..	..	..	..	..
Brazil	..	..	..	..	..	..	..	..	..	..	..	..	..	..
China	..	..	..	..	..	..	..	..	..	..	..	..	..	..
India	..	..	..	..	..	..	..	..	..	..	..	..	..	..
Indonesia	..	..	..	..	..	..	..	..	..	..	..	..	..	..
Russian Federation	..	..	..	..	..	..	..	..	..	..	..	..	..	..
South Africa	..	..	..	..	..	..	..	..	..	..	..	..	..	..

Note: Detailed metadata:
http://stats.oecd.org/OECDStat_Metadata/ShowMetadata.ashx?Dataset=NAAG_2015_NOV15&Lang=en&Coords=[INDICATOR].[DBTS11GOSC]

1. Information on data for Israel: http://dx.doi.org/10.1787/888932315602

32. Debt to equity ratio in financial corporations

Table 32.1. **Financial corporations debt**

Ratio of debt to equity, number of times

	2000	2001	2002	2003	2004	2005	2006	2007	2008	2009	2010	2011	2012	2013
Australia	5.4	5.0	5.4	5.7	5.6	5.4	5.4	5.8	7.9	7.4	8.5	9.6	9.2	8.6
Austria	3.7	3.9	3.8	3.6	3.4	2.4	2.4	2.3	3.2	2.6	2.6	2.7	2.5	2.4
Belgium	2.6	2.6	3.0	3.0	2.7	2.7	2.5	2.4	3.1	2.6	2.5	2.6	2.7	2.4
Canada	1.6	2.1	2.2	2.0	1.9	1.9	1.8	1.7	2.3	1.9	1.7	1.8	1.7	1.6
Chile	..	..	..	..	..	10.9	9.4	8.1	7.6	7.2	7.9	8.2	8.9	8.3
Czech Republic	11.4	13.5	15.3	7.6	7.0	7.3	7.4	7.2	8.2	7.2	6.4	7.1	6.2	6.1
Denmark	2.1	2.9	3.6	3.5	3.4	2.6	2.4	2.7	4.1	3.2	2.9	2.9	2.9	2.7
Estonia	2.6	2.6	2.4	3.0	2.4	2.9	4.5	4.3	4.6	5.0	4.4	4.4	4.3	3.8
Finland	4.2	4.4	4.7	3.9	3.5	2.9	2.6	2.7	4.1	4.1	3.9	5.3	4.9	3.7
France	2.9	3.1	3.4	3.2	3.1	3.0	2.9	3.5	4.7	4.1	4.3	5.3	4.9	4.5
Germany	4.8	5.4	7.0	6.1	6.2	5.5	5.2	5.3	7.6	6.5	6.1	6.4	5.7	4.9
Greece	2.2	2.9	4.0	3.3	3.1	3.0	3.0	3.2	12.2	9.2	17.3	26.5	10.6	8.8
Hungary	2.5	1.5	1.6	1.9	2.1	1.6	1.6	1.3	1.5	1.6	1.4	1.4	1.3	1.4
Iceland	..	..	..	3.9	2.9	2.8	2.8	2.8	6.9	11.9	8.4	7.8	8.9	8.4
Ireland	..	1.6	1.6	1.8	2.0	2.1	2.0	2.1	3.0	2.6	2.1	1.7	1.4	1.1
Israel[1]	..	19.2	28.6	15.7	11.9	10.6	11.1	10.9	24.7	7.3	5.8	7.5	7.1	6.7
Italy	1.8	2.4	3.1	2.9	3.0	2.9	2.9	4.0	8.2	7.6	9.8	12.9	13.2	10.4
Japan	19.9	21.3	24.9	15.0	13.9	8.8	9.3	11.1	14.6	11.9	11.6	11.8	9.3	8.5
Korea	..	..	..	..	..	..	..	..	..	..	..	7.0	6.6	6.5
Luxembourg	..	..	0.8	0.7	0.7	0.7	0.6	0.6	0.8	0.6	0.4	0.7	0.7	0.6
Mexico	..	..	..	2.8	2.6	2.3	1.8	1.9	2.0	1.9	2.0	2.0	1.9	2.0
Netherlands	2.6	2.8	3.3	3.3	3.3	3.3	3.0	2.7	2.8	2.2	2.1	2.0	1.9	1.6
New Zealand	..	..	..	..	..	..	..	..	..	..	..	..	..	..
Norway	8.1	9.1	9.9	9.3	7.8	7.0	6.3	6.2	11.1	7.8	6.5	7.2	5.1	4.5
Poland	..	..	..	5.0	3.8	3.4	2.8	2.7	4.9	4.3	3.8	4.6	4.0	3.6
Portugal	3.8	3.7	3.9	3.3	2.9	2.7	2.4	2.6	3.1	3.1	3.4	4.7	4.5	4.2
Slovak Republic	21.7	23.4	20.8	16.1	14.0	16.7	13.6	11.3	14.1	14.1	12.3	12.6	11.9	10.2
Slovenia	..	5.8	6.0	5.7	5.5	6.3	5.5	5.0	7.4	7.4	7.3	8.2	8.3	6.8
Spain	3.2	3.5	4.1	3.8	3.6	3.8	3.8	4.4	6.7	6.2	7.0	7.6	7.9	5.9
Sweden	2.6	2.9	3.6	3.1	3.0	2.9	2.7	3.0	4.7	3.5	3.2	3.5	3.1	2.8
Switzerland	2.8	3.2	3.9	3.5	3.2	3.0	2.6	2.8	3.2	2.7	2.7	2.9	2.9	..
Turkey	..	..	..	..	..	..	..	..	..	3.7	3.5	5.5	4.5	6.7
United Kingdom	6.2	6.9	8.8	8.2	8.3	8.2	7.7	8.5	11.4	8.2	7.4	8.3	7.6	6.7
United States	2.7	2.9	3.2	3.0	2.9	2.9	2.7	2.8	3.5	2.9	2.8	2.9	2.6	2.3
Euro area	..	..	..	..	..	..	..	..	..	..	..	..	..	..
OECD-Total	..	..	..	..	..	..	..	..	..	..	..	..	..	..
Brazil	..	..	..	..	..	..	..	..	..	..	..	..	..	..
China	..	..	..	..	..	..	..	..	..	..	..	..	..	..
India	..	..	..	..	..	..	..	..	..	..	..	..	..	..
Indonesia	..	..	..	..	..	..	..	..	..	..	..	..	..	..
Russian Federation	..	..	..	..	..	..	..	..	..	..	..	..	..	..
South Africa	..	..	..	..	..	..	..	..	..	..	..	..	..	..

Note: Detailed metadata:
http://stats.oecd.org/OECDStat_Metadata/ShowMetadata.ashx?Dataset=NAAG_2015_NOV15&Lang=en&Coords=[INDICATOR].[DBTEQS12]

1. Information on data for Israel: http://dx.doi.org/10.1787/888932315602

Table 33.1. Leverage of the banking sector

Ratio of selected assets to equity, number of times

	2000	2001	2002	2003	2004	2005	2006	2007	2008	2009	2010	2011	2012	2013
Australia	3.6	3.4	3.7	3.8	4.0	3.9	3.8	3.9	6.6	5.2	5.6	6.2	5.7	5.0
Austria	12.6	16.6	16.8	14.2	12.0	9.6	9.2	7.5	10.5	7.9	7.0	8.3	7.5	7.2
Belgium	14.3	12.8	17.1	17.7	15.4	14.6	13.2	13.3	24.2	18.6	15.9	17.5	13.9	12.8
Canada	1.7	2.3	2.6	2.3	2.2	2.2	2.1	2.0	2.8	2.4	2.1	2.3	2.2	2.1
Chile	..	..	..	..	..	32.2	28.0	22.4	15.9	23.6	30.1	24.9	31.3	25.6
Czech Republic	27.7	22.5	35.1	12.7	11.4	12.0	12.4	11.5	12.5	10.8	8.8	10.4	9.8	10.1
Denmark	..	..	..	8.2	9.9	7.2	8.0	10.5	16.6	10.7	10.2	10.4	12.3	9.7
Estonia	4.2	4.2	3.5	3.4	2.7	3.6	8.1	8.2	7.4	9.7	8.5	9.3	8.1	7.6
Finland	7.7	6.7	7.7	7.2	7.5	6.6	6.6	7.8	9.4	8.5	9.8	12.8	12.3	8.9
France	10.7	11.2	12.1	11.5	10.6	10.4	9.5	13.3	22.7	15.7	15.8	21.2	17.8	15.8
Germany	15.2	16.6	22.6	19.7	19.8	17.4	14.9	14.8	27.2	22.0	23.1	24.9	22.9	20.8
Greece	4.9	6.2	9.0	7.3	6.1	5.0	4.4	4.2	17.2	11.9	25.6	42.1	12.9	11.5
Hungary	11.6	11.2	9.6	8.4	7.1	7.1	6.8	7.7	13.3	11.0	11.9	12.3	12.3	12.4
Iceland	..	..	..	..	..	..	..	..	..	..	..	..	..	..
Ireland	..	10.1	11.5	11.8	12.4	13.9	14.6	17.6	26.8	19.1	17.9	12.4	10.6	8.2
Israel[1]	..	22.1	36.3	22.3	17.5	12.8	13.4	13.1	30.5	9.1	6.7	10.3	10.3	11.3
Italy	3.5	5.6	7.1	5.7	5.4	4.3	3.9	6.1	20.9	15.8	22.7	39.9	33.8	23.0
Japan	30.1	28.4	35.2	18.3	17.4	10.5	12.5	16.1	21.2	17.1	17.6	17.8	12.7	11.6
Korea	..	..	..	..	..	..	..	..	..	..	..	13.8	12.8	12.7
Luxembourg	..	..	35.1	25.4	26.0	28.9	28.1	30.6	22.8	19.2	22.4	24.4	22.8	20.8
Mexico	..	..	..	..	..	..	..	..	..	..	..	..	..	..
Netherlands	11.5	14.3	15.9	15.9	15.9	14.9	15.6	13.4	22.8	19.8	19.5	21.0	19.6	19.1
New Zealand	..	..	..	..	..	..	..	..	..	..	..	..	..	..
Norway	24.5	24.5	24.2	28.8	25.3	28.1	32.5	35.7	46.6	36.3	32.9	33.0	21.5	18.9
Poland	..	..	..	8.2	5.4	4.9	4.0	4.1	8.4	6.7	6.6	8.6	7.3	6.2
Portugal	8.5	9.2	11.0	11.2	12.0	10.9	9.4	9.8	16.9	15.1	16.8	20.4	16.8	16.5
Slovak Republic	64.9	69.3	47.9	40.7	39.5	305.5	232.9	41.7	42.0	47.9	35.5	29.3	30.8	21.6
Slovenia	..	8.8	10.1	10.8	10.9	11.9	11.9	11.3	12.7	12.0	11.6	13.3	14.3	11.5
Spain	6.3	7.6	10.6	9.8	9.4	9.5	8.5	10.2	18.4	13.2	15.8	15.2	15.9	10.8
Sweden	5.2	4.8	6.4	5.5	5.4	5.3	5.1	6.1	12.2	8.0	6.8	7.9	6.9	5.8
Switzerland	..	..	..	..	..	..	..	..	..	..	..	..	..	..
Turkey	..	..	9.8	6.6	5.6	3.3	4.3	3.5	7.6	4.2	4.1	6.4	5.3	8.1
United Kingdom	23.6	25.8	28.5	32.4	34.9	40.1	43.8	49.4	51.5	46.6	43.6	37.4	34.0	33.3
United States	8.1	8.5	8.8	7.9	7.1	7.3	7.0	8.5	11.2	9.8	9.1	9.6	8.6	8.3
Euro area	..	..	..	..	..	..	..	..	..	..	..	..	..	..
OECD-Total	..	..	..	..	..	..	..	..	..	..	..	..	..	..
Brazil	..	..	..	..	..	..	..	..	..	..	..	..	..	..
China	..	..	..	..	..	..	..	..	..	..	..	..	..	..
India	..	..	..	..	..	..	..	..	..	..	..	..	..	..
Indonesia	..	..	..	..	..	..	..	..	..	..	..	..	..	..
Russian Federation	..	..	..	..	..	..	..	..	..	..	..	..	..	..
South Africa	..	..	..	..	..	..	..	..	..	..	..	..	..	..

Note: Detailed metadata: http://stats.oecd.org/OECDStat_Metadata/ShowMetadata.ashx?Dataset=NAAG_2015_NOV15&Lang=en&Coords=[INDICATOR].[LEVS121_2_3]

1. Information on data for Israel: http://dx.doi.org/10.1787/888932315602

34. Share of profit and labour in value added

Table 34.1. Margin rates and labour share, non-financial sector

Gross operating surplus and compensation of employees as a percentage of net value added

	Compensation of employees							Net operating surplus						
	2007	2008	2009	2010	2011	2012	2013	2007	2008	2009	2010	2011	2012	2013
Australia	..	..	..	..	..	..	..	..	..	..	..	..	..	..
Austria	62.0	64.5	68.0	67.2	66.8	68.6	70.1	35.9	33.3	29.6	30.4	30.7	28.8	27.0
Belgium	73.9	76.4	80.4	78.2	79.0	80.8	81.2	28.7	26.5	23.1	25.9	25.5	23.4	23.3
Canada	..	..	..	..	..	..	..	..	..	..	..	..	..	..
Chile	..	..	..	..	..	..	..	..	..	..	..	..	..	..
Czech Republic	63.8	66.0	69.5	70.3	70.1	71.4	72.2	37.7	35.5	32.7	31.5	31.4	30.3	29.4
Denmark	74.9	77.3	82.6	76.5	75.9	76.9	76.8	25.1	22.6	18.2	24.2	24.4	23.3	23.1
Estonia	60.8	67.9	73.2	65.5	59.6	60.5	61.2	39.3	32.3	27.0	35.5	41.3	40.4	39.6
Finland	64.9	67.4	76.6	73.5	74.3	78.1	77.9	35.8	33.4	24.5	27.7	26.9	23.2	23.2
France	77.0	78.0	81.2	81.3	81.2	82.4	82.9	18.7	17.8	14.0	15.0	14.5	13.0	12.0
Germany	65.4	67.6	72.5	70.1	69.7	71.9	71.9	35.7	33.6	28.9	31.2	31.4	29.0	29.0
Greece	50.0	49.0	50.6	56.2	58.1	55.7	51.4	50.4	51.3	49.8	44.3	43.0	44.7	48.7
Hungary	67.7	67.9	70.9	68.3	67.9	69.6	65.8	32.3	32.7	29.9	32.0	32.6	30.6	33.7
Iceland	..	..	..	..	..	..	..	..	..	..	..	..	..	..
Ireland	53.8	60.2	58.0	52.2	46.7	46.9	45.8	44.7	38.0	40.1	46.2	51.9	51.8	52.8
Israel[1]	65.6	65.4	62.4	62.5	63.6	61.5	60.8	31.1	31.5	34.7	34.5	33.4	35.7	36.8
Italy	63.6	65.3	69.5	69.5	70.0	72.3	72.9	32.1	30.9	27.3	27.1	26.4	23.4	23.2
Japan	..	..	..	..	..	..	..	..	..	..	..	..	..	..
Korea	..	..	..	59.1	60.4	62.2	62.5	..	..	..	39.7	38.3	36.5	36.2
Luxembourg	..	..	..	..	..	..	..	..	..	..	..	..	..	..
Mexico	27.1	26.4	30.7	28.1	26.5	26.1	27.7	71.8	72.6	68.0	70.7	72.4	72.9	71.3
Netherlands	65.2	66.2	71.0	68.9	69.1	69.8	69.6	35.2	34.4	30.3	31.8	31.6	30.8	30.7
New Zealand	51.9	55.5	54.4	53.1	53.2	54.8	..	43.4	39.8	40.4	41.8	41.6	40.1	..
Norway	50.1	47.9	57.3	54.2	52.3	52.7	54.9	50.4	52.3	43.5	46.7	48.6	48.1	45.9
Poland	62.8	64.5	58.6	58.9	57.8	57.8	58.6	35.6	33.8	40.1	39.7	40.8	40.9	40.5
Portugal	75.4	78.0	75.8	74.9	75.8	73.7	70.4	24.7	21.8	24.0	25.2	24.3	26.2	28.9
Slovak Republic	58.8	59.0	69.5	65.4	65.9	64.7	65.8	42.6	43.5	32.8	36.9	35.2	36.1	35.3
Slovenia	79.5	81.1	89.3	90.7	87.8	88.1	85.7	19.5	18.8	12.3	10.9	11.9	11.3	13.9
Spain	75.2	73.1	72.5	72.7	73.5	71.7	70.7	25.4	27.2	27.7	27.7	26.8	28.2	29.0
Sweden	61.0	63.0	69.0	63.7	64.9	67.9	68.6	27.8	25.2	19.2	25.5	24.4	20.9	20.1
Switzerland	84.8	84.7	89.0	83.4	85.4	86.9	88.5	17.3	16.3	12.2	17.6	15.8	14.4	12.5
Turkey	..	..	..	..	..	..	..	..	..	..	..	..	..	..
United Kingdom	71.7	71.4	74.4	72.3	71.0	71.8	70.7	25.9	26.1	22.7	24.7	26.0	25.2	26.3
United States	70.2	71.0	71.2	68.0	68.0	67.4	67.7	19.7	18.9	18.5	21.8	21.8	22.6	22.3
Euro area	68.7	70.3	74.0	72.8	72.7	73.9	73.8	30.3	28.7	24.8	26.3	26.3	24.8	24.9
OECD-Total	..	..	..	..	..	..	..	..	..	..	..	..	..	..
Brazil	..	..	..	..	..	..	..	..	..	..	..	..	..	..
China	..	..	..	..	..	..	..	..	..	..	..	..	..	..
India	..	..	..	..	..	..	..	..	..	..	..	..	..	..
Indonesia	..	..	..	..	..	..	..	..	..	..	..	..	..	..
Russian Federation	63.6 |	61.1	70.1	62.4	63.1	63.9	65.7	34.8 |	30.6	23.8	31.1	29.7	35.0	33.0
South Africa	..	58.6	59.8	59.8	58.7	59.6	61.6	..	39.8	38.6	38.7	39.5	38.7	36.4

Note: Detailed metadata:
http://stats.oecd.org/OECDStat_Metadata/ShowMetadata.ashx?Dataset=NAAG_2015_NOV15&Lang=en&Coords=[INDICATOR].[D1SB1NS11]

1. Information on data for Israel: http://dx.doi.org/10.1787/888932315602

Table 34.2. **Margin rates and labour share of financial corporations**

Gross operating surplus and compensation of employees as a percentage of net value added

	Compensation of employees							Net operating surplus						
	2007	2008	2009	2010	2011	2012	2013	2007	2008	2009	2010	2011	2012	2013
Australia	..	..	..	..	..	..	..	..	..	..	..	..	..	..
Austria	66.4	69.1	76.9	77.9	74.6	79.7	77.4	30.2	27.4	19.2	18.1	16.9	10.3	12.8
Belgium	75.6	85.2	68.0	57.7	55.6	54.9	56.6	19.4	8.9	27.3	37.0	36.7	34.0	33.2
Canada	..	..	..	..	..	..	..	..	..	..	..	..	..	..
Chile	..	..	..	..	..	..	..	..	..	..	..	..	..	..
Czech Republic	51.8	46.2	41.0	38.3	40.7	46.5	43.6	46.2	51.9	57.2	58.7	56.5	49.9	56.0
Denmark	61.6	56.1	59.6	56.7	60.4	54.1	56.7	34.0	39.7	36.6	39.2	35.9	42.4	39.7
Estonia	37.7	32.8	48.5	44.1	44.4	42.8	44.7	57.7	65.0	51.3	54.9	53.2	57.1	55.3
Finland	53.7	59.6	62.8	68.6	66.2	66.8	73.8	46.3	40.4	37.2	31.4	33.8	33.2	22.8
France	69.6	72.1	72.2	62.6	65.8	69.1	64.1	22.0	19.0	19.0	30.0	25.8	22.2	27.7
Germany	67.5	75.4	65.1	64.3	70.8	71.7	74.2	32.2	24.3	34.6	35.5	28.1	27.1	24.8
Greece	61.1	62.6	62.0	59.2	58.9	53.6	54.5	37.0	35.3	35.9	39.3	38.7	43.8	43.1
Hungary	62.0	67.3	60.2	60.5	55.9	61.2	63.5	38.0	32.0	39.3	23.7	28.1	21.5	20.6
Iceland	..	..	..	..	..	..	..	..	..	..	..	..	..	..
Ireland	37.0	40.8	41.0	38.3	41.8	41.9	48.9	61.4	57.4	57.6	60.8	57.5	56.8	49.7
Israel[1]	47.1	47.7	40.1	40.6	39.0	40.9	41.2	46.7	46.4	54.0	53.7	55.0	53.3	53.1
Italy	49.0	50.4	53.7	52.2	50.5	50.6	46.0	45.2	44.1	41.1	42.3	43.9	43.6	46.6
Japan	..	..	..	..	..	..	..	..	..	..	..	..	..	..
Korea	..	..	..	45.4	43.2	43.7	46.7	..	..	..	54.1	56.4	55.8	52.8
Luxembourg	..	..	..	..	..	..	..	..	..	..	..	..	..	..
Mexico	24.9	26.2	25.7	26.2	27.3	27.5	25.4	72.5	71.1	71.4	70.6	69.2	68.9	71.1
Netherlands	73.0	71.3	51.1	43.6	46.3	42.5	46.0	25.8	27.7	48.1	55.7	53.0	55.9	52.1
New Zealand	52.7	47.3	37.4	45.1	43.9	42.3	..	38.7	45.0	57.2	48.1	49.7	49.2	..
Norway	45.6	50.3	44.1	44.8	46.9	39.1	35.6	57.1	52.6	58.7	58.3	56.5	63.9	67.0
Poland	44.2	48.3	48.5	45.3	41.5	47.5	44.7	54.7	50.3	49.9	53.4	56.5	50.1	52.8
Portugal	37.2	35.6	41.5	45.1	41.3	48.5	57.3	61.7	63.3	57.2	53.5	55.8	47.7	38.1
Slovak Republic	58.3	65.1	51.7	44.7	44.0	48.8	45.8	37.1	29.8	43.2	51.0	52.4	40.2	42.5
Slovenia	63.4	60.5	57.9	56.9	56.5	73.2	78.3	34.3	38.5	42.2	42.8	42.7	25.3	18.9
Spain	49.0	47.8	45.6	61.7	65.3	61.8	72.0	50.3	51.4	53.2	35.7	31.2	28.3	19.5
Sweden	56.7	56.7	46.7	51.7	48.4	46.0	43.6	31.8	31.4	43.8	36.4	40.5	42.1	45.3
Switzerland	50.5	51.4	60.0	63.4	61.5	62.5	59.7	49.6	48.7	40.1	36.8	38.6	37.5	40.3
Turkey	..	..	..	..	..	..	..	..	..	..	..	..	..	..
United Kingdom	58.8	58.0	52.0	58.7	57.3	58.2	52.6	39.8	40.2	46.5	36.3	40.4	39.3	45.1
United States	71.0	86.8	65.6	66.1	66.8	62.7	57.6	23.2	5.4	27.7	27.5	27.2	31.9	37.3
Euro area	59.6	62.4	59.3	58.0	60.2	60.8	60.9	37.0	34.2	37.4	38.7	35.6	33.8	33.5
OECD-Total	..	..	..	..	..	..	..	..	..	..	..	..	..	..
Brazil	..	..	..	..	..	..	..	..	..	..	..	..	..	..
China	..	..	..	..	..	..	..	..	..	..	..	..	..	..
India	..	..	..	..	..	..	..	..	..	..	..	..	..	..
Indonesia	..	..	..	..	..	..	..	..	..	..	..	..	..	..
Russian Federation	..	46.6	38.7	44.5	47.1	44.8	41.2	..	48.6	57.0	50.8	47.7	50.1	54.3
South Africa	..	47.5	49.4	51.4	51.5	50.4	51.4	..	51.8	49.4	47.5	47.3	48.4	47.3

Note: Detailed metadata:
http://stats.oecd.org/OECDStat_Metadata/ShowMetadata.ashx?Dataset=NAAG_2015_NOV15&Lang=en&Coords=[INDICATOR].[D1SB1NS12]

1. Information on data for Israel: http://dx.doi.org/10.1787/888932315602

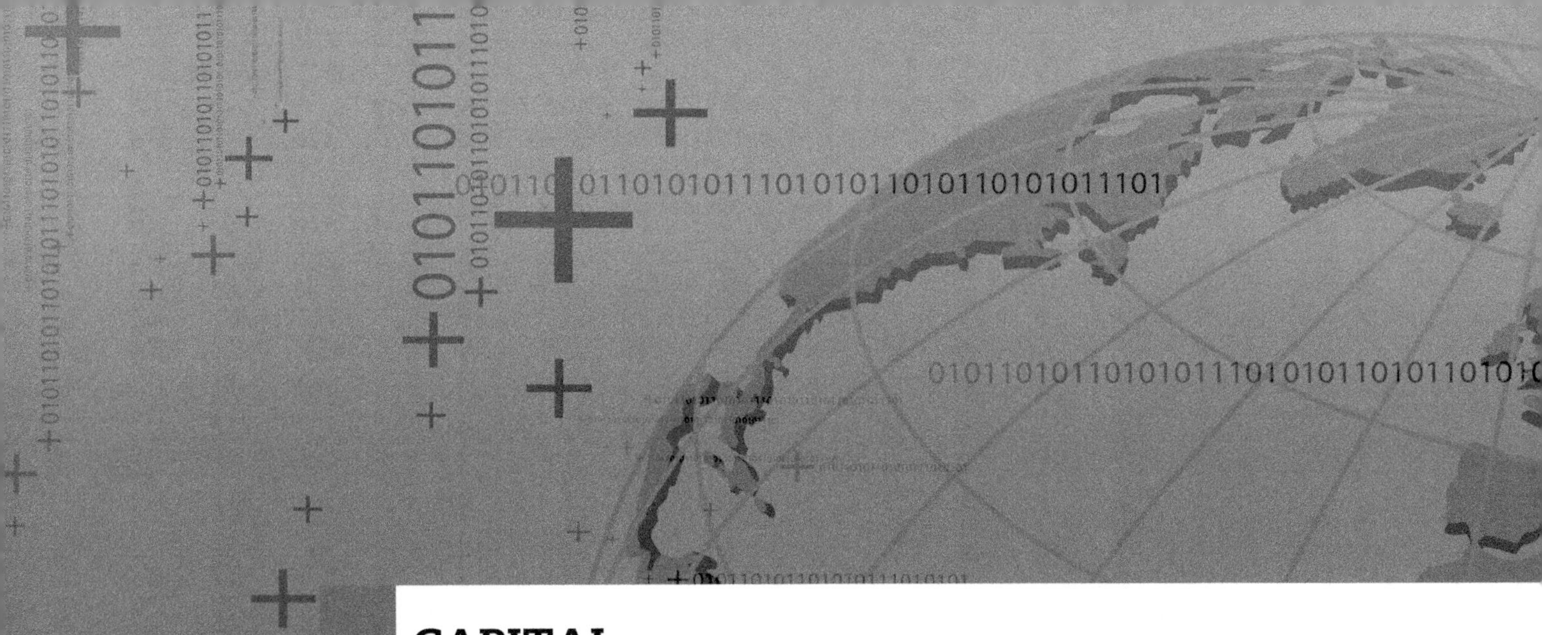

CAPITAL

35. Net capital stock

Table 35.1. **Net capital stock, volume**

Year 2010 = 100

	2000	2001	2002	2003	2004	2005	2006	2007	2008	2009	2010	2011	2012	2013
Australia	68.5	70.5	73.0	75.8	78.8	82.0	85.3	89.1	92.7	96.3	100.0	104.4	108.7	112.6
Austria	83.9	85.8	87.4	89.2	90.9	92.5	94.1	95.9	97.7	98.9	100.0	101.4	102.7	103.9
Belgium	65.7	68.5	70.6	71.9	75.3	79.3	83.2	89.0	93.9	98.9	100.0	103.9	107.9	110.9
Canada	..	..	..	..	..	..	..	..	..	..	..	..	..	..
Chile	..	..	..	..	..	..	..	..	93.2	97.7	100.0	106.3	113.6	120.1
Czech Republic	..	..	..	..	..	..	..	..	..	..	..	..	..	..
Denmark	98.1	98.3	98.0	98.2	98.0	98.2	98.9	98.4	97.8	98.7	100.0	98.9	97.8	97.2
Estonia	50.7	56.4	58.1	64.3	69.1	73.1	76.4	84.8	91.5	100.0	100.0	107.5	107.6	..
Finland	84.4	86.1	87.5	88.9	90.4	92.1	93.7	95.9	98.0	99.0	100.0	101.2	102.1	102.6
France	95.6	96.6	97.3	97.8	97.8	98.1	97.7	98.1	97.6	99.3	100.0	99.7	100.0	101.0
Germany	91.9	93.3	94.2	95.0	95.7	96.3	97.2	98.3	99.3	99.5	100.0	100.7	101.4	..
Greece	73.6	75.7	78.3	81.4	84.5	86.7	89.8	94.4	97.6	99.5	100.0	99.4	97.5	..
Hungary	86.6	87.7	89.2	90.3	91.9	93.5	95.1	96.8	98.7	99.7	100.0	100.2	100.2	..
Iceland	..	..	..	..	..	..	..	..	..	..	..	..	..	..
Ireland	..	..	..	..	..	..	..	..	..	..	..	..	..	..
Israel[1]	81.0	83.8	86.0	87.2	88.4	89.7	91.3	93.5	95.8	97.5	100.0	103.5	106.9	110.4
Italy	84.6	86.3	88.2	89.9	91.7	93.4	95.2	97.0	98.6	99.5	100.0	100.6	100.8	100.7
Japan	..	..	..	..	..	..	..	..	..	..	..	..	..	..
Korea	63.1	66.4	70.1	73.8	77.6	81.3	85.1	89.1	92.8	96.3	100.0	103.5	106.6	..
Luxembourg	..	..	..	..	..	..	..	..	..	..	..	..	..	..
Mexico	..	..	..	..	..	..	..	..	..	..	..	..	..	..
Netherlands	85.4	87.4	88.8	90.1	91.2	92.4	94.0	95.9	97.8	99.1	100.0	101.1	101.8	102.3
New Zealand	..	..	..	..	..	..	..	..	..	..	..	..	..	..
Norway	..	..	..	..	..	..	..	..	..	..	..	..	..	..
Poland	75.0	76.4	78.9	81.6	81.9	82.4	82.9	88.2	90.3	93.8	100.0	105.6	108.8	..
Portugal	..	..	..	..	..	..	..	..	..	..	..	..	..	..
Slovak Republic	..	..	..	..	86.6	89.0	91.2	92.7	95.3	99.4	100.0	102.8	103.0	105.2
Slovenia	82.6	84.3	85.5	86.7	87.9	89.7	92.2	95.8	98.4	99.8	100.0	99.8	99.2	..
Spain	..	..	..	..	..	..	..	..	..	..	..	..	..	..
Sweden	..	..	..	..	..	..	..	..	..	..	..	..	..	..
Switzerland	..	..	..	..	..	..	..	..	..	..	..	..	..	..
Turkey	..	..	..	..	..	..	..	..	..	..	..	..	..	..
United Kingdom	..	..	..	..	..	..	..	..	..	..	..	..	..	..
United States	82.4	84.6	86.5	88.5	90.7	92.8	95.1	97.2	98.7	99.3	100.0	100.8	101.7	102.8
Euro area	..	..	..	..	..	..	..	..	..	..	..	..	..	..
OECD-Total	..	..	..	..	..	..	..	..	..	..	..	..	..	..
Brazil	..	..	..	..	..	..	..	..	..	..	..	..	..	..
China	..	..	..	..	..	..	..	..	..	..	..	..	..	..
India	..	..	..	..	..	..	..	..	..	..	..	..	..	..
Indonesia	..	..	..	..	..	..	..	..	..	..	..	..	..	..
Russian Federation	..	..	..	..	..	..	..	..	..	..	..	..	..	..
South Africa	..	..	..	..	..	..	..	..	..	..	..	..	..	..

Note: Detailed metadata:
http://stats.oecd.org/OECDStat_Metadata/ShowMetadata.ashx?Dataset=NAAG_2015_NOV15&Lang=en&Coords=[INDICATOR].[AN11NVIXOB]

1. Information on data for Israel: http://dx.doi.org/10.1787/888932315602

Table 36.1. **Consumption of fixed capital**

Percentage of GDP

	2000	2001	2002	2003	2004	2005	2006	2007	2008	2009	2010	2011	2012	2013
Australia	16.3	16.1	16.0	15.8	15.9	15.9	16.0	15.9	16.0	16.2	15.6	15.4	15.9	16.4
Austria	16.3	16.6	16.7	17.0	16.9	16.8	16.6	16.4	16.7	17.6	17.5	17.3	17.6	17.8
Belgium	16.7	17.0	17.1	17.6	17.3	17.6	18.0	18.0	18.7	19.4	19.3	19.4	19.7	19.7
Canada	15.2	15.7	15.8	15.2	14.8	14.7	15.1	15.4	15.9	17.5	16.6	16.3	16.7	17.0
Chile	12.5 e	12.6 e	12.5 e	12.2 e	12.0 e	11.9 e	11.5 e	11.6 e	12.1 e	12.2 e	12.1 e	12.3 e	12.4 e	12.5 e
Czech Republic	22.9	22.4	21.9	21.8	21.0	20.5	20.1	19.9	20.2	21.4	21.5	21.5	21.8	22.2
Denmark	16.2	16.7	17.0	17.5	17.3	16.9	16.7	17.2	18.2	18.2	17.7	17.6	17.9	17.9
Estonia	12.5	11.9	12.1	12.5	13.0	12.7	12.6	12.7	14.0	16.8	16.2	14.8	14.7	15.3
Finland	16.9	17.1	17.1	17.2	17.3	17.6	17.6	17.4	17.9	19.6	18.9	18.6	19.2	19.3
France	15.2	15.4	15.6	15.8	15.9	16.1	16.4	16.5	17.1	17.8	17.7	17.8	18.0	18.1
Germany	16.7	16.8	17.0	17.1	17.0	17.1	16.8	16.8	17.2	18.3	17.8	17.6	17.9	17.9
Greece	12.5 e	12.7 e	12.5 e	13.7 e	13.4 e	13.7 e	13.5	13.6	14.3	15.5	16.6	18.1	19.4	19.1
Hungary	19.0	18.1	16.8	16.3	15.7	15.6	15.9	16.0	16.2	17.8	18.1	18.0	18.4	17.8
Iceland	12.4	13.1	13.0	13.0	12.5	12.6	13.6	13.9	16.3	18.6	18.0	17.1	17.1	16.4
Ireland	11.5	11.6	11.7	12.3	12.8	13.9	15.0	14.4	14.3	14.8	15.2	14.7	15.6	15.8
Israel[1]	13.4	14.1	14.9	15.1	15.3	15.5	15.0	14.8	14.4	14.4	13.6	13.3	13.6	13.1
Italy	14.7	14.8	15.1	15.2	15.3	15.5	15.6	15.7	16.2	17.2	17.4	17.7	18.3	18.4
Japan	20.3	20.3	20.4	20.1	20.0	20.1	20.5	20.7	21.7	22.7	21.5	21.6	21.2	21.2
Korea	17.1	17.4	16.8	17.1	17.2	17.3	17.3	17.1	18.4	19.3	18.3	18.9	19.4	19.5
Luxembourg	11.8	12.8	13.3	13.3	13.1	13.1	12.4	12.1	12.6	13.7	13.0	12.9	13.2	13.0
Mexico	10.2 e	10.5 e	10.5 e	10.7	10.5	10.3	10.1	10.1	10.5	12.1	11.3	11.1	11.4	11.4
Netherlands	15.6	15.8	16.2	16.5	16.4	16.3	15.9	15.7	15.8	16.9	16.9	16.7	16.7	16.8
New Zealand	14.7	14.4	14.0	13.6	13.6	13.9	14.4	14.0	15.2	15.5	14.8	14.4	14.4	13.9
Norway	15.1	15.3	15.7	15.3	14.6	13.8	13.5	14.1	14.1	16.3	15.9	15.6	15.5	15.7
Poland	14.0	14.3	14.3	14.4	13.8	13.6	13.4	12.7	12.2	11.7	11.2	10.8	11.0	11.3
Portugal	15.3	15.5	15.8	16.1	16.2	16.3	16.3	16.1	16.7	17.2	17.2	17.8	18.1	17.6
Slovak Republic	22.3	22.2	22.2	21.9	21.0	20.7	19.4	18.1	18.1	20.1	19.8	20.0	20.2	20.6
Slovenia	19.5	19.1	18.5	18.3	18.5	18.6	18.2	17.6	17.6	19.5	19.9	20.0	21.1	21.1
Spain	13.6	13.6	13.8	14.0	14.5	14.8	15.0	15.2	15.6	16.4	16.8	17.4	17.8	17.8
Sweden	15.4	16.0	16.2	15.8	15.5	15.6	15.4	15.4	16.1	17.6	16.7	16.4	16.8	16.7
Switzerland	20.2	20.8	21.4	21.6	21.3	21.0	20.5	20.2	20.4	21.4	20.8	20.7	20.7	20.9
Turkey	..	..	..	..	..	..	..	..	..	..	..	..	..	..
United Kingdom	13.7	14.0	14.3	14.4	14.3	14.1	14.3	14.3	13.5	13.9	13.4	13.3	13.3	13.3
United States	14.7	15.1	15.1	15.0	14.9	15.1	15.4	15.6	16.1	16.4	15.9	15.8	15.7	15.8
Euro area	..	..	15.8	16.0	16.0	16.2	16.2	16.2	16.6	17.6	17.5	17.6	17.9	17.9
OECD-Total	15.4 e	15.7 e	15.7 e	15.7 e	15.6 e	15.6 e	15.7 e	15.8 e	16.2 e	16.9 e	16.4 e	16.3 e	16.4 e	16.5 e
Brazil	..	..	..	..	..	..	..	..	..	..	..	..	..	..
China	..	..	..	..	..	..	..	..	..	..	..	..	..	..
India	..	..	..	..	9.9	9.9	9.7	9.7	10.1	10.0	..	..	..	..
Indonesia	..	..	..	..	..	..	..	..	..	..	..	..	..	..
Russian Federation	8.2 e	8.1 e	7.8	7.3	6.5	6.0	5.1	4.9	4.8	5.7	5.1	4.7	4.9	4.8
South Africa	13.4	13.4	13.2	12.9	12.2	12.0	12.3	12.5	13.3	13.7	13.2	12.5	12.7	13.0

Note: Detailed metadata:
http://stats.oecd.org/OECDStat_Metadata/ShowMetadata.ashx?Dataset=NAAG_2015_NOV15&Lang=en&Coords=[INDICATOR].[K1S]

1. Information on data for Israel: http://dx.doi.org/10.1787/888932315602

ANNEX A

Reference series

Table A.1. **Gross domestic product, 2010 prices and 2010 PPPs**

Billion US dollars

	2000	2001	2002	2003	2004	2005	2006	2007	2008	2009	2010	2011	2012	2013
Australia	691	718	740	771	796	819	850	882	897	914	936	971	995	1 020
Austria	302	306	311	313	321	328	339	352	357	343	350	360	363	364
Belgium	365	368	374	377	391	399	409	423	426	416	427	435	436	436
Canada	1 128	1 147	1 179	1 202	1 240	1 279	1 312	1 339	1 354	1 318	1 362	1 402	1 429	1 458
Chile	207	214	219	228	243	259	273	287	297	294	311	329	347	361
Czech Republic	207	214	217	225	236	251	269	283	291	277	283	289	286	285
Denmark	216	218	219	220	226	231	240	242	240	228	232	235	233	232
Estonia	20	22	23	25	26	29	32	34	32	27	28	30	32	32
Finland	174	178	181	185	192	197	205	216	217	199	205	211	208	205
France	2 068	2 108	2 132	2 149	2 209	2 245	2 298	2 352	2 357	2 287	2 332	2 381	2 385	2 401
Germany	2 961	3 012	3 012	2 990	3 025	3 047	3 159	3 262	3 298	3 112	3 239	3 358	3 372	3 382
Greece	271	282	293	310	325	327	346	357	356	341	322	293	271	263
Hungary	177	183	192	199	209	218	226	227	229	214	216	219	216	220
Iceland	9	10	10	10	11	12	12	13	13	13	12	13	13	13
Ireland	147	155	164	171	178	190	201	213	208	196	197	202	202	205
Israel[1]	160	161	161	163	171	178	189	200	206	209	221	232	238	246
Italy	1 994	2 030	2 035	2 038	2 070	2 090	2 132	2 163	2 141	2 023	2 058	2 070	2 012	1 976
Japan	4 005	4 019	4 031	4 099	4 195	4 250	4 322	4 417	4 371	4 129	4 321	4 302	4 377	4 448
Korea	977	1 021	1 097	1 129	1 184	1 231	1 294	1 365	1 404	1 413	1 505	1 561	1 596	1 643
Luxembourg	33	34	35	35	37	38	40	43	43	41	43	44	44	45
Mexico	1 432 e	1 432 e	1 443 e	1 463	1 524	1 571	1 649	1 703	1 726	1 644	1 730	1 798	1 870	1 897
Netherlands	653	667	668	669	683	698	722	749	762	733	743	756	748	744
New Zealand	105	109	114	119	124	128	132	136	133	133	135	138	141	144
Norway	246	251	255	257	267	274	281	289	290	286	287	290	298	300
Poland	541	548	559	579	609	631	670	718	746	766	794	834	847	857
Portugal	264	270	272	269	274	276	280	287	288	279	285	279	268	265
Slovak Republic	82	85	89	93	98	105	114	126	133	126	132	136	138	140
Slovenia	43	45	46	48	50	52	55	59	61	56	57	57	55	55
Spain	1 210	1 258	1 295	1 336	1 378	1 429	1 489	1 545	1 562	1 507	1 507	1 492	1 453	1 428
Sweden	318	323	329	337	352	362	379	392	389	369	391	402	401	406
Switzerland	334	339	339	339	349	360	374	390	399	390	402	409	413	421
Turkey	799	754	800	842	921	998	1 067	1 117	1 124	1 070	1 168	1 271	1 298	1 352
United Kingdom	1 921	1 974	2 023	2 091	2 143	2 207	2 266	2 324	2 313	2 216	2 250	2 295	2 322	2 372
United States	12 713	12 837	13 066	13 433	13 942	14 408	14 792	15 055	15 011	14 595	14 964	15 204	15 542	15 774
Euro area	10 726	10 953	11 057	11 131	11 382	11 572	11 946	12 308	12 365	11 800	12 042	12 239	12 141	12 106
OECD-Total	36 783 e	37 297 e	37 938 e	38 738	40 020	41 135	42 429	43 566	43 680	42 170	43 447	44 294	44 849	45 390
Brazil	1 937	1 962	2 022	2 047	2 163	2 231	2 320	2 459	2 583	2 577	2 772	2 880	..	..
China	4 470 e	4 840 e	5 280 e	5 809 e	6 395 e	7 119 e	8 021 e	9 157 e	10 039 e	10 964 e	12 110	13 236	14 249	..
India	..	..	..	..	..	..	..	..	..	..	..	..	..	..
Indonesia	1 209	1 253	1 309	1 372	1 441	1 523	1 606	1 708	1 811	1 896	2 017	2 142	2 271	2 398
Russian Federation	1 827 e	1 920 e	2 011	2 158	2 313	2 460	2 661	2 888	3 040	2 802	2 928	3 053	3 157	3 199
South Africa	425	437	453	466	487	513	542	571	589	580	598	617	631	645

Note: Detailed metadata:
http://stats.oecd.org/OECDStat_Metadata/ShowMetadata.ashx?Dataset=NAAG_2015_NOV15&Lang=en&Coords=[INDICATOR].[GDPVPVOB]

1. Information on data for Israel: http://dx.doi.org/10.1787/888932315602

The statistical data for Israel are supplied by and under the responsibility of the relevant Israeli authorities. The use of such data by the OECD is without prejudice to the status of the Golan Heights, East Jerusalem and Israeli settlements in the West Bank under the terms of international law.

Table A.2. **Gross domestic product per capita, OECD = 100**

Based on current PPPs

	2000	2001	2002	2003	2004	2005	2006	2007	2008	2009	2010	2011	2012	2013
Australia	112	113	115	117	116	116	116	116	114	121	121	121	118	118
Austria	118	115	117	117	117	114	116	115	118	120	119	121	121	119
Belgium	113	113	115	113	110	108	108	108	109	111	112	113	112	110
Canada	116	116	115	117	116	118	116	115	115	114	114	114	114	114
Chile	38	38	39	39	40	42	48	49	47	48	52	56	57	58
Czech Republic	65	68	69	71	72	73	75	78	78	79	77	79	77	77
Denmark	118	117	118	114	114	112	114	114	117	117	119	119	117	116
Estonia	39	41	44	48	50	54	59	64	65	60	60	66	68	69
Finland	106	106	107	105	107	105	106	110	114	111	109	111	108	106
France	104	106	107	102	100	100	99	100	101	103	102	103	100	99
Germany	106	107	107	107	106	106	107	108	110	110	113	116	115	114
Greece	77	81	85	87	88	83	87	86	90	91	83	73	68	67
Hungary	48	53	56	57	57	57	57	57	60	62	62	62	61	62
Iceland	118	121	120	116	120	118	113	114	118	118	110	109	109	111
Ireland	118	123	129	131	132	133	136	137	126	124	123	126	123	124
Israel[1]	99	96	94	86	87	81	79	81	79	81	83	84	86	87
Italy	106	109	105	103	99	97	98	99	100	100	98	98	94	92
Japan	103	103	102	102	101	100	98	98	96	94	96	94	96	96
Korea	72	74	78	78	79	79	80	82	83	84	87	86	86	88
Luxembourg	225	217	222	221	226	220	238	243	244	237	241	250	246	247
Mexico	40 e	39 e	39 e	39	39	40	42	42	42	43	43	45	45	45
Netherlands	126	127	127	123	122	122	126	128	133	131	128	128	125	124
New Zealand	86	87	87	87	86	84	85	86	85	90	88	89	88	93
Norway	147	146	141	142	149	159	168	167	179	166	168	173	179	174
Poland	42 e	42 e	43 e	44 e	45 e	45 e	47 e	50 e	52 e	57 e	59 e	61 e	62 e	62 e
Portugal	71	72	72	72	70	72	74	74	75	77	77	74	73	73
Slovak Republic	44	47	49	51	52	54	58	63	68	68	69	69	70	70
Slovenia	71	73	75	76	78	78	80	81	85 |	81	79	78	77	76
Spain	87	90	92	92	91	91	95	96	97	97	92	90	87	86
Sweden	117	115	115	117	118	113	116	119	120	117	119	120	118	118
Switzerland	136	136	135	132	130	128	133	139	144	147	146	150	150	150
Turkey	37	33	32	32	35	37	40	41	43	43	46	49	48 e	49 e
United Kingdom	109	111	113	113	114	114	114	110	108	107	102	101	101	102
United States	145	144	143	144	144	145	143	141	139	139	138	137	138	139
Euro area	100	102	102	100	99	98	100	101	103	103	102	102	100	99
OECD-Total	100	100	100	100	100	100	100	100	100	100	100	100	100	100
Brazil	36	35	35	35	35	35	35	36	38	39	40	41	..	..
China	11	12	13	14	15	16	18	20	21	24	26	28	29	31
India	..	..	..	..	9	10	10	11	11	13	..	..	..	..
Indonesia	20 e	20 e	20 e	21 e	21 e	21 e	21 e	22 e	23	24	24	25 e	25 e	27 e
Russian Federation	27 e	28 e	30	34	35	39	46	49	58	57	58	62	65 e	67 e
South Africa	31	31	32	32	32	33	33	34	34	34	34	34	34	34

Note: Detailed metadata:
http://stats.oecd.org/OECDStat_Metadata/ShowMetadata.ashx?Dataset=NAAG_2015_NOV15&Lang=en&Coords=[INDICATOR].[GDPHCPIXOE]

1. Information on data for Israel: http://dx.doi.org/10.1787/888932315602

Table A.3. **Gross domestic product per capita, 2010 constant prices and PPPs**

US dollars

	2000	2001	2002	2003	2004	2005	2006	2007	2008	2009	2010	2011	2012	2013
Australia	36 148	37 077	37 788	38 917	39 728	40 394	41 285	42 021	41 863	41 894	42 253	43 169	43 489	43 842
Austria	37 633	37 996	38 435	38 553	39 348	39 918	41 042	42 389	42 908	41 180	41 876	42 910	43 042	42 920
Belgium	35 589	35 756	36 220	36 349	37 511	38 088	38 785	39 804	39 783	38 575	39 276	39 636	39 423	39 248
Canada	36 757	36 974	37 601	37 982	38 811	39 660	40 290	40 702	40 738	39 182	40 055	40 836	41 131	41 475
Chile	13 427	13 711	13 924	14 292	15 129	15 892	16 628	17 312	17 706	17 351	18 173	19 040	19 869	20 486
Czech Republic	20 177	20 891	21 284	22 049	23 128	24 552	26 157	27 454	27 909	26 401	26 941	27 524	27 244	27 096
Denmark	40 551	40 739	40 785	40 838	41 814	42 707	44 182	44 358	43 775	41 322	41 812	42 119	41 686	41 321
Estonia	14 495	15 508	16 559	17 895	19 145	21 054	23 357	25 313	24 022	20 526	21 070	22 729	23 988	24 456
Finland	33 529	34 316	34 808	35 418	36 701	37 593	38 967	40 814	40 917	37 354	38 296	39 099	38 359	37 754
France	33 967	34 380	34 513	34 550	35 253	35 552	36 144	36 770	36 637	35 378	35 896	36 463	36 362	36 442
Germany	36 032	36 576	36 513	36 237	36 669	36 945	38 357	39 658	40 157	38 014	39 622	41 061	41 158	41 187
Greece	25 112	25 942	26 861	28 350	29 711	29 801	31 391	32 337	32 143	30 680	28 961	26 355	24 564	23 951
Hungary	17 294	18 001	18 861	19 643	20 658	21 601	22 458	22 589	22 818	21 354	21 562	22 003	21 743	22 215
Iceland	33 407	34 190	34 045	34 772	37 203	38 985	39 494	42 261	41 817	39 873	38 592	39 236	39 489	40 642
Ireland	38 541	40 161	41 809	42 708	43 818	45 555	47 184	48 324	46 271	43 247	43 223	44 174	44 115	44 634
Israel[1]	25 446	24 904	24 380	24 215	24 997	25 627	26 627	27 751	28 084	27 943	28 948	29 847	30 147	30 552
Italy	35 026	35 624	35 638	35 498	35 791	35 916	36 487	36 799	36 133	33 960	34 396	34 465	33 339	32 590
Japan	31 575	31 613	31 637	32 112	32 844	33 266	33 808	34 510	34 134	32 250	33 748	33 651	34 316	34 929
Korea	20 774	21 554	23 027	23 585	24 648	25 562	26 755	28 086	28 673	28 740	30 465	31 353	31 927	32 711
Luxembourg	75 046	75 811	77 730	77 823	80 157	81 456	84 315	89 911	87 604	81 396	84 440	84 623	81 996	83 394
Mexico	14 195 e	14 020 e	13 951 e	13 969	14 388	14 664	15 215	15 509	15 509	14 570	15 139	15 539	15 975	16 022
Netherlands	41 014	41 570	41 345	41 268	41 969	42 768	44 208	45 739	46 341	44 363	44 752	45 276	44 640	44 291
New Zealand	27 209	27 896	28 739	29 513	30 218	30 897	31 383	32 017	31 237	30 820	30 942	31 415	31 916	32 393
Norway	54 806	55 677	56 153	56 347	58 246	59 374	60 288	61 460	60 882	59 174	58 775	58 578	59 397	59 119
Poland	14 150 e	14 328 e	14 628 e	15 164 e	15 949 e	16 523 e	17 559 e	18 832 e	19 570 e	20 066 e	20 612 e	21 639 e	21 972 e	22 269 e
Portugal	25 700	26 015	26 072	25 732	26 135	26 287	26 647	27 257	27 272	26 435	26 924	26 471	25 508	25 359
Slovak Republic	15 205	15 771	16 487	17 378	18 282	19 434	21 068	23 327	24 603	23 201	24 325	25 164	25 509	25 841
Slovenia	21 855	22 470	23 296	23 944	24 973	25 927	27 297	29 033	29 945 |	27 344	27 586	27 710	26 906	26 585
Spain	29 833	30 866	31 251	31 656	32 154	32 737	33 567	34 158	33 978	32 492	32 361	31 918	31 061	30 656
Sweden	35 812	36 274	36 906	37 646	39 119	40 060	41 703	42 805	42 236	39 707	41 727	42 517	42 082	42 245
Switzerland	46 075	46 540	46 269	45 952	46 938	48 080	49 725	51 350	51 894	50 172	51 121	51 670	51 699	52 012
Turkey	12 437	11 570	12 121	12 594	13 600	14 561	15 379	15 909	15 816	14 853	16 001	17 182	17 326 e	17 843 e
United Kingdom	32 621	33 392	34 079	35 056	35 741	36 529	37 246	37 903	37 418	35 598	35 859	36 263	36 448	37 003
United States	45 018	45 007	45 377	46 221	47 540	48 677	49 503	49 903	49 292	47 503	48 302	48 704	49 419	49 784
Euro area	33 404	33 990	34 134	34 171	34 751	35 132	36 098	36 984	36 963	35 163	35 797	36 293	35 910	35 741
OECD-Total	31 856 e	32 080 e	32 396 e	32 845 e	33 700 e	34 399 e	35 234 e	35 908 e	35 724 e	34 252 e	35 053 e	35 520 e	35 757 e	35 987 e
Brazil	11 168	11 154	11 343	11 333	11 824	12 049	12 385	12 981	13 485	13 314	14 179	14 592	..	..
China	3 526 e	3 793 e	4 111 e	4 496 e	4 920 e	5 444 e	6 102 e	6 930 e	7 560 e	8 216 e	9 031	9 824	10 523	..
India	..	..	..	..	..	..	..	..	..	..	..	..	..	..
Indonesia	5 892	6 023	6 207	6 415	6 645	6 926	7 212	7 571	7 926	8 196	8 489	8 785 e	9 199 e	9 595 e
Russian Federation	12 464 e	13 154 e	13 842	14 919	16 054	17 143	18 602	20 224	21 295	19 623	20 498	21 355	22 050 e	22 399 e
South Africa	9 639	9 749	9 963	10 126	10 450	10 855	11 307	11 748	11 951	11 597	11 772	11 967	12 044	12 117

Note: Detailed metadata:
http://stats.oecd.org/OECDStat_Metadata/ShowMetadata.ashx?Dataset=NAAG_2015_NOV15&Lang=en&Coords=[INDICATOR].[GDPHVPVOB]

1. Information on data for Israel: http://dx.doi.org/10.1787/888932315602

Table A.4. **Gross domestic product per capita, OECD = 100 in 2010**

Based on 2010 constant prices and PPPs

	2000	2001	2002	2003	2004	2005	2006	2007	2008	2009	2010	2011	2012	2013
Australia	103	106	108	111	113	115	118	120	119	120	121	123	124	125
Austria	107	108	110	110	112	114	117	121	122	117	119	122	123	122
Belgium	102	102	103	104	107	109	111	114	113	110	112	113	112	112
Canada	105	105	107	108	111	113	115	116	116	112	114	116	117	118
Chile	38	39	40	41	43	45	47	49	51	49	52	54	57	58
Czech Republic	58	60	61	63	66	70	75	78	80	75	77	79	78	77
Denmark	116	116	116	117	119	122	126	127	125	118	119	120	119	118
Estonia	41	44	47	51	55	60	67	72	69	59	60	65	68	70
Finland	96	98	99	101	105	107	111	116	117	107	109	112	109	108
France	97	98	98	99	101	101	103	105	105	101	102	104	104	104
Germany	103	104	104	103	105	105	109	113	115	108	113	117	117	117
Greece	72	74	77	81	85	85	90	92	92	88	83	75	70	68
Hungary	49	51	54	56	59	62	64	64	65	61	62	63	62	63
Iceland	95	98	97	99	106	111	113	121	119	114	110	112	113	116
Ireland	110	115	119	122	125	130	135	138	132	123	123	126	126	127
Israel[1]	73	71	70	69	71	73	76	79	80	80	83	85	86	87
Italy	100	102	102	101	102	102	104	105	103	97	98	98	95	93
Japan	90	90	90	92	94	95	96	98	97	92	96	96	98	100
Korea	59	61	66	67	70	73	76	80	82	82	87	89	91	93
Luxembourg	214	216	222	222	229	232	241	256	250	232	241	241	234	238
Mexico	40 e	40 e	40 e	40	41	42	43	44	44	42	43	44	46	46
Netherlands	117	119	118	118	120	122	126	130	132	127	128	129	127	126
New Zealand	78	80	82	84	86	88	90	91	89	88	88	90	91	92
Norway	156	159	160	161	166	169	172	175	174	169	168	167	169	169
Poland	40 e	41 e	42 e	43 e	45 e	47 e	50 e	54 e	56 e	57 e	59	62 e	63 e	64 e
Portugal	73	74	74	73	75	75	76	78	78	75	77	76	73	72
Slovak Republic	43	45	47	50	52	55	60	67	70	66	69	72	73	74
Slovenia	62	64	66	68	71	74	78	83	85 |	78	79	79	77	76
Spain	85	88	89	90	92	93	96	97	97	93	92	91	89	87
Sweden	102	103	105	107	112	114	119	122	120	113	119	121	120	121
Switzerland	131	133	132	131	134	137	142	146	148	143	146	147	147	148
Turkey	35	33	35	36	39	42	44	45	45	42	46	49	49 e	51 e
United Kingdom	93	95	97	100	102	104	106	108	107	102	102	103	104	106
United States	128	128	129	132	136	139	141	142	141	136	138	139	141	142
Euro area	95	97	97	97	99	100	103	106	105	100	102	104	102	102
OECD-Total	91 e	92 e	92 e	94 e	96 e	98 e	101 e	102 e	102 e	98 e	100	101 e	102 e	103 e
Brazil	32	32	32	32	34	34	35	37	38	38	40	42	..	..
China	10 e	11 e	12 e	13 e	14 e	16 e	17 e	20 e	22 e	23 e	26	28	30	..
India	..	..	..	..	..	..	..	..	..	..	..	..	..	..
Indonesia	17	17	18	18	19	20	21	22	23	23	24	25 e	26 e	27 e
Russian Federation	36 e	38 e	39	43	46	49	53	58	61	56	58	61	63 e	64 e
South Africa	27	28	28	29	30	31	32	34	34	33	34	34	34	35

Note: Detailed metadata:
http://stats.oecd.org/OECDStat_Metadata/ShowMetadata.ashx?Dataset=NAAG_2015_NOV15&Lang=en&Coords=[INDICATOR].[GDPHVPIXOEOB]

1. Information on data for Israel: http://dx.doi.org/10.1787/888932315602

Table A.5. **Actual individual consumption, current prices and current PPPs**

Billion US dollars

	2000	2001	2002	2003	2004	2005	2006	2007	2008	2009	2010	2011	2012	2013
Australia	373	393	424	443	476	490	514	552	561	575	605	639	665	693
Austria	161	163	175	181	189	192	206	210	218	220	229	237	244	247
Belgium	196	202	218	215	225	226	235	242	258	260	274	288	299	303
Canada	597 e	626 e	656 e	686 e	725 e	767 e	797 e	850 e	879 e	876 e	922 e	956 e	980 e	1 011 e
Chile	93 e	97 e	101 e	107 e	118 e	130 e	150 e	165 e	178	178	199	230	251	271
Czech Republic	112	120	128	134	142	145	152	163	163	169	173	181	184	188
Denmark	101	102	112	108	115	116	125	132	139	139	145	149	155	156
Estonia	10	10	12	13	14	15	17	19	19	17	18	19	20	21
Finland	82	84	92	95	101	105	112	121	131	130	136	144	150	152
France	1 142	1 220	1 322	1 294	1 348	1 392	1 453	1 529	1 591	1 593	1 660	1 704	1 747	1 763
Germany	1 568	1 626	1 699	1 757	1 805	1 893	1 971	2 027	2 112	2 097	2 218	2 310	2 410	2 429
Greece	159	175	198	199	210	214	227	241	265	262	254	234	219	220
Hungary	92	99	113	119	122	125	130	133	138	136	140	146	148	150
Iceland	6	6	6	7	7	8	8	9	9	8	8	8	9	9
Ireland	64	68	75	80	85	91	98	107	108	103	106	106	106	108
Israel[1]	92	98	105	103	111	114	118	131	133	138	146	157	166	173
Italy	1 068	1 139	1 132	1 154	1 176	1 208	1 282	1 344	1 426	1 401	1 481	1 495	1 483	1 471
Japan	2 092	2 175	2 312	2 405	2 500	2 648	2 733	2 837	2 892	2 889	3 020	3 120	3 274	3 355
Korea	503	541	603	607	629	666	716	771	806	814	864	915	956	982
Luxembourg	12	12	14	14	14	14	15	15	16	16	16	17	18	18
Mexico	758 e	792 e	831 e	866	936	1 005	1 105	1 168	1 248	1 178	1 264	1 361	1 452	1 495
Netherlands	336	349	383	372	387	395	422	445	468	459	454	463	469	463
New Zealand	58	61	65	68	73	76	81	87	91	92	96	100	104	108
Norway	87	91	99	104	112	115	123	134	140	142	150	154	163	167
Poland	319	330	365	368	390	401	430	484	524	551	600	641	681	692
Portugal	136	142	152	155	162	176	186	194	204	200	208	207	210	212
Slovak Republic	43	48	53	53	57	61	67	76	85	86	91	92	95	97
Slovenia	25	26	28	29	30	31	32	34	37	36	37	38	39	38
Spain	633	681	757	764	812	853	921	968	1 012	981	994	993	1 007	1 002
Sweden	169	172	186	190	198	199	210	225	237	237	245	254	262	266
Switzerland	154	161	171	170	178	180	188	202	216	220	225	234	246	252
Turkey	455 e	441 e	469 e	481 e	542 e	602 e	650 e	697 e	767 e	774 e	871 e	972 e	1 000 e	1 049 e
United Kingdom	1 241	1 313	1 425	1 462	1 588	1 642	1 728	1 764	1 776	1 735	1 685	1 703	1 782	1 814
United States	7 413	7 769	8 083	8 496	9 030	9 608	10 162	10 659	10 975	10 826	11 200	11 693	12 100	12 516
Euro area	..	..	..	..	..	..	..	..	..	..	..	..	..	..
OECD-Total	20 349 e	21 333 e	22 564 e	23 300 e	24 606 e	25 903 e	27 366 e	28 733 e	29 824 e	29 539 e	30 733 e	31 961 e	33 094 e	33 892 e
Brazil	..	..	..	..	..	..	..	..	..	..	..	..	..	..
China	..	..	..	..	..	..	..	..	..	..	..	..	..	..
India	..	..	..	..	..	..	..	..	..	..	..	..	..	..
Indonesia	..	..	..	..	..	..	..	..	..	..	..	..	..	..
Russian Federation	637 e	703 e	843	898	1 019	1 137	1 359	1 569	1 864	1 833	1 946	2 176	2 440	2 686
South Africa	238	250	260	272	298	324	350	382	396	396	404	437	462	482

Note: Detailed metadata:
http://stats.oecd.org/OECDStat_Metadata/ShowMetadata.ashx?Dataset=NAAG_2015_NOV15&Lang=en&Coords=[INDICATOR].[P41CPC]

1. Information on data for Israel: http://dx.doi.org/10.1787/888932315602

Table A.6. **Actual individual consumption, 2010 prices and PPPs**

Billion US dollars

	2000	2001	2002	2003	2004	2005	2006	2007	2008	2009	2010	2011	2012	2013
Australia	427	441	459	483	505	520	543	567	572	585	605	622	633	646
Austria	198	200	203	206	210	215	220	223	226	228	229	232	234	234
Belgium	239	242	244	246	250	252	256	261	266	268	274	276	278	280
Canada	690 e	708 e	732 e	752 e	774 e	799 e	829 e	861 e	887 e	892 e	922 e	939 e	956 e	974 e
Chile	122 e	126 e	128 e	134 e	143 e	153 e	164 e	176 e	184	184	199	205	199	188
Czech Republic	132	137	143	150	154	157	162	167	172	172	173	173	171	172
Denmark	123	124	127	128	133	137	141	143	145	143	145	145	145	145
Estonia	12	13	14	15	16	18	20	21	21	18	18	18	19	20
Finland	107	110	113	117	121	125	129	133	135	133	136	139	140	139
France	1 384	1 417	1 449	1 474	1 504	1 539	1 571	1 609	1 619	1 629	1 660	1 671	1 674	1 685
Germany	2 081	2 112	2 102	2 109	2 117	2 129	2 158	2 167	2 190	2 204	2 218	2 249	2 271	2 287
Greece	203	211	221	232	239	249	256	266	275	270	254	230	211	205
Hungary	120	125	134	145	148	152	155	154	153	144	140	141	138	139
Iceland	7 e	7 e	7 e	7 e	8 e	9 e	9 e	9 e	9 e	8 e	8 e	8 e	8 e	8 e
Ireland	77	82	85	88	92	97	103	110	110	106	106	105	104	104
Israel[1]	106	110	112	112	117	121	126	136	138	140	146	151	155	161
Italy	1 386	1 404	1 409	1 422	1 438	1 457	1 477	1 493	1 482	1 465	1 481	1 478	1 427	1 395
Japan	2 716	2 766	2 803	2 821	2 856	2 902	2 932	2 964	2 947	2 941	3 020	3 040	3 112	3 174
Korea	609 e	644 e	698 e	697 e	701 e	731 e	768 e	807 e	821 e	828 e	864 e	892 e	911 e	930 e
Luxembourg	13	13	14	14	14	15	15	15	16	16	16	16	17	17
Mexico	990 e	1 014 e	1 029 e	1 050	1 106	1 153	1 214	1 249	1 274	1 199	1 264	1 324	1 386	1 417
Netherlands	399	408	416	419	422	426	438	447	453	452	454	456	451	446
New Zealand	69	71	75	79	83	88	89	93	92	94	96	98	100	103
Norway	107	110	114	118	123	128	134	140	143	145	150	153	157	160
Poland	416	425	441	448	467	479	501	532	564	584	600	614	619	627
Portugal	185	187	189	190	194	198	200	204	207	204	208	200	190	188
Slovak Republic	60	63	66	68	70	74	78	85	90	90	91	89	89	89
Slovenia	29	30	31	32	33	33	34	36	37	37	37	37	37	35
Spain	782	809	837	859	898	938	974	1 010	1 013	992	994	972	936	907
Sweden	202	205	210	214	218	223	228	235	236	238	245	249	250	254
Switzerland	194	198	200	201	205	208	210	215	217	221	225	227	233	238
Turkey	589 e	552 e	579 e	633 e	701 e	754 e	791 e	835 e	833 e	818 e	871 e	936 e	935 e	983 e
United Kingdom	1 385	1 437	1 493	1 546	1 599	1 647	1 678	1 724	1 721	1 682	1 685	1 690	1 721	1 753
United States	9 185	9 428	9 673	9 953	10 307	10 648	10 952	11 191	11 166	11 023	11 200	11 409	11 601	11 854
Euro area	..	..	..	..	..	..	..	..	..	..	..	..	..	..
OECD-Total	25 336 e	25 929 e	26 555 e	27 172 e	27 974 e	28 779 e	29 562 e	30 282 e	30 416 e	30 155 e	30 733 e	31 187 e	31 509 e	31 957 e
Brazil	..	..	..	..	..	..	..	..	..	..	..	..	..	..
China	..	..	..	..	..	..	..	..	..	..	..	..	..	..
India	..	..	..	..	..	..	..	..	..	..	..	..	..	..
Indonesia	..	..	..	..	..	..	..	..	..	..	..	..	..	..
Russian Federation	943 e	1 021 e	1 099	1 173	1 296	1 437	1 589	1 787	1 954	1 866	1 946	2 059	2 185	2 273
South Africa	272	282	293	302	320	337	364	388	397	389	404	422	435	447

Note: Detailed metadata:
http://stats.oecd.org/OECDStat_Metadata/ShowMetadata.ashx?Dataset=NAAG_2015_NOV15&Lang=en&Coords=[INDICATOR].[P41VPVOB]

1. Information on data for Israel: http://dx.doi.org/10.1787/888932315602

Table A.7. **Population, national concept**

Thousands

	2000	2001	2002	2003	2004	2005	2006	2007	2008	2009	2010	2011	2012	2013
Australia	19 120	19 361	19 582	19 804	20 024	20 283	20 591	20 979	21 423	21 827	22 144	22 482	22 878	23 271
Austria	8 012	8 042	8 082	8 118	8 169	8 225	8 268	8 295	8 322	8 341	8 361	8 389	8 426	8 477
Belgium	10 246	10 281	10 330	10 373	10 417	10 474	10 543	10 622	10 707	10 790	10 883	10 978	11 054	11 105
Canada	30 686	31 021	31 358	31 642	31 938	32 242	32 571	32 888	33 246	33 629	34 005	34 343	34 752	35 154
Chile	15 398	15 572	15 746	15 919	16 093	16 267	16 433	16 598	16 763	16 929	17 093	17 267	17 450	17 640
Czech Republic	10 273	10 224	10 201	10 202	10 207	10 234	10 267	10 323	10 430	10 491	10 517	10 497	10 509	10 511
Denmark	5 338	5 357	5 376	5 390	5 403	5 419	5 437	5 460	5 493	5 523	5 547	5 570	5 591	5 613
Estonia	1 401	1 393	1 384	1 375	1 366	1 359	1 351	1 343	1 338	1 336	1 333	1 330	1 325	1 320
Finland	5 176	5 188	5 201	5 213	5 228	5 246	5 266	5 289	5 313	5 339	5 363	5 388	5 414	5 439
France	60 872	61 317	61 764	62 202	62 661	63 133	63 574	63 967	64 324	64 655	64 974	65 294	65 595	65 881
Germany	82 188	82 340	82 482	82 520	82 501	82 464	82 366	82 263	82 120	81 875	81 757	81 779	81 917	82 103
Greece	10 806	10 862	10 902	10 928	10 955	10 987	11 020	11 048	11 078	11 107	11 121	11 105	11 045	10 965
Hungary	10 211	10 188	10 159	10 130	10 107	10 087	10 071	10 056	10 038	10 023	10 000	9 972	9 920	9 893
Iceland	281	285	288	289	293	296	304	311	319	319	318	319	321	324
Ireland	3 804	3 864	3 932	3 997	4 067	4 160	4 270	4 400	4 496	4 539	4 560	4 577	4 590	4 602
Israel[1]	6 304	6 457	6 591	6 714	6 837	6 961	7 088	7 219	7 351	7 482	7 621	7 763	7 907	8 056
Italy	56 942	56 980	57 100	57 413	57 845	58 191	58 428	58 787	59 242	59 578	59 830	60 060	60 339	60 646
Japan	126 831	127 132	127 400	127 634	127 734	127 755	127 838	127 980	128 045	128 034	128 043	127 831	127 552	127 333
Korea	47 008	47 357	47 622	47 859	48 039	48 138	48 372	48 598	48 949	49 182	49 410	49 779	50 004	50 220
Luxembourg	437	442	447	452	459	466	473	481	489	498	508	519	532	545
Mexico	100 896	102 122	103 418	104 720	105 952	107 151	108 409	109 787	111 299	112 853	114 256	115 683	117 054	118 395
Netherlands	15 922	16 043	16 147	16 223	16 276	16 317	16 341	16 378	16 440	16 526	16 612	16 693	16 752	16 800
New Zealand	3 865	3 900	3 970	4 045	4 101	4 148	4 197	4 235	4 271	4 318	4 363	4 393	4 418	4 460
Norway	4 491	4 513	4 539	4 565	4 591	4 622	4 661	4 706	4 769	4 827	4 889	4 953	5 019	5 080
Poland	38 256 e	38 251 e	38 232 e	38 195 e	38 180 e	38 161 e	38 132 e	38 116 e	38 116 e	38 153 e	38 517 e	38 526 e	38 534 e	38 502 e
Portugal	10 290	10 363	10 420	10 459	10 484	10 503	10 522	10 543	10 558	10 568	10 573	10 558	10 515	10 457
Slovak Republic	5 401	5 380	5 379	5 379	5 382	5 387	5 391	5 397	5 406	5 418	5 430	5 398	5 406	5 413
Slovenia	1 989	1 992	1 995	1 996	1 997	2 001	2 008	2 019	2 022 |	2 042	2 049	2 053	2 057	2 060
Spain	40 554	40 766	41 424	42 196	42 859	43 663	44 361	45 236	45 983	46 368	46 563	46 736	46 766	46 593
Sweden	8 872	8 896	8 925	8 958	8 994	9 030	9 081	9 148	9 220	9 299	9 378	9 449	9 519	9 600
Switzerland	7 249	7 280	7 334	7 388	7 438	7 482	7 525	7 589	7 680	7 775	7 856	7 912	7 997	8 089
Turkey	64 252	65 133	66 008	66 873	67 723	68 566	69 395	70 215	71 095	72 050	73 003	73 950	74 899 e	75 774 e
United Kingdom	58 886	59 113	59 366	59 637	59 950	60 413	60 827	61 319	61 824	62 260	62 759	63 285	63 705	64 106
United States	282 398	285 225	287 955	290 626	293 262	295 993	298 818	301 696	304 543	307 240	309 808	312 172	314 499	316 839
Euro area	321 103	322 245	323 927	325 755	327 537	329 385	330 934	332 789	334 519	335 585	336 387	337 229	338 086	338 725
OECD-Total	1 154 656 e	1 162 637 e	1 171 054 e	1 179 434 e	1 187 533 e	1 195 824 e	1 204 198 e	1 213 291 e	1 222 713 e	1 231 193 e	1 239 444 e	1 247 003 e	1 254 261 e	1 261 268 e
Brazil	173 448	175 885	178 276	180 619	182 911	185 151	187 335	189 463	191 532	193 544	195 498	197 397	..	..
China	1 267 430	1 276 270	1 284 530	1 292 270	1 299 880	1 307 560	1 314 480	1 321 290	1 328 020	1 334 500	1 340 910	1 347 350	1 354 040	1 360 720
India	..	..	..	..	1 089 000	1 106 000	1 122 000	1 138 000	1 154 000	1 170 000	1 194 623 e	1 210 980 e	1 227 193 e	1 243 337 e
Indonesia	205 132	207 995	210 898	213 841	216 826	219 852	222 747	225 642	228 523	231 370	237 641	243 802 e	246 864 e	249 866 e
Russian Federation	146 597	145 977	145 307	144 649	144 067	143 519	143 050	142 805	142 742	142 785	142 850	142 961	143 170 e	142 834 e
South Africa	44 108	44 801	45 448	46 034	46 641	47 270	47 922	48 597	49 296	50 021	50 772	51 550	52 356	53 192

Note: Detailed metadata:
http://stats.oecd.org/OECDStat_Metadata/ShowMetadata.ashx?Dataset=NAAG_2015_NOV15&Lang=en&Coords=[INDICATOR].[POPNC]

1. Information on data for Israel: http://dx.doi.org/10.1787/888932315602

Table A.8. **Purchasing power parities for GDP**

National currency per US dollar

	2000	2001	2002	2003	2004	2005	2006	2007	2008	2009	2010	2011	2012	2013
Australia	1.31	1.33	1.34	1.36	1.37	1.39	1.40	1.43	1.48	1.44	1.50	1.51	1.52	1.52
Austria	0.900	0.917	0.896	0.883	0.874	0.886	0.856	0.867	0.852	0.844	0.841	0.835	0.839	0.844
Belgium	0.891	0.885	0.865	0.877	0.896	0.900	0.882	0.887	0.874	0.858	0.854	0.840	0.843	0.850
Canada	1.23	1.22	1.23	1.23	1.23	1.21	1.21	1.21	1.23	1.20	1.22	1.24	1.25	1.25
Chile	286	292	299	307	321	334	322	326	343	353	357	348	350	355
Czech Republic	14.2	14.2	14.3	14.0	14.3	14.3	14.0	13.9	14.3	13.9	14.0	13.4	13.4	13.4
Denmark	8.40	8.46	8.30	8.52	8.40	8.59	8.32	8.23	8.01	7.83	7.76	7.60	7.66	7.67
Estonia	0.455	0.477	0.477	0.480	0.486	0.502	0.520	0.555	0.549	0.524	0.524	0.524	0.539	0.551
Finland	0.994	1.011	1.003	1.009	0.975	0.977	0.949	0.941	0.918	0.903	0.911	0.908	0.918	0.932
France	0.939	0.918	0.905	0.936	0.940	0.923	0.902	0.893	0.882	0.861	0.857	0.844	0.853	0.854
Germany	0.966	0.955	0.942	0.916	0.896	0.867	0.837	0.831	0.812	0.809	0.796	0.784	0.786	0.794
Greece	0.678	0.671	0.660	0.688	0.695	0.714	0.699	0.719	0.701	0.697	0.702	0.700	0.688	0.645
Hungary	107.8	110.6	114.9	120.3	126.3	128.6	128.4	131.3	129.4	125.6	125.5	124.8	127.9	129.3
Iceland	84.3	88.9	91.3	94.4	94.2	99.1	107.1	113.1	117.4	125.0	131.8	134.8	136.7	138.2
Ireland	0.961	0.992	1.004	1.013	1.006	1.010	0.984	0.958	0.952	0.892	0.843	0.832	0.832	0.832
Israel[1]	3.449	3.425	3.463	3.628	3.534	3.717	3.789	3.716	3.867	3.964	3.971	3.945	3.964	4.006
Italy	0.817	0.807	0.845	0.853	0.872	0.867	0.833	0.817	0.789	0.779	0.780	0.769	0.764	0.762
Japan	155	150	144	140	134	130	125	120	117	115	112	107	105	104
Korea	747	757	770	792	794	789	772	770	786	825	841	855	860	860
Luxembourg	0.939	0.948	0.934	0.941	0.922	0.953	0.914	0.924	0.906	0.907	0.922	0.894	0.898	0.915
Mexico	6.09	6.30	6.55	6.80	7.17	7.13	7.19	7.35	7.47	7.43	7.67	7.67	7.93	8.04
Netherlands	0.892	0.906	0.902	0.926	0.909	0.896	0.868	0.857	0.842	0.841	0.849	0.830	0.830	0.829
New Zealand	1.44	1.47	1.47	1.50	1.51	1.54	1.48	1.51	1.49	1.47	1.49	1.49	1.48	1.47
Norway	9.12	9.17	9.11	9.10	8.98	8.90	8.69	8.78	8.75	8.96	9.01	8.98	8.90	9.20
Poland	1.84	1.86	1.83	1.84	1.86	1.87	1.84	1.84	1.86	1.86	1.82	1.83	1.83	1.82
Portugal	0.699	0.705	0.708	0.705	0.716	0.684	0.661	0.660	0.649	0.633	0.632	0.620	0.593	0.589
Slovak Republic	0.525	0.521	0.528	0.554	0.572	0.566	0.555	0.546	0.533	0.511	0.510	0.518	0.519	0.513
Slovenia	0.531	0.565	0.588	0.614	0.611	0.612	0.607	0.629	0.634	0.644	0.641	0.630	0.615	0.608
Spain	0.734	0.739	0.733	0.752	0.759	0.765	0.735	0.728	0.720	0.709	0.717	0.704	0.688	0.680
Sweden	9.13	9.34	9.35	9.32	9.10	9.38	9.08	8.88	8.77	8.92	9.00	8.85	8.82	8.81
Switzerland	1.85	1.84	1.77	1.77	1.75	1.74	1.66	1.60	1.55	1.52	1.51	1.43	1.40	1.38
Turkey	0.283	0.428	0.613	0.772	0.812	0.831	0.847	0.864	0.890	0.912	0.941	0.992	1.051	1.112
United Kingdom	0.64	0.63	0.63	0.64	0.63	0.64	0.63	0.65	0.65	0.66	0.69	0.70	0.70	0.70
United States	1	1	1	1	1	1	1	1	1	1	1	1	1	1
Euro area	0.876	0.868	0.866	0.870	0.869	0.857	0.829	0.822	0.806	0.795	0.793	0.782	0.781	0.781
OECD-Total	..	..	..	..	..	..	..	..	..	..	..	..	..	..
Brazil	0.77	0.82	0.90	1.00	1.05	1.09	1.13	1.16	1.23	1.31	1.40	1.47	1.52	1.61
China	2.74	2.74	2.71	2.73	2.84	2.86	2.88	3.02	3.19	3.15	3.32	3.51	3.51	3.52
India	10.13	10.22	10.44	10.63	10.94	11.05	11.41	11.75	12.52	13.18	14.19	15.11	15.91	16.76
Indonesia	1 509.79	1 686.98	1 759.40	1 819.59	1 922.48	2 129.69	2 357.25	2 554.84	2 960.70	3 181.20	3 402.69	3 606.57	3 699.95	3 803.35
Russian Federation	7.30	8.32	9.27	9.87	11.55	12.74	12.61	13.98	14.34	14.02	15.82	17.35	18.04	18.43
South Africa	2.77	2.92	3.19	3.30	3.41	3.49	3.60	3.79	4.02	4.32	4.60	4.77	4.90	5.11

Note: Detailed metadata:
http://stats.oecd.org/OECDStat_Metadata/ShowMetadata.ashx?Dataset=NAAG_2015_NOV15&Lang=en&Coords=[INDICATOR].[PPPGDP]

1. Information on data for Israel: http://dx.doi.org/10.1787/888932315602

Table A.9. **Purchasing power parities for actual individual consumption**

National currency per US dollar

	2000	2001	2002	2003	2004	2005	2006	2007	2008	2009	2010	2011	2012	2013
Australia	1.31	1.32	1.31	1.34	1.33	1.37	1.42	1.43	1.46	1.50	1.51	1.51	1.51	1.51
Austria	0.872	0.889	0.847	0.848	0.841	0.864	0.845	0.862	0.856	0.863	0.849	0.857	0.855	0.865
Belgium	0.860	0.865	0.822	0.856	0.853	0.886	0.891	0.903	0.897	0.899	0.891	0.880	0.875	0.880
Canada	1.21	1.21	1.22	1.23	1.21	1.21	1.23	1.22	1.24	1.27	1.26	1.27	1.28	1.29
Chile	334	342	348	351	344	346	331	335	352	358	364	353	354	356
Czech Republic	12.8	12.7	12.7	12.8	12.9	13.1	13.1	13.1	14.0	13.8	13.6	13.2	13.1	13.0
Denmark	8.27	8.48	8.08	8.57	8.53	8.86	8.65	8.48	8.38	8.39	8.35	8.24	8.13	8.17
Estonia	0.405	0.433	0.421	0.436	0.444	0.477	0.505	0.545	0.555	0.541	0.531	0.539	0.542	0.555
Finland	1.009	1.033	0.993	1.019	0.997	1.006	0.987	0.962	0.945	0.952	0.950	0.954	0.945	0.954
France	0.885	0.866	0.830	0.880	0.879	0.888	0.887	0.882	0.875	0.871	0.862	0.858	0.849	0.853
Germany	0.924	0.922	0.889	0.877	0.864	0.840	0.827	0.820	0.807	0.819	0.794	0.787	0.775	0.787
Greece	0.672	0.657	0.622	0.668	0.675	0.711	0.714	0.726	0.710	0.720	0.715	0.715	0.701	0.659
Hungary	94.4	99.9	101.0	109.9	114.6	119.7	121.2	125.4	126.6	125.1	122.0	122.0	124.1	124.8
Iceland	84.4	91.0	91.9	95.8	96.3	100.3	106.2	109.5	120.0	132.1	133.8	135.7	137.1	140.1
Ireland	0.948	0.987	0.990	1.004	1.006	1.015	1.027	1.033	1.048	1.001	0.943	0.953	0.944	0.945
Israel[1]	3.769	3.742	3.691	3.754	3.669	3.744	3.856	3.799	4.007	4.002	4.074	4.038	4.006	4.089
Italy	0.823	0.803	0.834	0.849	0.864	0.874	0.857	0.844	0.813	0.817	0.791	0.800	0.795	0.791
Japan	161	156	147	140	135	129	126	122	119	116	113	109	106	105
Korea	742	769	774	796	801	809	804	801	816	837	840	850	849	852
Luxembourg	0.925	0.940	0.891	0.910	0.923	1.001	0.975	1.004	0.997	1.022	1.053	1.043	1.032	1.051
Mexico	5.75	6.07	6.20	6.53	6.72	6.84	6.79	6.96	7.09	7.43	7.64	7.69	7.86	8.04
Netherlands	0.834	0.851	0.821	0.869	0.855	0.861	0.848	0.839	0.829	0.843	0.867	0.866	0.862	0.876
New Zealand	1.40	1.40	1.41	1.44	1.44	1.49	1.46	1.45	1.43	1.47	1.47	1.48	1.47	1.46
Norway	9.31	9.48	9.20	9.30	9.22	9.50	9.43	9.31	9.46	9.72	9.78	9.92	9.79	10.05
Poland	1.73	1.77	1.71	1.73	1.76	1.80	1.79	1.73	1.76	1.79	1.73	1.74	1.71	1.69
Portugal	0.700	0.707	0.697	0.706	0.709	0.689	0.680	0.685	0.679	0.673	0.669	0.651	0.612	0.606
Slovak Republic	0.472	0.469	0.460	0.498	0.523	0.526	0.535	0.524	0.521	0.517	0.500	0.506	0.503	0.498
Slovenia	0.514	0.547	0.553	0.590	0.598	0.613	0.612	0.629	0.642	0.667	0.662	0.656	0.637	0.632
Spain	0.706	0.704	0.673	0.706	0.720	0.739	0.736	0.750	0.745	0.749	0.751	0.750	0.723	0.712
Sweden	9.02	9.23	8.97	9.15	9.08	9.36	9.25	9.08	8.92	9.15	9.29	9.26	9.15	9.27
Switzerland	1.89	1.87	1.76	1.80	1.77	1.79	1.76	1.70	1.64	1.63	1.63	1.59	1.54	1.53
Turkey	0.273	0.397	0.542	0.715	0.779	0.818	0.874	0.917	0.922	0.944	0.969	1.016	1.069	1.138
United Kingdom	0.62	0.61	0.60	0.62	0.60	0.62	0.62	0.64	0.66	0.67	0.72	0.74	0.73	0.74
United States	1	1	1	1	1	1	1	1	1	1	1	1	1	1
Euro area	0.844	0.836	0.814	0.835	0.835	0.836	0.828	0.825	0.813	0.818	0.804	0.803	0.792	0.794
OECD-Total	..	..	..	..	..	..	..	..	..	..	..	..	..	..
Brazil	..	..	..	..	..	..	..	..	..	..	..	..	..	..
China	..	..	..	..	..	..	..	..	..	..	..	..	..	..
India	..	..	..	..	..	..	..	..	..	..	..	..	..	..
Indonesia	..	..	..	..	..	..	..	..	..	..	..	..	..	..
Russian Federation	6.00	7.14	7.59	8.58	9.67	10.96	11.25	12.06	12.71	13.66	14.37	14.84	14.93	15.10
South Africa	2.85	3.00	3.27	3.37	3.49	3.56	3.68	3.85	4.11	4.36	4.67	4.77	4.93	5.13

Note: Detailed metadata:
http://stats.oecd.org/OECDStat_Metadata/ShowMetadata.ashx?Dataset=NAAG_2015_NOV15&Lang=en&Coords=[INDICATOR].[PPPP41]

1. Information on data for Israel: http://dx.doi.org/10.1787/888932315602

Table A.10. **Exchange rates**

National currency per US dollar

	2000	2001	2002	2003	2004	2005	2006	2007	2008	2009	2010	2011	2012	2013
Australia	1.72	1.93	1.84	1.54	1.36	1.31	1.33	1.20	1.19	1.28	1.09	0.97	0.97	1.04
Austria	1.085	1.118	1.063	0.886	0.805	0.804	0.797	0.731	0.683	0.720	0.755	0.719	0.778	0.753
Belgium	1.085	1.118	1.063	0.886	0.805	0.804	0.797	0.731	0.683	0.720	0.755	0.719	0.778	0.753
Canada	1.49	1.55	1.57	1.40	1.30	1.21	1.13	1.07	1.07	1.14	1.03	0.99	1.00	1.03
Chile	540	635	689	691	610	560	530	522	522	561	510	484	486	495
Czech Republic	38.6	38.0	32.7	28.2	25.7	24.0	22.6	20.3	17.1	19.1	19.1	17.7	19.6	19.6
Denmark	8.08	8.32	7.89	6.59	5.99	6.00	5.95	5.44	5.10	5.36	5.62	5.37	5.79	5.62
Estonia	1.084	1.117	1.062	0.886	0.805	0.804	0.797	0.731	0.683	0.719	0.755	0.719	0.778	0.753
Finland	1.085	1.118	1.063	0.886	0.805	0.804	0.797	0.731	0.683	0.720	0.755	0.719	0.778	0.753
France	1.085	1.118	1.063	0.886	0.805	0.804	0.797	0.731	0.683	0.720	0.755	0.719	0.778	0.753
Germany	1.085	1.118	1.063	0.886	0.805	0.804	0.797	0.731	0.683	0.720	0.755	0.719	0.778	0.753
Greece	1.072	1.118	1.063	0.886	0.805	0.804	0.797	0.731	0.683	0.720	0.755	0.719	0.778	0.753
Hungary	282.2	286.5	257.9	224.3	202.7	199.6	210.4	183.6	172.1	202.3	207.9	201.1	225.1	223.7
Iceland	78.6	97.4	91.7	76.7	70.2	63.0	70.2	64.1	87.9	123.6	122.2	116.0	125.1	122.2
Ireland	1.085	1.118	1.063	0.886	0.805	0.804	0.797	0.731	0.683	0.720	0.755	0.719	0.778	0.753
Israel[1]	4.077	4.206	4.738	4.554	4.482	4.488	4.456	4.108	3.588	3.932	3.739	3.578	3.856	3.611
Italy	1.085	1.118	1.063	0.886	0.805	0.804	0.797	0.731	0.683	0.720	0.755	0.719	0.778	0.753
Japan	108	122	125	116	108	110	116	118	103	94	88	80	80	98
Korea	1 131	1 291	1 251	1 192	1 145	1 024	955	929	1 102	1 277	1 156	1 108	1 126	1 095
Luxembourg	1.085	1.118	1.063	0.886	0.805	0.804	0.797	0.731	0.683	0.720	0.755	0.719	0.778	0.753
Mexico	9.46	9.34	9.66	10.79	11.29	10.90	10.90	10.93	11.13	13.51	12.64	12.42	13.17	12.77
Netherlands	1.085	1.118	1.063	0.886	0.805	0.804	0.797	0.731	0.683	0.720	0.755	0.719	0.778	0.753
New Zealand	2.20	2.38	2.16	1.72	1.51	1.42	1.54	1.36	1.42	1.60	1.39	1.27	1.23	1.22
Norway	8.80	8.99	7.98	7.08	6.74	6.44	6.41	5.86	5.64	6.29	6.04	5.60	5.82	5.88
Poland	4.35	4.09	4.08	3.89	3.66	3.24	3.10	2.77	2.41	3.12	3.02	2.96	3.26	3.16
Portugal	1.085	1.118	1.063	0.886	0.805	0.804	0.797	0.731	0.683	0.720	0.755	0.719	0.778	0.753
Slovak Republic	1.528	1.605	1.505	1.221	1.071	1.030	0.986	0.820	0.709	0.720	0.755	0.719	0.778	0.753
Slovenia	0.929	1.013	1.003	0.864	0.803	0.804	0.797	0.731	0.683	0.720	0.755	0.719	0.778	0.753
Spain	1.085	1.118	1.063	0.886	0.805	0.804	0.797	0.731	0.683	0.720	0.755	0.719	0.778	0.753
Sweden	9.16	10.33	9.74	8.09	7.35	7.47	7.38	6.76	6.59	7.65	7.21	6.49	6.78	6.51
Switzerland	1.69	1.69	1.56	1.35	1.24	1.25	1.25	1.20	1.08	1.09	1.04	0.89	0.94	0.93
Turkey	0.625	1.226	1.507	1.501	1.426	1.344	1.428	1.303	1.302	1.550	1.503	1.675	1.796	1.904
United Kingdom	0.66	0.69	0.67	0.61	0.55	0.55	0.54	0.50	0.54	0.64	0.65	0.62	0.63	0.64
United States	1	1	1	1	1	1	1	1	1	1	1	1	1	1
Euro area	1.085	1.118	1.063	0.886	0.805	0.804	0.797	0.731	0.683	0.720	0.755	0.719	0.778	0.753
OECD-Total	..	..	..	..	..	..	..	..	..	..	..	..	..	..
Brazil	1.83	2.35	2.92	3.08	2.93	2.43	2.18	1.95	1.83	2.00	1.76	1.67	1.95	2.16
China	8.28	8.28	8.28	8.28	8.28	8.19	7.97	7.61	6.95	6.83	6.77	6.46	6.31	6.20
India	44.94	47.19	48.61	46.58	45.32	44.10	45.31	41.35	43.51	48.41	45.73	46.67	53.44	58.60
Indonesia	8 421.78	10 260.90	9 311.19	8 577.13	8 938.85	9 704.74	9 159.32	9 141.00	9 698.96	10 389.90	9 090.43	8 770.43	9 386.63	10 461.24
Russian Federation	28.13	29.17	31.35	30.69	28.81	28.28	27.19	25.58	24.85	31.74	30.37	29.38	30.84	31.84
South Africa	6.94	8.61	10.54	7.56	6.46	6.36	6.77	7.05	8.26	8.47	7.32	7.26	8.21	9.66

Note: Detailed metadata:
http://stats.oecd.org/OECDStat_Metadata/ShowMetadata.ashx?Dataset=NAAG_2015_NOV15&Lang=en&Coords=[INDICATOR].[EXC]

1. Information on data for Israel: http://dx.doi.org/10.1787/888932315602

ANNEX B

The 2008 SNA – changes from the 1993 SNA

For all OECD countries except Chile, Japan, and Turkey, indicators presented in this publication are based on the 2008 System of National Accounts (2008 SNA). This new set of standards for the compilation of national accounts finalised in 2009 was adopted by most OECD countries by the end of 2014. The 2008 SNA includes a number of changes to the 1993 SNA, some of which have a large impact on the indicators presented in this publication and therefore are discussed below.

Changes affecting whole economy levels of income, etc.

In situations like this when changes in international standards are actually implemented in the national accounts, countries tend to take advantage of the unique situation and make changes to improve all their compilation methods - therefore also implementing various improvements in sources and estimation methodologies. It is important to underline that the impact of the latter "statistical benchmark revision" could be higher than the impact of the changeover in standards. The overall impact on the levels of Gross Domestic Product (GDP), resulting from (i) the changes due to the implementation of the new standards, and (ii) the statistical benchmark revision is 3.8 %-points on average for the OECD for the year 2010. It ranges from 0.2 %-points for Luxembourg to 7.6 %-points for the Netherlands and 7.8% for Korea. For the OECD as a whole, the average impact of the changeover to the SNA 2008 amounts to 3.1 %-points, while the impact of the statistical benchmark revision accounts for 0.7 %-points, or 17% of the total impact, with a wide variation across countries.

A statistics brief on the general impact of the changeover to 2008 SNA is available at *www.oecd.org/std/na/new-standards-for-compiling-national-accounts-SNA2008-OECDSB20.pdf*

Research and experimental development: R&D is recognised for the first time as a produced asset. This also means that payments for the acquisition of patents, treated as acquisition or disposal of non-produced, non-financial assets in the 1993 SNA, will be treated as transactions in produced assets, R&D. This also has implications for sectorial gross value added as the 2008 SNA recommends that a separate establishment is distinguished for R&D producers when possible (see: *OECD Handbook on Deriving Capital Measures of Intellectual Property Products* : *www.oecd.org/std/na/44312350.pdf*). The inclusion of R&D as a capital asset represents the largest change due to the implementation of the 2008 SNA on GDP levels for all OECD countries, varying between 0.5% for Luxembourg and Poland and up to 4.0% for Finland and Sweden.

Under the 1993 SNA expenditure on R&D by government already adds to government output (which is estimated on a sum of costs basis) and subsequently as general government final consumption. So, for government the direct impact of the capitalisation mainly involves a reclassification of expenditure from government final consumption to government gross fixed capital formation. Indirectly, however, government output and hence GDP, will increase as part of the costs of government include an imputation for depreciation; which now includes a component for the capital stock of R&D by government.

Weapons systems: Military weapons systems such as vehicles, warships, etc. used continuously in the production of defence (and deterrence) services are recognised as fixed assets in the 2008 SNA (the 1993 SNA recorded these as fixed assets only if they had dual civilian use and as intermediate consumption otherwise). Some single-use items such as certain types of ballistic missiles with a highly destructive capability, but which provide ongoing deterrence services, are also recognised as fixed assets in the 2008 SNA. Because most if not all of these expenditures are carried out by government (whose output is typically valued by summing costs) GDP will only increase by the related new consumption of fixed capital. The impact on the GDP level as a result of the recognition of military weapons systems as capital expenditures varies across countries ranging from having no impact for countries such as Ireland or New Zealand to 0.5% and 0.6% for the United States and Greece, respectively for the year 2010. The impact on the OECD as a whole is 0.3% on average for the year 2010.

Financial Intermediation Services Indirectly Measured (FISIM): The method recommended in the 2008 SNA for the calculation of FISIM implies several changes from that in the 1993 SNA. For example, it explicitly recommends that FISIM only applies to loans and deposits provided by/deposited with financial institutions, and that for financial intermediaries all loans and deposits are included, not just those of intermediated funds. In addition, the 2008 SNA no longer allows countries to record FISIM as a notional industry.

Financial services: The 2008 SNA defines financial services more explicitly to ensure that services, such as financial risk management and liquidity transformation, are captured.

Output of Central Banks: The 2008 SNA has provided further clarification on the calculation of FISIM in calculating the output of Centrals Banks. Where Central Banks lend or borrow at rates above or below the effective market lending/borrowing rate, the 2008 SNA recommends the recording of a tax or subsidy from the counterpart lender/borrower to/from government to reflect the difference between the two rates. Correspondingly, a current transfer (the counterpart to the tax/subsidy) is recorded between government and the Central Bank. These flows will have an impact on the distribution of income in national income compared to the 1993 SNA treatment.

Output of non-life insurance services: The methodology used to indirectly estimate this activity in the 1993 SNA (premiums plus premium supplements minus claims) could lead to extremely volatile (and negative) series in cases of catastrophic losses. The 2008 SNA recommends a different indirect approach to measurement that better reflects the pricing structures used by insurance companies and the underlying provision of insurance services per se. The approach can be simply described as an ex ante expectation approach. Output is equal to premiums plus expected premium supplements minus expected claims. The 2008 SNA also recommends that exceptionally large claims, following a catastrophe, are recorded as capital rather than current transfers which will have an impact on (particularly sectorial) estimates of disposable income.

Valuation of output for own final use: The 2008 SNA recommends that estimates of output for own final use should include a component for the return to capital as part of the sum of costs approach when comparable market prices are not available. However, no return to capital should be included for non-market producers.

Costs of ownership transfer: The 1993 SNA recommended that these costs (treated as GFCF in the accounts) should be written off over the life of the related asset. The 2008 SNA instead recommends that these costs are written off over the period the asset is expected to be held by the purchaser. This will impact on measures of net income and only marginally on gross measures, reflecting the calculation of output for own final use and government output (which is calculated as the sum of costs including depreciation).

Re-allocating income, etc. across categories

Goods sent abroad for processing: The 2008 SNA recommends that imports and exports are recorded on a strict ownership basis. This means that the values of a flow of goods moving from one country (that retains ownership of the goods) to another, providing processing services, should not be recorded. Only the charge for the processing service should be recorded in the trade statistics. The 1993 SNA imputed an effective change of ownership.

Merchanting : Under the Balance of Payments Manual 5th Edition (BPM5) merchanting – the purchase and subsequent resale of goods abroad without substantial transformation and without the goods entering or exiting the territory of the merchant – is classified as a services transaction. This treatment causes global imbalances in goods and services because the merchant records an export of a service at the same time as the country acquiring the good records an import of a good. Therefore, the 2008 SNA and BPM6 recommend classifying merchanting as a component of trade in goods. The acquisition of goods by the merchant are recorded as negative exports of the merchant's economy and the subsequent resale of goods by the merchant are recorded as a positive exports. The difference between sales and purchases of merchanted goods is recorded under a new category "Net exports of goods under merchanting" of the merchant's economy.

(Pensions) Defined benefit schemes: The 1993 SNA stated that actual social contributions by employers and employees should reflect the amounts actually paid. The 2008 SNA differs, recognising that the amounts actually set aside may not match the liability to the employees. As such, the 2008 SNA recommends that the employer's contribution should reflect the increase in the net present value of the pension entitlement plus costs charged by the pension fund minus the employee's own contributions. This change will result in a shift of income between gross operating surplus and compensation of employees and between institutional sectors (corporations/government and households).

In some cases, a defined benefit pension plan may be underfunded implying the pension plan has insufficient financial assets to earn the returns that are necessary to meet promised future benefits. The promised future benefits are assets of the household sector and liabilities of the pension schemes, or the employer if there is no autonomous scheme. According to the 1993 SNA, only the funded component of pension plans should be reflected in liabilities. However, the new 2008 SNA recognizes the importance of the liabilities of employers' pension schemes, regardless of whether they are funded or unfunded. For pensions provided by government to their employees, countries have some flexibility in the recording of the unfunded liabilities in the set of core tables. However, the full range of information is required in a new standard table (SNA Table 17.10) that shows the liabilities and associated flows of all private and public pension schemes, whether funded or unfunded, including social security.

Ancillary activities: The 2008 SNA recommends that if the activity of a unit undertaking purely ancillary activities is statistically observable (separate accounts, separate location) it should be recognised as a separate establishment.

Holding companies: The 2008 SNA recommends that holding companies should always be allocated to the financial corporations sector even if all their subsidiary corporations are non-financial corporations. The 1993 SNA recommended that they were assigned to the institutional sector in which the main group of subsidiaries was concentrated.

Exceptional payments from public corporations: The 2008 SNA recommends that these should be recorded as withdrawals from equity when made from accumulated reserves or sales of assets. The 1993 SNA treated such transactions as dividends.

Exceptional payments from governments to quasi-public corporations: The 2008 SNA recommends that these should be treated as capital transfers to cover accumulated losses and as additions to equity when a valid expectation of a return in the form of property income exists. The 1993 SNA treated all such payments as additions to equity.

ORGANISATION FOR ECONOMIC CO-OPERATION AND DEVELOPMENT

The OECD is a unique forum where governments work together to address the economic, social and environmental challenges of globalisation. The OECD is also at the forefront of efforts to understand and to help governments respond to new developments and concerns, such as corporate governance, the information economy and the challenges of an ageing population. The Organisation provides a setting where governments can compare policy experiences, seek answers to common problems, identify good practice and work to co-ordinate domestic and international policies.

The OECD member countries are: Australia, Austria, Belgium, Canada, Chile, the Czech Republic, Denmark, Estonia, Finland, France, Germany, Greece, Hungary, Iceland, Ireland, Israel, Italy, Japan, Korea, Luxembourg, Mexico, the Netherlands, New Zealand, Norway, Poland, Portugal, the Slovak Republic, Slovenia, Spain, Sweden, Switzerland, Turkey, the United Kingdom and the United States. The European Union takes part in the work of the OECD.

OECD Publishing disseminates widely the results of the Organisation's statistics gathering and research on economic, social and environmental issues, as well as the conventions, guidelines and standards agreed by its members.

OECD PUBLISHING, 2, rue André-Pascal, 75775 PARIS CEDEX 16
(30 2015 07 1 P) ISBN 978-92-64-24679-9 – 2015

www.ingramcontent.com/pod-product-compliance
Lightning Source LLC
LaVergne TN
LVHW081418110826
845149LV00010B/1781
* 9 7 8 9 2 6 4 2 4 6 7 9 9 *